Archaeological Site Museums in Latin America

Cultural Heritage Studies

UNIVERSITY PRESS OF FLORIDA

Florida A&M University, Tallahassee
Florida Atlantic University, Boca Raton
Florida Gulf Coast University, Ft. Myers
Florida International University, Miami
Florida State University, Tallahassee
University of Central Florida, Orlando
University of Florida, Gainesville
University of North Florida, Jacksonville
University of South Florida, Tampa
University of West Florida, Pensacola

CULTURAL HERITAGE STUDIES

Edited by Paul Shackel, University of Maryland

The University Press of Florida is proud to announce the creation of a new series devoted to the study of cultural heritage. This thematic series brings together research devoted to understanding the material and behavioral characteristics of heritage. The series explores the uses of heritage and the meaning of its cultural forms as a way to interpret the present and the past. The series highlights important scholarship related to America's diverse heritage.

Books include important theoretical contributions and descriptions of significant cultural resources. Scholarship addresses questions related to culture and describes how local and national communities develop and value the past. The series includes works in public archaeology, heritage tourism, museum studies, vernacular architecture, history, American studies, and material cultural studies.

Heritage of Value, Archaeology of Renown: Reshaping Archaeological Assessment and Significance, edited by Clay Mathers, Timothy Darvill, and Barbara J. Little (2005)

Archaeology, Cultural Heritage, and the Trade in Antiquities, edited by Neil Brodie, Morag M. Kersel, Christina Luke, and Kathryn Walker Tubb (2006)

Archaeological Site Museums in Latin America, edited by Helaine Silverman (2006)

Authors interested in contributing to the Cultural Heritage Study Series
should send inquiries to:
Paul A. Shackel
Department of Anthropology
1111 Woods Hall
University of Maryland
College Park, MD 20742
Phone 301-405-1422
Fax 301-314-8305
Email: Pshackel@anth.umd.edu

Archaeological Site Museums
in Latin America

EDITED BY HELAINE SILVERMAN

FOREWORD BY PAUL SHACKEL

University Press of Florida
Gainesville/Tallahassee/Tampa/Boca Raton
Pensacola/Orlando/Miami/Jacksonville/Ft. Myers

A record of cataloging-in-publication data is available from the
Library of Congress.
ISBN 0-8130-3001-3

The University Press of Florida is the scholarly publishing agency
for the State University System of Florida, comprising Florida A&M
University, Florida Atlantic University, Florida Gulf Coast University,
Florida International University, Florida State University, University
of Central Florida, University of Florida, University of North Florida,
University of South Florida, and University of West Florida.

University Press of Florida
15 Northwest 15th Street
Gainesville, FL 32611-2079
http://www.upf.com

For Edward M. Bruner, a pioneer in the anthropology of tourism

Contents

Illustrations

Tables

Foreword

The museum is a very interesting component of the archaeological site, and Helaine Silverman has brought together professionals who share compelling stories about their experiences working with site museums in Latin America. In this region many important archaeological sites have museums, and for some local communities it is a status symbol to be associated with a place that is considered so important that it attracts tourists to their homeland. The authors describe in detail the negotiations and struggles within Latin America to make local interpretation a part of the national heritage. Negotiations can be between archaeologists and the local community, the local community and the federal government, the federal government and archaeologists, and sometimes local community and local community. The authors provide case studies that show how archaeologists can work with communities in Latin America to make the local past a part of the public memory.

While the New Archaeology placed academically trained professionals as gatekeepers of archaeological knowledge, archaeologists are increasingly relying on community input for their projects. This changing perspective in the discipline is paralleled by changes in anthropology as a whole, and although the discipline has changed significantly, archaeologists are only beginning to realize the importance of community involvement. Community participation means that scientists are no longer the cultural brokers, and practitioners are beginning to recognize that many histories can exist in any one place. These stories of the past are continually being shaped and reconstructed. Archaeologists are in a good place to address these changing perspectives, and they need to respond effectively to these challenges and opportunities. The authors in this volume are part of a larger trend in community archaeology approaches (Derry and Malloy 2003; Dongoske et al. 2000; Shackel and Chambers 2004; Swidler et al. 1997; Watkins 2000), and their work is timely and groundbreaking.

As communities in developing countries embrace site museums, they are using for their own means and goals a vehicle once used to reinforce their oppression and subordination. Site museums are becoming a platform to express regional identity, and they are a device with which local communities can negotiate goods and services from the central government. The archaeologist plays a significant role in protecting and interpreting archaeological resources, but the local Latin American communities are gaining greater sovereignty over how their past is treated and interpreted. This volume provides important and thought-provoking case studies that allow others involved in community museums to see how professionals worked with local communities to develop site museums and interpret their past.

Historian Eric Hobsbawm (1983: 13) writes, "The history which became part of the fund of knowledge or the ideology of nation, state or movement is not what has actually been preserved in popular memory, but what has been selected, written, pictured, popularized and institutionalized by those whose function it is to do so." Traditions, meanings, and memories are invented, and they become legitimate through repetition or a process of formalization and ritualization characterized by reference to the past. By implying continuity with the past, these traditions reinforce values and behavior (Hobsbawm 1983: 1–5).

Those working with site museums struggle with the idea of presenting the community's heritage. Heritage often means integrity, authenticity, and stability; it is a way for communities to make a claim to a past and assert themselves on the present political and social landscape. The case studies in this volume offer very interesting perspectives about the control over the past and the meaning it has to local Latin American communities. Academics are critical about which stories should be told about the past. Is the story about art history or anthropology; is it about the elite or the everyday life of people; is it about the thrill of archaeological discovery, or should it be the story of ruin, decay, and antiquity? These are the issues that the authors grapple with in the case studies. These are the tensions that any museum faces when deciding which past to present.

The development of these community museums is also tied to issues of heritage tourism. Tourism changes the economy of a community. While professionals need to think about making their projects sustainable, they also need to weigh other impacts to the site and think about the potential damage to a site, the ecological impacts, and the change of local traditions. Tourism development comes at a price; while everyone touts the economic viability of tourism, the real economic impact is still not completely understood.

The articles assembled in this volume address very timely issues of heritage, tourism, identity, authenticity, cultural expression, power, ownership of the past, and the role of the archaeologist in the discourse of the past. The authors wrestle with the issue of objectivity. Future generations need to think about how these museums can be used in a broader social and political context. While the museum displays are often about the accomplishments of descendants and a connection to a glorious past, they can also be used as a platform to discuss inequalities and call for social justice. *Archaeological Site Museums in Latin*

America introduces valuable case studies related to site museums at archaeological sites. The volume makes a valuable contribution to understanding the dialogue between groups and the creation of a past.

Paul A. Shackel, Series Editor

Preface

This volume originated as a symposium at the Sixty-ninth Annual Meeting of the Society for American Archaeology, held in Montreal in 2004. For several years I had been aware of the remarkable activities of various colleagues who, with their own funds or donations, had undertaken to leave a lasting contribution in the areas in which they were conducting long-term fieldwork by constructing site museums. Yet archaeological site museums are poorly represented in the abundant literature on museums. I convened the symposium to offer colleagues a chance to share experiences and bring larger professional attention to site museums as a first line of defense in cultural heritage protection and as a feasible source of employment and revenue in rural areas. The session went so well and was so enthusiastically received by the large public in attendance that I decided to invite participants to publish their papers. The new Cultural Heritage Studies series of the University Press of Florida is an ideal venue for our work.

The contributors to *Archaeological Site Museums in Latin America* are united by their commitment to archaeology in the public interest. This concept advocates an ethical engagement with the living communities in and around which archaeologists conduct their projects as well as a critical understanding of the current and historical social, political, and economic contexts of our field investigations. The framework for our applied archaeology is site museums. Many of the authors (Cyphers, Paredes and coauthors, Hastorf, Stothert, Weinstein, Castillo, McEwan, Elera and Shimada, Onuki) have actually built or rehabilitated site museums and/or created a development project at one. Three other authors comment critically on existing site museums, applying the concept of museum in usual (Manzanilla, Mortensen) and expanded (Silverman) manners. And one author (Jennings) describes how an entire landscape is being converted into a kind of site museum by adventure travel companies.

I believe that *Archaeological Site Museums in Latin America* is the first volume to specifically deal with *archaeological* site museums and to ground (literally and figuratively) them at their point of origin: the sites that generate the collections that traditionally have ended up in large regional and national museums away from the communities. What makes the volume special is the very newness of site museums as a heritage management strategy. These museums are becoming didactic and conservation forces in their own right. All of the chapters address this issue.

Latin America is fascinating as the geographical fulcrum for these case studies because of its enormous range of archaeological sites, from single burials to entire pre-Columbian cities. As such, our case studies constitute what is essentially a handbook for archaeologists and heritage managers—a "how to," "what to expect" and "what not to" primer that can readily be incorporated into courses on museums, heritage, and ethics.

The interdisciplinary field of museum studies came to the fore in the 1980s and has been growing ever since. Its principal weakness, in my opinion, is that it is a critical discipline. Museum scholars are overwhelmingly talkers (theoreticians), not doers. In contrast, many of the archaeologists who have contributed to *Archaeological Site Museums in Latin America* are extraordinary because they have figured out for themselves how to build (literally, with adobe bricks or wood panels or cement) a museum structure and how to display objects. They also are exemplary because in each case their undertakings have involved significant interaction with the local community in a highly equitable rather than top-down endeavor. This volume privileges "doing" while also being moderated by critical commentary (see especially Manzanilla, Mortensen, Silverman, Coben, Pyburn). This volume has a laudatory balance between practical application and theoretical appreciation.

I am grateful to the symposium participants—including the two discussants—for writing up their fascinating oral presentations as equally stimulating chapters. I also express my thanks to Paul Shackel and John Byram for providing us with the opportunity to open a dialogue on this very important aspect of cultural heritage management.

PART 1

Introduction

Archaeological Site Museums in Latin America

HELAINE SILVERMAN

Introduction

Over the past twenty years, museums have been receiving critical attention from scholars in various disciplines. Among the many topics considered in the literature are the history of museums, museums and nationalism, museum architecture, the relationship between museums and tourism, and museums as contested spaces of class display, identity formation, public culture, and representation. However, within the burgeoning field of museum studies, scant attention has been directed to archaeological site museums. Most revealing of this situation is the fact that the International Council of Museums (ICOM) has offered only a skeletal definition, dating to 1982, stating that the archaeological site museum is a museum located "at the point where excavations have taken place" (cited in Hudson 1987: 144). Other kinds of site museums recognized by ICOM are ethnographical, ecological, and historical. All of these site museums are supposed to protect natural or cultural property, moveable and immovable, on its original site and to "acquire, conserve and communicate material evidence of people and their environment" (Article 2, ICOM Statutes, 1989, 1995, 2001).

The recent interest taken by the United Nations Educational, Scientific and Cultural Organization (UNESCO) in site museums of all kinds—archaeological, historic, urban, natural—is therefore most welcome. In his editorial for a thematic issue (called "The Site Museum") of UNESCO's journal, *Museum International,* Gadi Mgomezulu (2004), director of UNESCO's Division of Cultural Heritage, contemplates the complexities of site museums, archaeological and otherwise:

> [They] do not exist in isolation; they take on meaning in a web of interpretative and exhibition systems that are primarily developed within museal institutions. . . . [T]he site [i]s a space and the museum [i]s a place which produces knowledge and which is symbolic of the relationship between societies and their heritage at a given moment. . . . [T]he museum simultaneously anchors this relationship and functions as a mediation

zone . . . a museum is not only an instrument which explains the site in a static relationship that is updated according to the rhythm of new museographic developments. The site and the museum each designate a space of heritage whose limits adapt and transform themselves, occasionally overlapping when a heritage space takes on the characteristics of a museum.

I extrapolate from his remarks that the key issue for archaeological site museums—specifically the concern of the present volume—is their imbrication of heritage, cultural mediation, and representation. The case studies of almost all of the authors in *Archaeological Site Museums in Latin America* illustrate this point.

As commonly understood by archaeologists, an archaeological site museum (henceforth referred to as a site museum) is a building located at an archaeological site in which exemplary excavated materials from the site, and perhaps from related sites, are displayed, accompanied by explanatory texts that interpret the site and its archaeological culture for the public. Barbara Kirshenblatt-Gimblett observes, "The museum is an integral part of the site. The museum does for the site what it cannot do for itself. It is not a substitute for the site but part of it, for the interpretive interface shows what cannot otherwise be seen. It offers virtualities in the absence of actualities" (1998: 169). Other features of site museums may include laboratory and storage facilities. They may or may not have an organized educational program. They may or not have housing for a resident archaeologist and/or site protection personnel.

The location of these museums runs the gamut from world-famous monumental sites (such as Teotihuacan, San Lorenzo, Copán) to sites having much less striking—albeit archaeologically important—material evidence (such as the Vegas occupation of the Santa Elena Peninsula in Ecuador). In this volume the contributors amplify the concept of site museum to encompass not just buildings with displays pertaining to a site or group of related sites but also buildings whose exhibits address broad regional prehistories, as well as entire historic districts and even landscapes that are scripted as museums by particular agents.[1]

The site museums discussed in this volume include some of the greatest sites of Latin America (Figure 1.1). These sites are and will grow as tourist destinations because they are part of the ineluctable process of globalization within which the heritage and tourism industry operates. Site museums in Latin America are particularly interesting because of the frequent tension they embody—narrative as well as real—between perceived pre-Hispanic glory, the usually disadvantaged situation of the local and/or descendant communities, and the pressure for development, often in the form of tourism. The contributors to this volume

Figure 1.1a. Location of site museums discussed in this volume in Central America. Map by Steven J. Holland.

consider a range of site museums and the uneasy as well as successful engagements occurring among diverse local and outside interest groups.

Ethical Considerations

The field of archaeology has become increasingly self-critical and self-reflexive as it interrogates its own practices. At the international level this is seen most noticeably in the meetings and publications of the World Archaeological Congress (for example, the One World Archaeology series beginning with the 1986 meeting in Southampton; see, as examples, Bond and Gilliam 1994; Gathercole and Lowenthal 1990; Layton 1989a, 1989b) and the Society for American Archaeology in the United States (for example, the SAA Committee on Ethics, Committee on Native American Relations, Committee on Repatriation, Public Education Committee; see Lynott and Wylie 2000; Zimmerman et al. 2003a; see also, inter alia, Kohl and Fawcett 1995; Shackel and Chambers 2004; Vitelli 1996). Beyond anthropological archaeology per se, a range of ethical issues has been raised by the field of critical museum studies, in which the representa-

Figure 1.1b. Location of site museums discussed in this volume in South America.
Map by Steven J. Holland.

tion of O/others and relationships with living and descendant communities are among the most salient for archaeologists.

We, as archaeologists, should be informed and enthusiastic about archaeological site museums because, among other reasons, they have the potential to fulfill six of the eight principles of archaeological ethics guiding the Society for American Archaeology (Lynott 1997). Indeed, the museum work or museum critiques of the contributors to this volume specifically engage these principles in the following way:

Principle 1. Site museums can promote local stewardship of the archaeological record.

Principle 2. Site museums should function in consultation with affected groups.

Principle 4. Site museums fulfill the mission of public education and outreach.

Principle 6. Site museums present the knowledge of archaeological investigation to the public in accessible form.

Principle 7. Site museums can function as appropriate depositories of materials and records.

Principle 8. Site museums can sponsor training workshops that teach contemporary standards of professional practice to the local community so that local individuals and organizations are able to appropriately conduct any program of research they initiate or in which they participate.

Each author is well aware that "today's archaeology calls for 'active ethics': the awareness that essentially everything we do as professionals has ethical implications" (Zimmerman et al. 2003b: xvi). Moreover, many of these archaeologists are proactive, not only aware of the ethical implications of their actions but also actively seeking to better the circumstances of the communities in and around which they work.

Site Museums and Site Protection

In compliance with SAA Ethical Principle #1, site museums can promote stewardship of the archaeological record. In so doing, they should function in consultation with affected groups, in compliance with SAA Ethical Principle #2. But the process may go awry. Here are four true stories from Peru that concern the relationship between site museums and site protection. I offer them as lessons.

Story 1: one site museum, widespread looting

In 1914 Max Uhle, the German father of Peruvian archaeology, lamented, "As soon as I had left the scene [the Ica Valley in 1901 and Nazca region in 1905] of my last explorations, my workingmen, who had become quite experts, under my training, continued alone and in secret to search for this valuable and rare pottery [Nasca, dating to circa A.D. 1–750]. Thus a vast amount of this beautiful ware was unearthed and found its way to Lima, where all was greedily acquired by dealers. Many additional cemeteries were located by these huaqueros [tomb robbers] and entirely rifled" (Uhle 1914: 8). Twelve years later, looting was so intense that it prompted Julio C. Tello, the Peruvian father of Peruvian archaeology, to comment in a letter dated 29 October 1926: "In the short space of 25 years [since Uhle's discovery of the Nasca style], the looters have opened about 30,000 tombs. Their vandalized trophies are found dispersed all over the world as mere curiosities. They have lost, perhaps forever, their historical and scientific value" (cited in Tello and Mejía Xesspe 1967: 156). Archaeological excavations have an afterlife that can be either advantageous or deleterious, depending on the decisions made by archaeologists once a project has ended.

The only site museum in the valleys of the Río Grande de Nazca heartland where ancient Nasca society flourished (see Silverman and Proulx 2002 for overview) is the Maria Reiche Museum, dedicated to the life and discoveries of the German investigator of the region's geoglyphs, with an accompanying exhibition of archaeological materials from the major ancient cultures of the area.[2] Neither the Maria Reiche Museum nor the small municipal and private museums in the towns of Nazca and Palpa or the major regional museum in the city of Ica are thus far having an ameliorative role with regard to the area's unabated looting (notwithstanding looting's diminishing returns, caused by a century of exploitation), despite their admirable public outreach.

Story 2: a site museum, rare looting, but no research

Between 1925 and 1930, one of the most important archaeological sites in Peru was excavated by a team from Peru's national museum. The site is Paracas (actually composed of five distinct loci; see Silverman 1991), dating to circa 200 B.C.–A.D. 200 and famous for its exquisite textiles. In 1930 a military revolution overthrew the government and shut down the archaeological project as the political winds of favor shifted. In the absence of an archaeological project, the site was immediately devastated by looters.

In 1964 a site museum was created by the wealthy Swiss archaeologist Frederic Engel, who was working at the site and in the region. No other archaeologist has excavated at Paracas since Engel, and empirical knowledge about the in situ Paracas habitation zones and cemeteries has not advanced, although the material culture has been continuously studied by many scholars. Looting virtually ceased with the construction of the museum.[3]

Story 3: site versus local population versus major museum versus site museum

In February 1987 a small group of looters living in the northern coastal village of Sipán discovered a gold-filled royal tomb in a prehistoric mound alongside their homes. Infighting led to rumors of their discovery leaking to the police, who then informed the director of the regional museum, Dr. Walter Alva. Looted materials from the tomb that had not yet been sold to the illicit antiquities market indicated the extraordinary wealth of what had been plundered. As has been dramatically recounted in the popular press (Alva 1988; Kirkpatrick 1992; Nagin 1990), a real shootout determined whether the academic field of archaeology or the shadowy world of the looters would control the site. Within days of the confiscation of the artifacts still in the village, a police presence was established on the mound, and Dr. Alva began a salvage excavation. Scientific excavation proceeded thereafter. Dr. Alva's results are so important that they have revolutionized Mochica (the name of the ancient society to which the remains pertain, circa A.D. 200–750) archaeology. In addition to the permanent police station, a rustic site museum was created at Sipán to inform visitors and presumably educate the local people. In November 2002, a state-of-the-art museum for the spectacular remains excavated at Sipán was inaugurated in Lambayeque, the provincial capital, located thirty-five kilometers away from the site of origin. It is ironic that the April 2004 issue of *Art News* (cover, page 99; it is a magazine devoted to the sale of art and education of collectors) heralds the Royal Tombs of Sipán Museum as one of "the top ten museums (you never heard of)," while page 8 contains a full-page color ad for an exhibition sale of pre-Columbian pottery at a Chicago art gallery. The recent history of Sipán and its two museums is poignant and illuminating in this context. The local population at Sipán still protests their poor share of the wealth generated by the site in their backyard (see Silverman 2005a).

Story 4: a site museum integrates the local community and furthers archaeological research and community development

An example is found at Kuntur Wasi, an important Formative period site in the northern highlands. Prior to the arrival of the Japanese Archaeological Mission of the University of Tokyo in 1988, there had been several interventions in the site (excavation by a Peruvian team in 1946, topographic mapping in 1982–83, analysis of the 1946 ceramic collections: see discussion in Onuki et al. 1995: 3).

As it did elsewhere in Peru in its prior projects, the Japanese Mission made a long-term fieldwork commitment to the site. What makes the Kuntur Wasi archaeological project extraordinary (beyond the always high quality of the Japanese Mission's research) is the social commitment that it simultaneously tendered to the local community, resulting in the creation of a community-based, decision-making, not-for-profit Kuntur Wasi Cultural Association and a superb co-managed site museum (Onuki in this volume).[4] Today, the site museum is the pride of the community as well as a source of gradually increasing income and modernization. Despite the repeated discovery of gold-filled tombs at Kuntur Wasi (dating to circa 800 B.C.) by the Japanese Mission, there has been no looting at the site, nor has the museum suffered any loss despite housing more than two hundred gold artifacts in addition to outstanding pottery; there are also in situ carved stone monoliths.

These four scenarios illustrate four different directions that cultural patrimony preservation can take with and without the presence of site museums. I could provide other examples, but these suffice to show the range from least to most successful outcome for both the ancient people (that is, preservation of the archaeological site) and the living local community. As the remarkable initiatives of various of this volume's contributors clearly demonstrate, site museums can play a positive determinant role in the survival of the material record and betterment of the lives of the community around it, making local people true stakeholders. Thus, site preservation matters. Beyond giving archaeologists access to a database with which to reconstruct the past, archaeological sites can be deployed in the present as sources of employment, local and regional development, and proud identity. Site museums are on the front line of these endeavors, since archaeological sites cannot speak for themselves.[5]

Site Museums and Development

In large and small, thriving and would-be urban centers around the world, museums have been seized upon as a sign of cities' promising futures and facilitator of their economic present. Speaking of heritage in general, Kirshenblatt-Gimblett (1998: 155) notes its role as "an instrument of urban redevelopment." The boom in signature architect-designed museum buildings (Henderson 2001) is inextricably linked to municipal plans for development (Solomon 2001). Museums are "premier attractions. Museums are not only destinations on an itinerary: they are also nodes in a network of attractions that form the recreational geography of a region and, increasingly, the globe" (Kirshenblatt-Gimblett 1998: 132).

In a greatly scaled-down form, this is what archaeologists and local communities are quite literally banking on with site museums.[6] Site museums can generate and support sustainable, income-producing activities in an expanding tourism circuit or corridor—and employment diminishes the need for looting. Site museums can function as economic motors for their region. Indeed, starting from the premise that cultural tourism was already unstoppable and would continue to grow exponentially, the 1976 International Seminar on Contemporary Tourism and Humanism (organized by the International Council on Monuments and Sites, or ICOMOS) specifically recognized that archaeological sites can be a source of economic benefit and cultural education in their regions, and ICOMOS argued for better management (also see the 1967 Norms of Quito [ICOMOS 1967]).

The issue is not just the conundrum of indigenous people in a postcolonial small-scale community seizing on the Western-in-origin concept of a museum as a sign of their engagement with modernity and as a facilitator of their construction of identity (see Hastorf's discussion of Chiripa in chapter 7), it is that museums actually can generate revenue and development through their insertion into the global economy. Indeed, developing countries present their museums to diplomats and visiting foreign entrepreneurs as an assurance of their political stability, cultural worth, and amenable climate for investment. Visiting tourists pay entrance fees, need guides, consume soda and chips sold in kiosks by residents, have their vehicles washed by local teenage boys after the dusty ride, adventurously stay in family-run local lodgings, eat in a local restaurant, and want souvenirs (another form of heritage consumption; for a larger discussion see Lury 1997). Thus, just before the gala inauguration of the Royal Tombs of Sipán Museum in 2002, a proposal for an adjacent open-air Mochica artisans village was approved by the Ministry of Trade and Tourism and is now functioning. Lambayeque artists/artisans sell to tourists their own replicas of ancient Mochica pottery, textiles, and metalwork, along with ethnographic crafts, thereby achieving employment and income.

The ability of site museums to promote development, however, should be constrained by what Kirshenblatt-Gimblett (1998: 171) calls a "responsibility to their 'product' that distinguishes them from market-driven amusement, whose primary responsibility is profitability. They are responsible for giving form and space to concerns animating public life in the communities they serve." The site museums discussed in this volume are philosophically and pragmatically in agreement with Kirshenblatt-Gimblett's admonishment.

It is also important to bear in mind that development predicated upon site museums in Latin America is a different process with a radically dissimilar social and historical context than the one problematized by Hewison (1987) in his famous discussion of Britain's heritage industry. Hewison attributes extensive recent museum growth in the United Kingdom to a replacement of "the real industry upon which this country's economy depends. Instead of manufacturing goods, we are manufacturing heritage. . . . The reason for the growth of this new force is [that] this country is gripped by the perception that it is in decline" (Hewison 1987: 9). In the case of the towns near the archaeological sites treated by this volume's contributors, they have not declined. Rather, they have not been thriving centers for centuries or millennia. In Latin America the issue is not to put heritage on display so as "to give dying economies and dead sites a second life as exhibitions of themselves" (Kirshenblatt-Gimblett 1998: 7). Instead, these site museums are intended to assist the development of long-marginalized regions while valorizing and enabling the local population to define its own identity/ies.

Site Museums and the Construction of Identity

Construction of identity is a leitmotif coursing through technical discussions of cultural heritage management (for example, 1996 ICOMOS Declaration of San Antonio; 2001 UNESCO Universal Declaration on Cultural Diversity; see Cleere 1989: 8) in addition to ethnographic studies of appropriations of the past in local communities whose prehistories (antecedent or merely geographically sedimented) are deemed "greater" or more "glorious" than their current socio-economic reality (for example, Silverman 2002). For instance, the ICOMOS Declaration of San Antonio states that heritage sites can carry a deep spiritual message that sustains communal life, linking it to the ancestral past (ICOMOS 1996). The 2001 Universal Declaration on Cultural Diversity recognizes that "culture is at the heart of contemporary debates about identity, social cohesion, and the development of a knowledge-based economy" (International Journal of Cultural Property 2002).[7] Mgomezulu (2004), speaking of site museums in general, argues that by paying "particular attention to preserving or reinterpreting memories and history in relation to issues of the present . . . they contribute to developing cultural equilibriums which are necessary for managing and living in peace." He goes on to specifically observe that "[i]n Latin America, more than anywhere else, the integration of local communities and cultural minorities into the life of the museum [is] one of the most important factors in changing the missions of the museum and its reorientation toward socio-economic objectives." This is well documented in *Archaeological Site Museums in Latin America*.

If we accept the premise that construction of a strong (albeit invented) identity is important for an emotionally fulfilling life (not to mention the economic perquisites discussed above), then site museums are important at the local and regional level because of the role they may play in identity construction. The "new museology" (Vergo 1989) is especially concerned with community development (Mayrand 1984, 1985) and recognizes the need for creation of local museums that "actually involve the community in developing an appreciation of its own places" (Walsh 1992: 161).

But identity construction and its related sense of place are not just phenomenological pleasantries, undertaken nostalgically and without cost. They are highly political, spatially assertive, and contestatory social acts (for example, Appadurai 1996). Way (1993: 125), for instance, has observed of regional and indigenous museums that "[t]o the extent that indigenous identity is not subsumed to national citizenship, these museums will reflect a discourse between nationalist representatives in museum administrations and representatives of the varieties of indigenous peoples within the national borders. In any event, such efforts depend on the tolerance of cultural pluralism and internal ethnic political stability." For Latin America I would rephrase Way's statement and apply it to site museums to mean that these museums, by their very location, are provincial and local: they are not in national capitals, and site preservation is such that they are typically in the countryside/nonurban areas where non-elites—often indigenous or descendants therefrom—reside and constitute the majority of the population. This essentially rural location is also the implicit premise of Riviére's (1985) "ecomuseums"[8] although this need not be the case (see, for example, Duitz 1992; González and Tonelli 1992; Jones 1992; Tchen 1992 [all of whom are dealing with urban community museums]; see also Hayden 1999).

Ecomuseums are implicated in the new museology, a museology that espouses "the idea of the 'active' museum—museums which are concerned with involving people in the processes of both representation and interpretation" (Walsh 1992: 162). Riviére (1985) argued that the ecomuseum is the mirror with which the emplaced local population views itself to discover its own historically contingent image/identity (that is, encompassing preceding peoples in the territory), and a mirror held up to visitors so that they will understand and respect this emplaced local population. It is very much a "social construction of space" paradigm in the sense of Lefebvre (1991). As explained by Walsh (1992: 164), "The ecomuseum is . . . concerned with the facilitation of an understanding, or awareness, of how places are a construction of human interaction with environments across time and space."

Marliac (1997) has suggested multifarious relationships between archaeology and development (understood as "in developing countries"). He sees identity as a core problem of development, arguing that any improvement in standard of living (usually the desired outcome of development) will necessarily be effected through sociocultural transformations impacting "people who possess an identity and a history" (Marliac 1997: 325). Because archaeology "rebuilds past societies as neither history nor ethnology can do, its intervention in development is clearly solicited" (Marliac 1997: 325–26). However, as is well known, the archaeological operationalization of the concept of identity is neither procedurally nor theoretically unambiguous (see, for example, Jones 1997; Olsen 2001; Shennan 1989b, to name only the most obvious examples), and a host of ethical dilemmas may result from the archaeological identity enterprise (for example, Barkan and Bush 2002; Meskell 1998; Schmidt and Patterson 1995), not to mention outcomes of outright violence (see, for example, Arnold 1992). Although Marliac strays from his title's topic, the issue is important, and Marliac is correct in recognizing the fundamental importance of identity construction as offered by archaeologists and as manipulated by a public.

Site museums can be a rallying point for the generation of local identity, and this is precisely what has happened in some of the case studies presented in this volume. For instance, the town of Chepén, near San José de Moro, has erected a life-size statue of the Priestess of San José de Moro excavated by Luis Jaime Castillo and Christopher B. Donnan (Donnan and Castillo 1992; see chapter 10, this volume). Chepén is claiming a Mochica identity; some townsfolk speak of the priestess as the fiancée of the excavated Lord of Sipán in Lambayeque (Krzysztof Makowski, personal communication, 2004), thereby generating a neo-Mochica territory and tourism corridor covering the northern range of the archaeological Mochica (see also chapter 13). In other areas, the living local community does not claim to be the descendant community of an archaeological civilization but takes significant pride of place based on the local pre-Columbian remains. Of course, in the cases of Copán (chapter 4), Kuntur Wasi (chapter 5), Pukara (chapter 6), Chiripa (chapter 7), and Cusco (chapter 11), many people living in and around the great archaeological sites are indeed the descendants of those who created the monuments.

Conclusion

Museums began in Europe as the famous cabinets of curiosities and were displays of elite knowledge and power (see, for example, Findlen 1994). Even as they and royal collections developed into modern museums, these museums remained elite private institutions until their democratization through, for instance, the French Revolution's Louvre (McClellan 1994) and the founding of Oxford's Ashmolean Museum (1683) and the British Museum (1759)—although admission to the English museums took some determination and perseverance even 123 years after being opened to the public (Ames 1992: 20); the Victorian disciplinary project resolved this problem, albeit through elaboration of the much-criticized exhibitionary complex (see Bennett 1995: 59–88). Stocking's (1985: 7) historical survey of museum development documents the establishment in Europe of a number of museums of a more anthropological nature during the first half of the nineteenth century, such as in Denmark (1816), Leiden (1837), and Petrograd (1836).

After the U.S. Civil War, there was a burst of art museum construction in the North, as exemplified by New York's Metropolitan Museum of Art (Duncan 1995: 48–71). Despite being virtual palaces built by the country's wealthy and powerful families, these fine art museums were public institutions, contradictions about access notwithstanding. With the interdigitation of the exhibitionary complex and the growth of anthropology, museums began a new phase of their existence in the United States, quickly evolving into such recognizable scientific (natural history, anthropology) institutions as the Field Museum of Natural History in Chicago, originally the Field Columbian Museum, arising out of the 1893 World's Columbian Exposition. But this was not the only influence on their formation. The U.S. Smithsonian National Museum of Natural History was founded in the 1850s explicitly as a research and educational institution (Ames 1992: 26). By contrast, Phineas T. Barnum's American Museum was intended to be a profit-making business venture (Ames 1992: 26). The two kinds of museums—art and natural history/anthropology—still dominate the cultural scene and coexist with moments of crossover and redundancy (as when the Metropolitan Museum of Art acquired the collections of the Museum of Primitive Art). The differences in their scripts are still notable, even outside the United States, as Manzanilla points out in her essay on Teotihuacan's site museums (chapter 2).

In the English-language literature, very little scholarship has been directed at Latin American museums of any kind (see, for example, Errington 1993, 1998; Florescano 1993). In general, independence from Spain led to the rapid establishment of national museums throughout Latin America as anticolonial statements of autonomy that reached back to the pre-Hispanic era to ground and legitimate the new nation-state. Florescano (1993: 87) is clear that in Mexico there was a "compulsive need to create a historical and cultural identity for the new nation" and that out of this arose "the idea of establishing a Mexican museum." The Mexican Revolution at the beginning of the twentieth century again created the need for a new national museum, for the oppressed indigenous peoples of Mexico had come to be seen as historical protagonists, and "pre-Hispanic civilization [was situated] at the very base of the history of Mexico" (Florescano 1993: 97, 98). Archaeological excavations at Teotihuacan were conducted "to bring out the founding nature and original character of the ancient indigenous civilizations" (Florescano 1993: 98). The great new Museo Nacional de Antropología, inaugurated in 1964, was the culmination of the Mexican Revolution ideology that "recognized the pre-Hispanic past in its historical and cultural development and in the traditions of indigenous and popular groups, values and symbols that identified them as the genuine part of the nation's soul" (Florescano 1993: 99).

In Peru, too, "antiquities . . . were in the thoughts of the founders of the nation, the sacred symbols of our history and basis of a national idea" (Ravines 1989: 23). Not only was the Inca past (at that time the many pre-Hispanic archaeological cultures were undifferentiated) mobilized for the construction of national identity, but less than one year after independence, a law was passed declaring that Peru's ancient monuments were property of the nation "because they pertain to the glory that is derived from them" (Supreme Decree Number 80, 2 April 1822, cited in Ravines 1989: 23).

Today, site museums in Latin America are being created and valorized as local iterations of these nationalist sentiments, as first lines of defense in the protection of cultural (archaeological) patrimony, and as new promoters of economic development in their immediate regions. Moreover, as the contributors to this volume recognize, archaeologists, local communities, and site museums are tightly enmeshed in crosscutting webs of intercultural understanding and misunderstanding pertaining to cultural heritage management, economic development, political empowerment, and production of personal and group identity. Our awareness and involvement is a fairly recent development in archaeological professional practice, and one that is so important that Shackel and Chambers (2004) specifically call it "public archaeology as applied anthropology" (also see comments by Castillo and Holmquist in chapter 10 and Pyburn in chapter 16). Archaeologists are increasingly associated with "community-based activities that seek to empower historically subordinated groups" (Shackel 2004: 1)—the kinds of groups that characterize the Latin American populations within which site museums are embedded.

Site museums are another fascinating stage in the centuries-old and varied history of museums around the world, exemplifying the remarkable flexibility of this institution. Negotiating the tensions between tradition and modernity and locality and globalization in the societies in which they are found, site museums offer a new perspective on some of the most important issues impacting Latin America and the developing countries of the world.

Notes

1. Thomas (2002: 132) says that "an archaeology museum is anything that publicly presents something important from the past. America contains thousands of such museums, from the largest urban natural history museums to major archaeological sites like Cahokia and Chaco Canyon."

2. Nasca written with an *s* refers to the archaeological culture. Nazca written with a *z* refers to the town and geographical area of the Río Grande de Nazca drainage.

3. In late July 2004, several pre-Nasca tombs, known as *cavernas,* were looted within throwing distance of the Paracas Site Museum. This looting, however, was quickly detected and found to be the work of an eccentric schoolteacher from the region, notorious to local archaeologists for more than fifteen years as an occasional *huaquero* (grave robber). This was an isolated instance.

4. The museum-community relationship at Kuntur Wasi can be positively compared to Riviére's (1985: 182) concept of "ecomuseum" as "an instrument conceived, fashioned and operated jointly by a public authority and a local population. The public authority's involvement is through the experts, facilities and resources it provides; the local population's involvement depends on its aspirations, knowledge and individual approach."

5. Kirshenblatt-Gimblett (1998: 168) argues that the "inability of sites to tell their own story authorizes the interpretation project itself." A site of extraordinary beauty such as Machu Picchu could be an exception. That site currently does not have a site museum. Indeed, I would argue that for tourists the essence of the visit to Machu Picchu is the emotional-aesthetic experience of it. In my observations, many tourists are not overly concerned with the archaeological details of the site. Indeed, that information may conflict with their own constructions and performances of meaning, particularly among those with New Age beliefs.

6. The Royal Tombs of Sipán Museum falls somewhat outside this parameter of "greatly scaled down" inasmuch as it is a multimillion-dollar state-of-the-art facility designed by a distinguished Peruvian architect, Celso Prado Pastor. The museum is at the heart of plans for a comprehensive north coast tourist circuit or corridor.

7. An excellent framing discussion on heritage and identity is provided by Lowenthal (1994). The relationship between cultural heritage and construction of identity/production of locality is contravened by documents such as the 1972 World Heritage Convention, which argue for the universality of cultural heritage (for discussions about "universality" see Cleere 2001 and Omland 1997, inter alia).

8. This is an infelicitous term because it suggests the meaning "ecological museums." In fact, the term *ecomuseum* refers to museums "concerned with the total ecology and environment, natural and human, of a defined locality" (Boylan 1990: 32). A good site museum would fulfill this mission. Thus, because of the semantic confusion created by the term *ecomuseum,* I will not use it.

PART 2

Site Museums at Monumental Sites/
Sites with Monuments

2

The Site Museums at Teotihuacan, Mexico

The View of Art Historians versus the View of Archaeologists

LINDA MANZANILLA

Introduction

Site museums are the first places where visitors to archaeological sites may have a glimpse of the culture, changes through time, and artifacts that serve to define the archaeological site. In central Mexico during the past three decades, site museums have been the locus of a battle between the view of the art historians and that of the archaeologists.

A large Classic period metropolis such as Teotihuacan in central Mexico is difficult to characterize, owing to its complexity. Teotihuacan was a vast, planned urban settlement, the capital of a particular type of state, a sacred city, a multiethnic settlement, a crafts center, and a site that monopolized basic resources such as obsidian (see, for example, Manzanilla 1997; Millon 1973; Pasztory 1997; Spence 2000). Teotihuacan has so many aspects and its monumental setting is so impressive that it is difficult to represent to the layperson.

In Mexico, from the time of the establishment of the National Museum of Anthropology in the Chapultepec area of Mexico City in 1964, a tradition began whereby museums could give an idea of the different cultures in a macro-area (see, for example, *Newsweek* 1971). The culture area concept prevailed in this type of museum. Nevertheless, many different and important aspects were left aside in this characterization: we may cite, for example, regional settlement patterns, the domestic domain, political organization, and the ritual sphere.

Some decades after the National Museum's inauguration, we see a change in this tradition to one that is more dominated by the art historians, in which little is said about processes and interrelationships and in which archaeological objects are displayed for the pleasure of admiring them, without attention to context, function, chronology, and associations. There is not one museum in Mexico that focuses on change through time, on the living conditions of the common people in the cities, on craft specialization and its importance in political economy, on social differentiation and ethnic affiliation.

Teotihuacan

The archaeological zone of Teotihuacan has two site museums (Figure 2.1). One of these is devoted to general issues and was a by-product of the 1992–94 project of the Instituto Nacional de Antropología e Historia (INAH, or National Institute of Anthropology and History), headed by Eduardo Matos (Figure 2.2; see also del Río Alvarez 2005; Advantage Mexico 2005 [on the map for this Web site, the site museum is identified as the Manuel Gamio Museum, after its early leading investigator]). Teotihuacan is advertised by the Mexican Tourism Board (2005) on that agency's official Web site in these terms: "The Museum of Teotihuacan Culture shows the various archaeological eras of Teotihuacan, as well as displaying beautiful pieces from the excavations and a scale-model that provides an overview of the archaeological features of this site." (Note, too, that this Web site erroneously identifies Teotihuacan as a site of Aztec civilization.)

The second museum at Teotihuacan (Figure 2.3; also see INAH Web site) was inaugurated a few years ago and is devoted to the extraordinary mural paintings at the site (see, for example, Pasztory 1976, 1988). It is called the Museum of Mural Painting and is advertised by the Mexican Tourism Board on that agency's official Web site as follows: "A new museum was created at entrance No. 3 to the archeological site of Teotihuacán. The purpose of the museum was specifically to conserve the 35 mural paintings found at the site. A notable example is part of the mural found in the Temple of Mythological Animals; this consists of colorful paintings of such fantastical animals as plumed serpents, jaguars, and fish with wings." From my perspective, both museums have a strong emphasis in single objects (the view of traditional art history) and practically no anthropological background. Below I review their contents and propose a new reorganization.

The Site Museum of Teotihuacan

Inside INAH, during the past decades, there have been different views concerning the placing of site museums. The most influential opinion states that site museums should not be very visible from the archaeological site and should be placed on the periphery of the archaeological zones. Nevertheless, INAH breaks its rules when dealing with macroprojects with large budgets. Thus, aberrant as it may be, Teotihuacan's site museum was built adjacent to the main monumental structure of the site, the enormous Pyramid of the Sun (Figure 2.1).

The site museum of Teotihuacan is organized in seven sectors. Sector 1 is devoted to the natural environment (plants and animals) as represented in ceramic vessels, stone sculptures, and mural paintings. Nothing is said about the paleoenvironment, the agricultural techniques of the Teotihuacanos, the subsis-

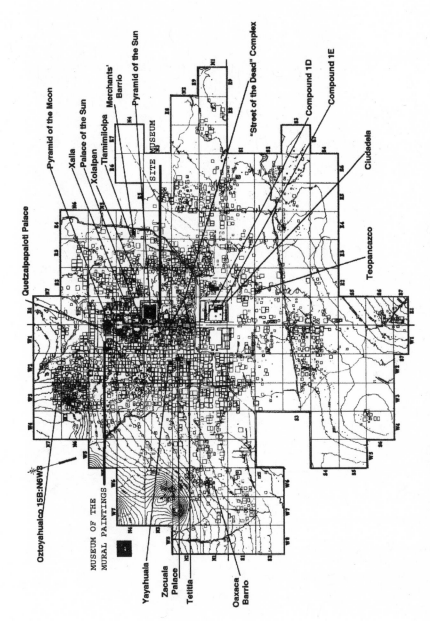

Figure 2.1. Location of Teotihuacan's two museums in the plan of the ancient urban center.

Figure 2.2. Teotihuacan's site museum: the Museum of Teotihuacan Culture. Photograph by Linda Manzanilla.

Figure 2.3. Museum of Mural Painting at Teotihuacan. Photograph by Linda Manzanilla.

tence base, and so forth. Sector 2 is related to the ceramic chronology (different periods with their ceramic forms and decorations), and nothing is said about ceramic production, the different elaboration techniques, the manufacturing districts (barrios) in the city, and so forth. Some instruments (such as polishers, molds, raw materials) are scattered throughout different halls. Sector 3 deals with industries in other media: obsidian, bone, antler, shell, and clay objects are displayed, but again, there is nothing about their processes or organization of production or the like. Sector 4 is the central hall. It has a huge model of the core of the city, with a glass pane through which the visitor may admire the Pyramid of the Sun. Even though the model is exceptional, it shows only the civic-administrative center of the city, and there is no explanation about the urban grid, the construction modules, the elements of urban planning, the drainage system, the multifamily apartment compounds, and the real extension of the city. Sector 5 presents some examples of burials and funerary offerings, particularly those of the Pyramid of the Feathered Serpent. Nothing is said about the different mortuary practices of the ethnic Zapotecs, Michoacanos, or Gulf Coast merchants who lived in the city, with respect to those of the local Teotihuacanos. Sector 6 is devoted to the main deities, but only the God of Thunder, the Fire God, and the Feathered Serpent are displayed. Nothing is said about the Water Goddess, the Butterfly God, or the patron gods of the most humble families that archaeologists have detected, nor are the domestic and state rituals discussed. Sector 7, the last sector, displays some objects from other Mesoamerican regions: Oaxaca, Michoacán, Veracruz, Puebla, and Maya. Nothing is said about the Granular ware and greenstones from Guerrero or about the objects coming from the Bajío and Zacatecas. There is no mention whatsoever about the so-called Teotihuacan enclaves in Matacapan, Veracruz, or Kaminaljuyú, Guatemala, or about different sites in Michoacán, about Chingú in the Tula Valley, or about the eighty sites in the Puebla-Tlaxcala Valley, for example.

Thus, visitors leave the site museum without knowing that this huge site was the capital of a state; that this state may have established enclaves in the rest of Mesoamerica to ensure the provisioning of sumptuary goods; that it was also a lively city, where different lineages or extended families inhabited the so-called apartment compounds, where there was family hierarchy as in a conical clan; that each individual household had a patron god and its own ritual courtyard but participated with other households in particular activities for the barrio and the urban setting.

Because I find the current exhibition script of the site museum lamentably deficient, I propose the following reorganization so as to provide a comprehensive view of Teotihuacan as a metropolis and the capital of a state.

- First, there would be an introductory hall where Teotihuacan is contextualized within the Mesoamerican Classic period; in addition to Teotihuacan I would illustrate other main Classic period states, such as Maya and Zapotec and the Teuchitlán tradition in western Mexico.
- Second, I'd have a chronological framework showing the main changes in urban planning and the different transformations in the industries and mural paintings.
- Third, the natural and cultural environment would be represented, including the subsistence of the Teotihuacanos, with a comprehensive view of the climate, soils, vegetation, fauna, forest management, and agricultural techniques; maps would be used for the presentation of some of this information.
- Fourth, I would show the different phases and elements of urban planning and the growth of the city by means of three-dimensional models of the different phases of growth.
- Fifth, we would see the architectural elements of Teotihuacan and the changes through time; drawings would depict the architectural characteristics of the site.
- Sixth, there would be a general view of the mural paintings, their techniques, and the scenes portrayed.
- Seventh, there would be a depiction of the craft activities and production areas for pottery, figurines, lithics, polished stone, worked bone, shell, and so forth. Some drawings would show the different phases of production of figurines, green obsidian blades, gray obsidian bifacials, San Martin Orange ware, *incensario* plaques, and other items.
- Eighth, the domestic domains and the social organization would be presented: the types of apartment compounds, what we know about life inside, and the problem of individuating the rulers' palaces (the latter issue may be represented by comparing the plans of apartment compounds such as Oztoyahualco 15B:N6W3, Tlamimilolpa, Xolalpan, Tetitla, Structure 1D in La Ciudadela, Xalla, and the Street of the Dead complex).
- Ninth, we would see the foreign barrios: the Oaxaca Barrio, the Merchants' Barrio, and the Michoacán sector, in terms of the type of house, the funerary practices, foreign materials, culinary activities, domestic cult, and so forth.
- Tenth, I would consider the exchange relations and the different Mesoamerican regions involved: raw materials, products, sites (maps would be used in this sector).
- Eleventh, the rulers of Teotihuacan would be introduced, in conjunction with a discussion about the different alternative sites: the so-called palaces in

the Ciudadela, the Street of the Dead complex, the Quetzalpapálotl Palace, and Xalla.

- Twelfth, there would be a presentation of ritual in the city and its different scales: the funerary and domestic domains; the barrio level; the state cult with its gods, practices, and ceremonies.
- Thirteenth, I'd show the encompassing nature of Teotihuacan state: the regional settlement pattern, enclaves, political alliances, coercive and conquest episodes, flow of prestige and sumptuary items.
- And finally, fourteenth, there would be a representation of the fall of the city and the Teotihuacan state system, followed by the post-Teotihuacan occupations of the valley.

The Museum of Mural Painting

The Museum of Mural Painting is the other museum at Teotihuacan. It has a more articulated structure than the site museum, although there are some issues missing in its discourse. This museum is more modern than the site museum in terms of its conception, for it utilizes videos, multimedia, and other devices to provide a better comprehension of the subjects presented there. Nevertheless, there is practically no explanation about the information that archaeologists derive about activities, social groups, and ritual themes at Teotihuacan from the scenes depicted in the mural paintings.

The organizational structure of this museum is not very clear. The first sector shows some murals and architectural representations as well as chronological data to illustrate the different layers where mural paintings were placed at the site, together with objects and models of sectors of the city that have no relation to mural paintings, such as the so-called Astronomical Cave. The second sector provides information about some painting techniques and mineral pigments used, together with female figurines and other objects. The third sector has some architectural models of complete apartment compounds, indicating the places where mural paintings were found, as well as some of the most outstanding complex scenes portrayed by the Teotihuacanos. But the explanatory texts say little about the interpretation of the murals. A very interesting area is a model, at a scale of 1:1, of the Eagles' Hall at Tetitla, with the original black background color. The next sector seems to be devoted to depictions of priests, with some theater-type censers on which priests are represented. There the problem is that some themes are chosen and others are left aside; we do not have a complete glimpse of the whole universe. The last sector displays different objects and mural paintings, as well as a three-dimensional model of the interpretation of the Mythological Animals mural painting.

I suggest a reorganization of this museum so as to create a more articulated discourse.

- Thus, first there should be a map showing the places where the mural paintings (replicated in the museum) come from, so that we may know the different sectors and contexts.

- Second, the construction and painting techniques, changes through time, and description of the different raw materials and their proveniences should be discussed.

- Third, there should be the representations and the description of the places where they are found: abstract motifs, plants, animals, human beings, processions, composite scenes.

- Fourth, we should see the mural paintings of the domestic domains, that is, the models of particular apartment compounds showing the placing of murals.

- Fifth, there should be the mural paintings of the public domains, as well as the type of representations.

- Sixth, I'd have interpretations of the processions, mythical scenes, possible titles, and so forth.

Conclusion

I have indulged myself in the hypothetical power with which to redesign the two museums at Teotihuacan. I propose to break with the traditional art historical view that characterizes the two museums at Teotihuacan. I argue that new presentations are needed that offer a more lively view of the site and more effectively present Teotihuacan's processes and relations. Such museological reorganizations will inform visitors about the dynamic life of Teotihuacan over the many centuries of its existence while stimulating the public to think more critically about the site and urbanism overall.

Now, in this concluding section, I briefly address the hard questions of how to go about achieving the goals I propose and overcoming the many obstacles that would stand in the way of such a change. In my opinion the more critical venue for change is the site museum rather than the Museum of Mural Painting, because the site museum is what introduces visitors to Teotihuacan as a Mesoamerican city and society. In my text above, I propose a script to situate Teotihuacan dynamically in the central highlands of Mexico. This new script would involve not only objects but also a plethora of supplemental didactic material such as three-dimensional dioramas, architectural models, reconstructive drawings for the walls, and state-of-the-art interactive information technology (recently, an interactive exhibition on Teotihuacan was co-organized by the

Universum Science Museum and the Institute for Anthropological Research at the Universidad Nacional Autónoma de México or UNAM). Indeed, the latter can provide the contextual information that I regard as necessary for understanding the site and that visitors could engage to varying depths of inquiry. The virtue of my scheme lies in its *optional* character. The less curious or more hurried visitor could still obtain an overview with little investment of intellectual energy, though the new organization of the script would convey a holistic and evolutionary essence not available in the current site museum. The more inquisitive and leisurely visitor could literally explore the site, taking several real and virtual routes.

Moreover, I observe above that the site museum is located intrusively and obtrusively in the ruins. In the best of all worlds, the existing site museum would be demolished and rebuilt outside the main protected Zones A and B, perhaps outside San Juan Teotihuacan (two kilometers away) to stimulate its economy by making townsfolk into stakeholders in the archaeological site through stimulation of local economic development, such as in restaurants and tourist souvenir shops and guided tours to the small colonial convent of Oxtotipac (founded in 1548), in addition to inducing tourists to enjoy its two spas and stay overnight at one of its two nice hotels.

Most countries outside the canonical developed world lack the financial resources to protect and display their cultural patrimony to best advantage. Such is not the case in Mexico, whose strong nationalist ideology implicates the pre-Columbian past. INAH, through budget negotiation with the federal government of Mexico and international agencies, could obtain the funds necessary to enact the suggestions I propose here. The investment would be well worthwhile because Teotihuacan's proximity to Mexico City engenders the site's inclusion in all day-trip tourist excursions from the capital. Entrance fees to the site and tourist purchases at a fine museum gift shop would eventually defray the cash outlay involved in construction of a new site museum.

Archaeologists should not restrict their activities to fieldwork. Site museums offer us an exciting and necessary opportunity for conveying to the public at large the significance of our research while contributing to the local and national economy. If coordination and cooperation can be achieved between the archaeologists and those in charge of the implementation of site museums (their architectural design, siting, landscaping, and script), then these museums can greatly enhance the tourist experience, which can only improve prospects for the future of archaeology itself.

3

Community Museums in the San Lorenzo Tenochtitlán Region, Mexico

ANN CYPHERS AND LUCERO MORALES-CANO

Introduction

Archaeological research in the San Lorenzo Tenochtitlán region[1] of the Texistepec municipality of the Mexican state of Veracruz (Figure 3.1) began in 1945 (Matthew Stirling 1955). However, despite the importance of the Olmec site of San Lorenzo, community museums were not founded in the towns of Tenochtitlán and Potrero Nuevo until fifty years later, notwithstanding community interest in a museum in Tenochtitlán during the late 1960s (Coe and Diehl 1980: I: 7). The long delay in creating them was due to several factors, which will be discussed below.

The San Lorenzo Tenochtitlán region is set amidst swamps and meandering rivers, so for many years the fluvial network was the only mode of transport and communication. Since the first archaeological discoveries in this key Olmec area, the Mexican government has not shown excessive interest in providing a communications infrastructure and urban services to this region, as has been done in other places with important archaeological sites. The principal government focus has been on the petroleum industry; consequently, little attention has been placed on the protection of the sites or the natural environment. This situation likely is attributable to the fact that this site complex lacks monumental masonry architecture and, as well, has served as a constant source of monumental stone art for large museums. In addition, the majority of the inhabitants, relatively recent immigrants to the area who make a living through farming and cattle ranching, have been financially and educationally unprepared to advance and mature development plans. Exceedingly difficult social relations and competition in the locality are accompanied by the illegal trafficking in Olmec artifacts.

What is the cultural patrimony for? Who is it for? These basic questions are cause for profound reflection. In this chapter we shall try to illustrate how the cultural patrimony of this region has been used in the past by giving a background of local history, followed by summaries of different attempts to establish community museums: an unsuccessful one at El Azuzul ranch and two others, both successful, in the villages of Potrero Nuevo and Tenochtitlán, respectively.

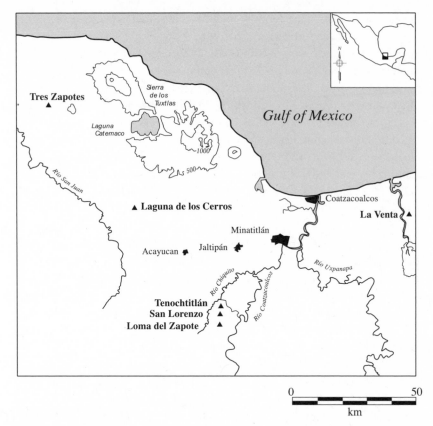

Figure 3.1. The southern Gulf Coast with the San Lorenzo Tenochtitlán region. Map by Steven J. Holland.

These events may contribute to an understanding of the problems and achievements surrounding the growth of community museums in the region. A proposal for the future joint protection of natural and archaeological assets in the region is also outlined.

Brief Historical Background

In the 1930s and 1940s, the feverishly booming petroleum industry in southern Veracruz and Tabasco promoted extensive exploration of regional oil deposits. This activity was in the hands of the English-controlled Aguila Company, and, as war loomed upon the international scene, the petroleum industry was nationalized by President Lázaro Cárdenas in 1938. The industry, with its heavy influx of foreigners, principally of English descent, created an aristocratic society in the region. Many men working in the industry adopted English customs, including the "hunt." However, the "hunt" was in search not of foxes but rather of jaguars, tapirs, and other fauna native to the tropical forest then covering a large portion of the southern Gulf Coast. Often organized in formal clubs, the hunters penetrated deep into virtually unknown upriver regions in the Isthmus of Tehuantepec. They sometimes came across archaeological pieces, which often were given or sold to eminent politicians, oil company executives, and collectors, such as Gustavo Corona and Diego Rivera. In those days, collecting antiquities was not illegal, and collectors likely had already removed small pieces from San Lorenzo by 1945, when the first archaeologist arrived. In this historical context, that the archaeologist, Matthew Stirling, received word of San Lorenzo at all is noteworthy, but thanks to certain circumstances, he was duly informed.

Matthew Stirling and his wife, Marion, became good friends with Margarita Bravo, a resident of Coatzacoalcos, when she joined their La Venta expedition as the translator assigned by Petróleos Mexicanos (PEMEX). When not in the field, these stylish young women corresponded about their friends, family, and, of course, fashion, a hot topic in the war years. They had discovered a craftsman in Coatzacoalcos who would make smart purses from crocodile skin, so they had their own designs made to order. Naturally, their correspondence intensified when orders were placed and received (Marion Stirling 1945).

As the Stirlings were finishing fieldwork in Chiapas in May of 1945, Marion received Margarita's letter about an order of purses. In it mention also was made of huge stone heads, like the ones from La Venta, that had been sighted by hunters near the Chiquito River (Marion Stirling 1945). Without hesitation, the Stirlings cancelled previous travel plans and rushed to Coatzacoalcos to follow up on the clues obtained from the hunter, Juan del Alto (Marion Stirling 1945, 1981).

After a grueling long trip on the narrow-gauge train from Coatzacoalcos and a long, evening horseback ride across swamps and rivers, Matt and Marion arrived at Tenochtitlán, a small village of huts with palm-thatch roofs, founded less than ten years earlier (Matthew Stirling 1955). In just a few days, the Stirlings found colossal heads and other stone monuments at the site of San Lorenzo. Matt returned in 1946 for another season of exciting discoveries, which *National Geographic* magazine colorfully spread across its lustrous pages (Matthew Stirling 1947). When the research was completed, the stone monuments remained at the site.

From 1946 to 1960, no archaeological work was conducted at San Lorenzo, but the monumental sculpture had attracted the attention of national and international museums. At that time the conditions for safeguarding the sculptures did not exist in the town, nor was there an adequate regional communication network. In addition, with the opening and furnishing of new museums in the country, little interest existed in developing any local infrastructure for housing the pieces. The people of Tenochtitlán grew increasingly aware of the importance of the sculpture as government officials began removing monuments for display in the Xalapa Museum (Xalapa—also written Jalapa—is the state capital). Their removal caused an uprising. As recounted by Coe and Diehl, "Resentment built to a high pitch, fanned by cleavages among the people of Tenochtitlán, a few of whom sided with the outsiders. The contingent from Jalapa had promised that a new schoolhouse would be built in return for the exportation of the monuments; the school having failed to materialize, there was a virtual revolt of the populace" (1980: II: 26). The army was sent to Tenochtitlán to quell the discontent created when the colossal head (San Lorenzo Monument 2) was removed from the site and taken to an exhibition in Houston, an event that occurred only a few years before Michael D. Coe began the Rio Chiquito Project in 1966.

What was the outcome? Although the rebellious townspeople stood up to the Mexican soldiers sent to quell them and ensure the removal of the monuments, in return for acquiescence, they received the school. This incident established a regional precedent in negotiations regarding the national patrimony, and to this day, people in the region hold archaeological pieces for ransom to obtain the kinds of services that the government should provide anyway.

In 1986, history repeated itself in several ways. Official representatives were sent to the site to remove the three colossal heads (Monuments 53, 61, and 66), which had been discovered in 1969, 1970, and 1982, respectively (Beverido 1970; Brüggeman and Hers 1970; Ruíz Gordillo 1982). However, the townspeople demanded electricity and that a dirt access road be built across the floodplains as preconditions for a "loan" of the three monuments to the Xalapa Museum of Anthropology. A contract was signed by both parties, and the pieces were removed. A hastily constructed, rambling mud-walled building, unworthy to be called a museum, was built on the campsite of the Instituto Nacional de Antropología e Historia (INAH, or National Institute of Anthropology and History). It rapidly deteriorated, and by 1990, when the San Lorenzo Tenochtitlán Archaeological Project (SLTAP) began, it housed only a few broken monuments, rats, cockroaches, bats, and spiders.

This historical perspective suggests that because the Olmec sculptures had no cultural value or traditional meaning for the local community, they were susceptible to removal and their original contexts to destruction (see Cleere 1989). In a sense, the sculptures were assigned a new significance by the local inhabitants when they traded the objects for services provided by the federal and state governments. As we shall see in the following examples, the effects of archaeological interest in this region include the local appropriation of pre-Hispanic pieces for use as powerful instruments of negotiation with the government. This type of reappropriation of the cultural patrimony by the local population may be essential in its eventual protection.

El Azuzul

In 1987 an important discovery made at the Loma del Zapote site, located a few miles south of Tenochtitlán, would affect the course of future events. Three complete Olmec sculptures—the impressive Azuzul twins and feline figure (León and Sánchez 1991–92)—were fortuitously discovered on a hillside that is part of a private ranch. The extraordinary sculptures were kept in a leaky shack on the ranch, and nearby communities formed a union to forcibly inhibit their removal by federal authorities. In 1992, the San Lorenzo Tenochtitlán Archaeological Project was invited to work there, in the hope that more pieces would be found. Fieldwork was able to add another feline to the corpus (Cyphers 1994, 2004). During its research there, the SLTAP made as many modifications to the shack as were allowed by the owner to keep slope wash from entering the shack and damaging the monuments.

All archaeological work there has been done in a menacing, high-caliber atmosphere. Political intrigue was put into action with the intention of keeping the sculptures on the ranch. Wondrous promises were heaped upon neighboring marginal communities that lack the most basic services, such as electricity and purified water, and these promises glorified the economic consequences of an Azuzul site museum, which allegedly would attract major businesses such as the Sheraton Hotel and Denny's restaurant, where everyone would be employed. At the same time, competition with Tenochtitlán and the other communities became tangible. Whereas the Azuzul museum never materialized, Tenochtitlán and Potrero Nuevo were successful in their efforts.

Potrero Nuevo

In 1990, the small village of Potrero Nuevo had only one stone monument (Loma del Zapote Monument 1) in its possession, and this sculpture rested uncovered and abandoned in a house lot. INAH commissioned Cyphers in 1992 to follow up on a lead about a newly discovered sculpture there. When she arrived, local people reluctantly took her to the spot where the decapitated human sculpture already was mounted on poles for its removal. Per INAH's instructions, she told them that the monument could be taken to their village for safekeeping (Cyphers 1992). They found themselves in a sticky situation when

Figure 3.2. The first community museum in Potrero Nuevo, built of wattle and daub with a palm-thatch roof. It unfortunately suffered irreparable damage from hogs scratching their backs against it. Photograph by Ann Cyphers.

pressured to allow the handsome stone torso to be moved to the Azuzul ranch, where the supposed museum, hotel, and franchise restaurant would be built. It took a great deal of courage for the local people to assume the responsibility for protecting the monument in their village. Perhaps as a consequence of their decision, village and *ejido* leaders were subject to intense harassment over the following years.

Of the three cases discussed in this chapter, the village of Potrero Nuevo, considered by many visitors to be the most "picturesque" because of its rustic homes, was the most disadvantaged because it lacked a decent access road, electricity, and running water. Nevertheless, these hardworking people were able to build the first community museum in the region, a typical mud-walled, thatched one-room building with a dirt floor (Figure 3.2), where they proudly placed the two monuments.

Tenochtitlán

In 1989, the Tenochtitlán ejido authorities welcomed the new phase of research represented by the SLTAP, which was programmed to start the following year. They anticipated the work and income it would provide for the town's youth. At the same time, they were concerned that stone monuments would be removed from their lands. They requested that any such discoveries remain in the ejido.

Figure 3.3. The discovery of the tenth colossal head at San Lorenzo was the final impetus for the completion of the Tenochtitlán Community Museum. Photograph by Ann Cyphers.

Given that nine colossal heads and numerous other stone monuments had already been removed to major museums, Cyphers was in complete agreement that any newly found sculptures should stay in Tenochtitlán, in the event that at some point the community might be able to benefit from their presence.

The first incentive for the community museum in Tenochtitlán came in 1993 from a government agency called Culturas Populares. But the ground plans for a modest building were rejected by the community, which had illusions of a grand museum. Tenochtitlán hoped that the Xalapa Museum of Anthropology would return the colossal heads after its ten-year contract expired, and the community trusted in the promise that any future discoveries would be housed in Tenochtitlán. Unfortunately, since the available funds were not sufficient for the larger version, only foundations and a few walls were completed, and the sculptures already located on the premises (for example, Monuments 13, 18, 30, 41, and 47) remained exposed to the elements.

In April 1994, a Sunday volunteer work program was initiated at the construction site to improve the conditions for housing the sculptures. Dirt floors were tamped, monuments were relocated, a semblance of order was created, and a great deal of bonding was achieved. The municipal president, Sergio Salomón, generously donated cement for the building. Little did we imagine that soon there would be a new and determinant impetus for the museum: a colossal head (Figure 3.3) that was discovered on May 3, 1994.[2]

The imminent approach of the rainy season necessitated removing the newly discovered head from its resting place at the bottom of a deep ravine, transporting it to the village, and obtaining permission for it to stay there permanently. In coordination with INAH and PEMEX, these objectives were achieved. Using steel cables and a large crane, a crew specialized in maneuvering heavy objects extracted the eight-ton head from the ravine and placed it on a low-bed truck for transport into town.

Unfortunately, owing to the fact that the roof of the community museum was incomplete and the colossal head unsheltered, it was in danger of being claimed by a large museum. In the absence of support from any formal sector, friends and members of the San Lorenzo Tenochtitlán Project pooled funds to buy and install galvanized roofing for the head and circumvent any outside attempt at removal. A few weeks later, with the unfailing support of Luis Vargas, then director of the Instituto de Investigaciones Antropológicas (IIA) of the Universidad Nacional Autónoma de México (UNAM), Cyphers sought funding from the university's rector, José Sarukhán, to complete the Tenochtitlán museum and build a permanent museum in the community of Potrero Nuevo. Funding was granted, and construction began in March of 1995, coinciding with the next field season at the site (Cyphers 2004).

The town was ecstatic, but others were not—perhaps because a museum in Tenochtitlán was perceived as an excellent excuse to remove the sculptures from the Azuzul ranch. Perhaps it was not totally coincidental that, at this time, Cyphers was denounced at the highest level of the Veracruz state government for the supposed nighttime robbery of a second colossal head (supposedly found next to the other one), which she purportedly removed from the ravine in a pick-up truck. Sensible INAH and UNAM authorities kept her from going to jail on the trumped-up charge.

Hence, the construction of the Tenochtitlán and Potrero Nuevo museums (Figures 3.4, 3.5) began in a climate of harassment. In addition, building them was no easy matter since there were no water lines in either town. Manual pouring of the cement roof in Tenochtitlán required conveying a seemingly infinite number of barrels of river water in the project truck. Construction materials had to be fetched from towns located two hours away. Nonetheless, because of the strong commitment of the master builder, masons, workmen, and project personnel, the museums were ready for inauguration in the summer of 1995 (Figure 3.6).

The inaugurations may have been the biggest formal social and political events ever witnessed by the approximately 1,200 inhabitants of these towns.

Figure 3.4. This second museum in Potrero Nuevo was built around the first museum to provide protection for the sculptures during construction activity. Photograph by Ann Cyphers.

Figure 3.5. Construction of the Tenochtitlán Community Museum. Drawing by Fernando Botas.

Figure 3.6. The Tenochtitlán Community Museum when finished in 1995. Photograph by Rogelio Santiago.

Included in the presidium were the UNAM rector, the director of the IIA, the state governor, and many local authorities (Figures 3.7, 3.8). After receiving the VIPs at the Canticas airport, the caravan of cars proceeded to the municipal capital, Texistepec—somehow slipping through a human net designed to block its arrival and cause the cancellation of the event. Allegedly, a group of disgruntled road workers intended to hold the UNAM rector and state governor ransom to get back pay. Luckily, the rector's entourage slipped through the net, the governor arrived by helicopter, and the inauguration proceeded. Hundreds

Figure 3.7. Inauguration of the Potrero Nuevo Community Museum, attended by UNAM representatives. Photograph courtesy of Marco Mijares, *Gaceta-UNAM*.

Figure 3.8. Inauguration of the Tenochtitlán Community Museum, officiated by the governor of the state of Veracruz and the rector of the UNAM, and presided over by the tenth colossal head. Photograph by Rogelio Santiago.

of people from the region and afar could not get to Tenochtitlán and Potrero Nuevo due to the blockade.

The Sequel

What has happened in these places since then? The protection of Olmec monuments was achieved, and Tenochtitlán and Potrero Nuevo take pride in their museums, which are visited every year by hundreds of national and international tourists (mostly during the months of least rainfall). However, the museums have not spontaneously generated any secondary productive activities despite intermittent attempts to encourage craft production. From the inhabitants' point of view, sporadic tourism—largely attributable to the dirt access roads and dramatic seasonal variations—cannot generate a reliable source of income. As long as ecologically destructive cattle production, the drug trade, and trafficking in archaeological pieces continue to be the local mainstays, little interest will be placed on the archaeological and natural potential of the region as an educational attraction for domestic and international tourists.

In addition, recent events in the region lead us to believe that there is a lack of political will to protect the archaeological patrimony and promote new lines of social and economic development in this region. Despite political statements and programs in favor of decentralization emanating from national levels, there is a tendency to concentrate archaeological pieces in the state and national capitals. Why is this so? The following account may shed some light on possible answers to this question in regard to the San Lorenzo Tenochtitlán region.

The local inhabitants relate that around 1999 negotiations for the removal of the Azuzul sculptures were initiated. We believe these accounts to be accurate, since the negotiation of archaeological pieces for personal or collective benefit unfortunately has become a time-honored tradition in the region. It leads us to believe that a private agreement also was reached in this case. Most people in Tenochtitlán were opposed to their removal and requested that the pieces be relocated in their community museum. Media protests, letters, and phone calls to authorities, all were to no avail.

However, certain events would dissipate the unity and cooperation in Tenochtitlán. When the next municipal president assumed office in 2000, he appointed a local representative (*agente municipal*) in Tenochtitlán, but the opposition forcibly took over the representative's duties and threw him in jail. Out of fear, no one protested. Carefully designed intrigue split the town along political party and religious lines, and by early 2001 many were intimidated into supporting the removal of the sculptures. Those who were not in favor received threats and physical violence. A state of siege existed in Tenochtitlán for more than a year, and organized endeavors to keep the sculptures in the region dissolved. In this way, a carefully designed, tense social climate opened the way for extracting the sculptures.

As the evening shadows fell on October 25, 2001, the sculptures furtively were prepared for removal. Packing the pieces in the dark must have been difficult, since the ranch had no electricity. Even more difficult may have been dragging them down the hill in pitch blackness to the waiting vehicle, which had arrived surreptitiously via the rutted back route. Just as they departed around midnight, a rare electrical failure luckily blanketed the region in darkness. Consequently, no one saw (or dared to see?) the vehicles pass through Tenochtitlán, and the sculptures arrived at the capital city the very next day, in the nick of time for the fifteenth anniversary celebration of the Xalapa Museum of Anthropology. A letter promising the construction of yet another school in Tenochtitlán was proffered.

Into the Future

After the removal of the first set of monuments from San Lorenzo in the 1960s, a growing awareness of the economic value of Olmec sculpture led to intense looting and sale of pieces, many of which ended up in international collections. Momentarily slowed by three research projects conducted between 1966 and

1970 and by the SLTAP (1990–present), this activity unfortunately continues despite the permanent presence of representatives of INAH.

Even with the existence of the community museums, the difficulty in protecting the national patrimony is aggravated by centripetal social forces, for example, the kin and political commitments of local people that inhibit them from exposing perpetrators of illegal acts. This—added to the extensive economic and political contacts of local looters with untrustworthy politicians, antiquities collectors, and purveyors of other illegal products—has increased the economic gain involved in looting.

Despite proximity to nearby petroleum complexes (Sánchez Salazar and Oropeza Orozco 2003), the San Lorenzo Tenochtitlán region is marginal in the national landscape. The region's inadequate insertion in the national economy is, for the most part, responsible for propagating the present ecological disaster. The extraction and production of oil products and cattle ranching have decimated the tropical paradise once enjoyed by ancient inhabitants (Sánchez Salazar and Oropeza Orozco 2003). In addition, looting and trafficking in archaeological materials foil the full germination of the seeds of pride in the Olmec culture and hence of any type of sociocultural identity (albeit adopted) related to them.

Is the development of a tourism industry the solution to this calamity? Tourism is a complex social phenomenon in which the national government usually plays the role of mediator between the tourist attraction and the local population. The government plans tourism in a unilateral fashion based on the cultural elements that it considers important. It generally does not take into account the local community or the long-term effects that tourism may have on the local inhabitants' identity (Greenwood 1989; Martínez and Morales 1999; Morales 1997; Morales-Cano and Mysyk n.d.; Stonich et al. 1995; UNESCO 1976; Whelan 1991). For example, the government may promote a cultural event as a tourist attraction, or (as in the past at San Lorenzo) it may extract those cultural elements that are attractive for developing other spaces, such as national and state museums. The result of this complex process may include social conflict and a struggle for power among the social actors involved.

Tourism is not entirely benevolent, as it is known to often bring damage to sites, increased pollution, water shortages, traffic, ecological destruction, and unfavorable changes in local traditions. The desire for economic development based on tourism, particularly in Third World countries, often carries a high cultural and social price. For the San Lorenzo Tenochtitlán region, as in all others, this question should be carefully evaluated.

From the perspective of local inhabitants, any development that brings an "improvement" in the quality of life (read as "monetary income, modern services, and products") is worthwhile. Such a viewpoint is rooted in poverty, landlessness, and out-migration. An operational definition of "improvement in quality of life" should integrate economic development perspectives while seeking to recapture local cultural traditions and reemphasize the importance of the natural environment.

In ecological terms, since the region already is devastated, an appropriate development program could include the restoration of the natural landscape, that is, the recovery of biodiversity. If such restoration were to be started at the archaeological site of San Lorenzo, a natural and archaeological preserve could be created. Such joint protection of the natural and archaeological heritage perhaps could eventually lead to environmental and cultural stability.

The success of any joint protection of the cultural patrimony and the natural environment depends on the possibilities for establishing diversified economic strategies for agricultural and forest production, along with the provision of services that can underwrite tourism and the expansion of the symbolic importance of both facets (Carabias et al. 1994; Cleere 1989; Morales-Cano 1999). The core of the archaeological zone should be subject to archaeological heritage management with a double purpose. The first includes the protection of the site, which should go hand in hand with educational programs emphasizing its importance for the local inhabitants and visitors. The second should be the ecological restoration of the site. Such an initiative would allow the site to guide the community in the establishment of diversified production strategies that are not damaging to the natural environment, such as in the application of new techniques of organic agricultural production, forestry exploitation, and the use of other resources that does not involve overexploitation. Morales-Cano personally has observed that such strategies have been successful in community organizations such as Tosepan Titataniske of Cuetzalan, located in the Sierra Norte of the state of Puebla, a local organization that received the Mexican national ecological merit award (Moguel and Toledo 2001; Jornada de Oriente 2001). They also have been viable in Cuyuxquihui, Veracruz (Omar Ruiz-Gordillo, personal communication, 2003). As in these places, the joint protection of the cultural and natural patrimony at San Lorenzo would provide beneficial environmental services such as the production of oxygen, carbon capture, the conservation of biodiversity, and aquifer recharge, among others.

Nondiversified economic development based principally on tourism has been shown to be inefficient (Daltabuit et al. 2000; Stonich 1998). A program of sustainable tourism involving carefully designed, planned, and executed social and economic development could avoid overloading and short-circuiting the delicate ecological system and archaeological remains. Steps toward achieving cultural and natural stability could include fomenting a sense of regional identity and providing alternatives for ecological production. Through a program of environmental restoration and archaeological preservation, new social and economic trends could be fashioned that would help arrest the increasing out-migration of local landless youth, who face perennial unemployment.

If development proposals originated in the community itself and if subsequent programs were executed by it, then perhaps the typically short-lived government programs could be avoided. For the community to apply new development mechanisms, it would need to build a diversified production base, which, in turn, would allow local residents to enter the service sector (such as tourism). The appropriation of the land by speculators should be avoided as much as possible.

One possible development scenario for San Lorenzo Tenochtitlán could involve the following: federal protection (which is the conventional means implemented by the Mexican government to protect sites) for at least 250 hectares of the 500-hectare extent of San Lorenzo; the diagnostic evaluation of the natural environment[3] and its eventual ecological restoration; educational programs for rescuing cultural traditions and fomenting environmental and archaeological consciousness; initiatives for establishing alternative economic activities for the local populace; and the encouragement of an archaeological-ecological tourist industry.

If these measures were taken, other possibilities for the eventual development of alternative economic activities for the local population might arise. In the long run, productive projects could be designed according to predetermined resource scheduling. Such activities could create new income possibilities while maintaining traditional activities and avoiding damage to the environment.

The careful preparation of a nondestructive development program would safeguard natural and cultural patrimony and buttress new lines of economic development at the same time that it would provide employment and wages. Importantly, the inevitable influx of national and international tourism could be controlled to avoid destruction and commercial intensification. There is little chance, given the regional geography (that is, wetlands), that any extensive polluting road network could be created, which is a blessing in many ways. The same is true for drinking water, a limited local resource, which puts a limit on certain tourist services, such as lodging. The legal framework for such a project is provided for by the Mexican Law of Ecological Equilibrium and the Federal Monument Law, but precise planning and determined, conscientious political backing are needed to meet the immense, but not insurmountable, challenge.

The purchase of the San Lorenzo site and its official declaration as national patrimony has been attempted unsuccessfully for the past ten years. This is a basic first step for any kind of development program. Since 1993, because of bureaucratic obstacles, not one of the four independent offers to underwrite the purchase has become a reality. It seems that this important site never will be protected unless there is political clout and resolve.

Back from the Future

Evidence since 2004 suggests that a new attitude toward the archaeological heritage is being forged in San Lorenzo Tenochtitlán. Six months after the rescue of a five-ton Olmec monument from looters in April 2004 by the SLTAP, Tenochtitlán vehemently refused to allow INAH to remove sculptures from its community museum to loan them to a foreign exhibit. Although not enough time has elapsed for us to determine whether this event was a watershed in the struggle to achieve patrimonial protection in the region, hopefully it may indicate the long-awaited blossoming of a sense of pride and identity, as well as custodial responsibility in the in situ preservation of the archaeological heritage.

In this context the Tenochtitlán and Potrero Nuevo site museums constitute an educational and community space accessible to all the inhabitants while providing adequate conditions for safeguarding the national patrimony. The children of these villages seem to recognize their importance more than their elders do—which is heartening, since they are the future. If their enthusiasm does not lessen as they face the problems of surviving in miniature "third worlds" inserted into a larger one,[4] these young people may well be the ones who, after weighing the consequences of the local historical events surrounding the national patrimony, will become the principal instruments of its protection. But we cannot wait for these children to grow up. Right now it is urgent that measures be taken to guarantee that the San Lorenzo Tenochtitlán region does not remain a remote quarry for handsome objects.

Acknowledgments

Many details of regional history have been gleaned from interviews with people living in Tenochtitlán, Jaltipán, Minatitlán, Coatzacoalcos, and other places. In particular, we would like to thank Carlos and Laura Bravo, Gustavo Corona, Carlos Godard, Juan Meléndez, and Anatolio Ramos for generously sharing the past and present with us. We thank Rogelio Santiago for assistance with the illustrations.

Notes

1. The term *San Lorenzo Tenochtitlán* was coined by Matthew Stirling (1955) to refer to a complex of sites. Recent research has been able to define the limits of four sites in this

complex: San Lorenzo, Loma del Zapote (which includes the village of Potrero Nuevo), Tenochtitlán (located under the modern town of the same name), and El Remolino (Cyphers 2004; Symonds et al. 2002).

2. This date is celebrated in Mexico as the "Day of the Mason, the Archaeologist and other 'related' professions."

3. The Texistepec municipality once had an ecosystem that Challenger (1998: 303) assigns to the *selva húmeda*. Today this fragile ecosystem has been destroyed by human activity. The most destructive processes are demographic, economic, and cultural pressures exercised by particularly unfavorable practices related to agriculture, cattle ranching, and the extraction and processing of petroleum and other natural resources. If the natural resources of this region were restored and protected, then there is a good chance that the jungle could be reinstated. The communities mentioned in the text are located in close proximity to one of the priority regions for conservation specified by the Comisión Nacional para el Conocimiento y Uso de la Biodiversidad de México (CONABIO). In fact, at one time the Texistepec municipality had the same ecosystem described as RTP-131 by the CONABIO. The Región Terrestre Prioritaria (RTP-131) refers to an area limited by the Sierra de los Tuxtlas and the Laguna del Ostión. It is the northern limit of tropical jungle on the continent, a zone of biogeographic contact, and its large number of vegetation types is associated with altitudinal gradient and special ecological processes. It is an area of latitudinal and altitudinal butterfly migration whose functional and structural integrity is threatened. The jungle is one of the final remaining relics of high evergreen jungle and has the highest precipitation levels in the country (4,700 mm annually). The region contains the greatest extension of *bosque enano* (dwarf forest) in Mexico. Within it, there also is a high deforestation index with a resulting fragmentation of ecosystems and the local extinction of birds, plants, and mammals. The CONABIO and Challenger (1998: 296) list the following species as threatened or in danger of extinction: *Galictis vittata, Phantera onca, Herpailurus yagouaround, Ateles geoffroyi, Alouata palliata, Lutra longicaudis, Leopardus pardalis, Tamandua mexicana, Cyclopes didactylus, Leopardus wiedii, Chironectes minimus, Coendou mexicanus, Anolis sericeus, Bothrops asper, Claudius angustatus, Crocodylus moreleti, Hyla picta, Iguana iguana,* and *Staurotypus triporcatus.*

4. Unless concerted action is taken to further the region's economic self-sufficiency, particularly with regard to the extraordinary archaeological heritage it possesses, the migration of young people to Mexico's urban areas and the United States in search of work will continue to drain the region of its future potential.

4

Experiencing Copán

The Authenticity of Stone

LENA MORTENSEN

Introduction

In the world of Maya archaeology and Maya archaeological tourism, the ancient site of Copán in western Honduras (Figure 4.1) is best known for the quantity and quality of sculpted stone that adorns its buildings and plazas. Stone also serves as the foundation for the ancient buildings as well as the public image of this important Maya archaeological park. The many ornate figures found throughout the archaeological park dominate visual representations of the site in public media and have become iconic of Copán itself (Figure 4.2). Not surprisingly, therefore, when tourists come to Copán, they expect to see the stone sculpture, and without this experience their visit feels incomplete. Stone has become the essence of an authentic Copán.

Today visitors to Copán can experience the site's famous stone sculpture in at least two settings: in situ in the archaeological park (Figure 4.3) or showcased (Figure 4.4) in the Copán Sculpture Museum, a recent addition to the park's attractions. Each environment provides a different experience for the visitor and a different medium for projecting an authentic Copán. However, both narrate Copán using a grammar based on stone, which leads to competing notions of authenticity. In this chapter I discuss the role of authenticity in the overwhelming emphasis on stone sculpture at Copán in its various presented contexts. I consider the ramifications of this emphasis for presenting the ancient Maya past, as well as the implications it holds for communities in the present.

The Prevalence of Stone

Copán was designated a United Nations Educational, Scientific and Cultural Organization (UNESCO) World Heritage Site in 1980, signaling its international status as a place of "outstanding universal value" (see UNESCO's Web site for criteria). Nearly a century and a half prior to that date, the govern-

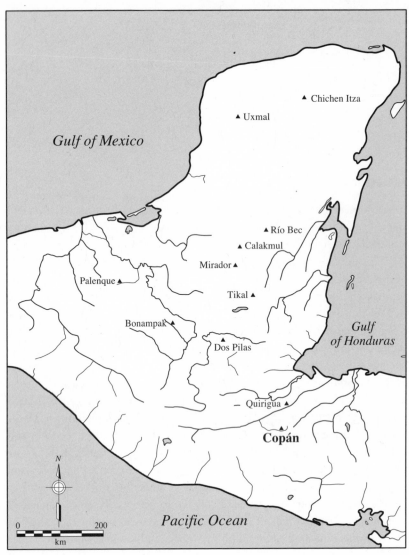

Figure 4.1. Location of Copán in the context of some of the principal Late Classic Maya sites (adapted from John S. Henderson's Map 10 in *The World of the Ancient Maya*, Cornell University Press, 1981). Map by Steven J. Holland.

Figure 4.2. Magazine ad featuring Copán stela.

ment of Honduras recognized Copán as a unique part of its historical territory and placed the site under special protection (Agurcia F. 1984: 12; Rubin de la Borbolla and Rivas 1953: 16). Today the site remains a central symbol in the country's national past (Mortensen 2001). Copán's national and international fame is predicated in large part on the sculptural works crafted by the hands of its ancient residents. Many would argue that sculpture is indeed Copán's defining and distinguishing feature.

The stelae of Copán, and the fallen stone sculptures that once decorated most of Copán's public architecture, are unique in the Maya area for their high-relief carved style, often described as "baroque." Artist Frederick Catherwood was one of the first to bring international attention to Copán's sculpture through his drawings in the famous travelogue from 1841, *Incidents of Travel in Central America, Chiapas and Yucatan* (Figure 4.3; see Stephens and Catherwood 1969). This publication introduced North American and European audiences to the eloquence and exoticness of Copán's sculpture; ever since, scholars, artists, and tourists have marveled at the level of detail, the fanciful design, and the often undecipherable imagery packed into the site's public art. These qualities have

Figure 4.3. Stela H, Great Plaza, Copán. First published in a lithograph by Frederick Catherwood, 1844.

Figure 4.4. Select sculpture pieces featured in the Copán Sculpture Museum. Photograph by Lena Mortensen.

made the stone sculpture emblematic of Copán. They are also the basis for an oft-rehearsed analogy that Copán, with its artistic genius, is the Paris of the ancient world.

The primacy of stone at Copán is constantly projected to an international audience through tourism media and subsequently reinforced in every guidebook and every tour of the site. Local residents have also internalized the association of Copán with stone, and they participate in its reproduction within the tourism sphere. One medium for this reproduction is through the creation of physical icons in the form of tourism souvenirs. Tourists can buy a variety of souvenirs at Copán, but by far the most popular are replicas of the stelae and other stone sculptures, often cast in concrete but also carved in stone by local artisans. Today, every souvenir boutique as well as itinerant vendor at Copán sells some form of stone or concrete curio, ranging from cheap molded figurines to highly detailed replicas wrought from the same stone used by the ancient Copánecos. Resident storekeepers and others involved in the tourism industry consider stone carving to be essentially the only local craft in the Copán area. It is also a relatively recent tradition. This increasingly popular activity of stone sculpting has developed in part as a response to the demand of rising levels of tourism at

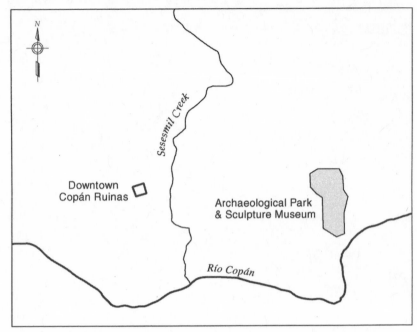

Figure 4.5. Location of contemporary settlement of Copán Ruinas, separated from the archaeological park and sculpture museum by Sesesmil Creek. Map by Steven J. Holland.

the site and consequently the growing market for these items. The past twenty-five years of research at Copán have produced a surplus of artisans who trained on archaeological projects at the site as illustrators or making replicas, and now translate their familiarity with archaeological detail into commercial success.

Residents of the small town of Copán Ruinas live next door to the archaeological site (Figure 4.5) and also use stone carvings (the replicas, that is) to represent Copán in noncommercial ways. Take for instance the example of a recent training and capacity-building program for guides and teachers in the Copán region. The program, funded by the World Bank loan project PROFUTURO,[1] was taught by professors from Honduran universities and administered by the local nonprofit Asociación Copán. At the close of the nine-month training, the group of some thirty local adult students got together to discuss gifts for the instructors, who by and large were Honduran but not from Copán. Without much discussion, the group easily agreed that the instructors should receive carved stone replicas made by a local artisan, as such items were clearly both appropriate as a symbol of Copán (even for fellow Hondurans) and distinguished enough to adequately represent their sincere gratitude.

One of the reasons why stone is famous at Copán is that it is perceived as the most expressive medium, and accessible medium, through which the ancient Maya "speak." For most visitors, and many residents, the sculptured artwork and script that has endured at the site is a form of communication that viscerally connects the past with the present. Most individuals interpret the symbols and signs according to decipherments offered by experts, transmitted through tour guides and tour books, and supplemented by their own experience and imagination. For art historians and epigraphers who undertake the inventive and frustrating task of unraveling the cosmological imagery and incomplete glyphs, the stones literally transmit the messages of their original authors, although always through the distorting lens of the present.

The semiofficial guidebook to the ruins of Copán is provocatively entitled *History Carved in Stone* (Fash and Agurcia F. 1998). This title is both a reference to the presumption that ancient Maya history is accessible through the recorded texts, of which Copán boasts many, and an explicit invocation of the site's most famous stone monument, the Hieroglyphic Stairway. This stairway is a series of over two thousand carved glyphs, the longest known text in the Americas, which was reconstructed largely out of sequence by the Carnegie Institute of Washington in the 1930s. According to Maya epigrapher David Stuart, the stairway text is concerned with the history of rulership at Copán and events during the reign of what is commonly referred to as Copán's "Dynasty" (Stuart 1996). The stairway continues to be one of the most popular and most important monuments at Copán and was specifically cited as grounds for granting Copán the status of a UNESCO World Heritage Site. In recommending Copán for inclusion on the World Heritage List, the advisory board evaluation conducted by the International Council on Monuments and Sites (ICOMOS) concluded, "Moreover, the lengthy hieroglyphic inscription on the Hieroglyphic Stairway is of considerable historic significance thus corresponding to criterion 6 [of the World Heritage Convention]" (ICOMOS 1979).

Stone at Copán, for all its notoriety and attention, is also a curious contradiction. The image of enduring stone forms a solid metaphor for the history of Copán's past. Stone is seen as permanent, unquestionable, even inalterable. It can, of course, also be seen as frozen, static, and cold. But most perceive the stone at Copán as remarkably alive—alive with imagery and detail, evocative to even the most reluctant imagination. Ironically, most of the stone used in Copán sculpture, a locally found green volcanic tuff, is notoriously soft and pliable when first quarried. This very quality of malleability is what allowed ancient sculptors to perform their craft fluidly. But this quality also makes the stones of Copán fragile: myriad environmental factors, as well as human ones, have rapidly deteriorated many stone carvings on site since their reexposure in the late nineteenth century. Deciding how to deal with preserving them has resulted in tension between the two museums, the topic to which I now turn.

Site Museum: The Copán Sculpture Museum

The Copán Sculpture Museum opened with great fanfare in 1996. Touted as a "world class museum," the sculpture museum grew out of the Copán Mosaics Project, a collaborative effort begun in 1985 and sponsored by the Honduran government to document, conserve, store, and, when possible, reconstruct disarticulated sculptural facades and monuments at the site (Fash and Fash 1997). The sculpture museum is a two-story structure, built into an earthen mound on park grounds, specifically designed to reflect "central concepts of the Maya worldview" (Fash and Fash 1996b). The museum accomplishes this through poetic details in the architectural and exhibition concepts. For instance, the four-sided main building is oriented according to the four cardinal directions, reflecting the horizontal ordering of the ancient Maya world. Exhibits are grouped topically and spatially to mimic the ancient Maya worldview of a vertical axis that connected the human world with the supernatural ones above and below. Additionally, a large opening in the center of the roof floods the entire museum with natural light, exposing the exhibits to the timeless cycle of the seasons that ancient and contemporary residents share.

As an extension of the Copán site, and a monument to its most famous products, the Copán Sculpture Museum has become a new focus for the continuous political project of centering Honduras' multicultural present in the ancient Maya past. Fostering a stronger sense of national identity was an explicit goal of all those involved with the museum's conception, including former Honduran president Rafael Leonardo Callejas, an important advocate for the project (Fajardo 1997; Fash and Fash 1997). Not surprisingly, therefore, the museum has also been the frequent backdrop for political spectacle, providing a photo opportunity for many visiting dignitaries, and more recently, the site of President Ricardo Maduro's inauguration banquet (for example, Docter 2002). With its high profile, it serves as a concentrated arena for staging the local context of global heritage, bolstering Honduras' symbolic currency as a nation with an internationally noteworthy past.

The museum has received high accolades from academic experts, as well as undistinguished travelers, who label it "one of a kind" in the Maya world. But reactions to the museum are not uniform. In addition to accolades the museum has also generated controversy and discord. The source of both the controversy and the praise are the same: varying perspectives on the stone sculpture that it houses. The museum was originally conceived as a way to both safeguard and showcase sculpture from the site, a goal agreed upon by conservation experts, concerned archaeologists, government officials responsible for the management of the country's cultural patrimony, and even the president of Honduras. But deciding to what extent pieces of sculpture should be removed from their on-site locations and placed in the museum was another matter altogether.

Take for example the case of the Hieroglyphic Stairway. In February of 1997, a group of site managers from Central American World Heritage Sites met in Copán to discuss and compare the problems of managing sites in the area. One topic of discussion was conservation of stone sculpture—in particular, what to do about the continuing deterioration of the Hieroglyphic Stairway, arguably the most important monument at Copán. Original plans for the sculpture museum had always included housing the stairway and replacing its on-site location with a replica. However, the participants at this meeting concluded that such action might conflict with the authenticity provisions of the World Heritage Convention and its operational guidelines (Esteban 1997; see UNESCO Web site). Further study was recommended, and a follow-up meeting of experts was called for that summer to discuss exactly what should be done about the stairway.

The first *reunión de expertos* (meeting of experts), held in July 1997, included North American and Honduran archaeologists, conservators, site managers, and representatives from Honduran government agencies, such as the Institute of Anthropology and History and the Institute of Tourism. As discussed elsewhere by Rosemary Joyce (n.d.), a North American Mayanist who participated in this meeting, the proposal to remove the Hieroglyphic Stairway from its on-site location again met with skepticism from a variety of representatives. According to Joyce, one representative from the Institute of Tourism argued that such a change would compromise the authenticity of the site. Another representative from an international museum argued that a "decaying original" was preferable to a "pristine replica" in terms of the experience of the site (Joyce n.d.). Of course, the proposal to relocate the stairway to the new sculpture museum in the first place came out of concern for maintaining the stairway's integrity and ultimately its authenticity as a source of information about the ancient Maya past. The group concluded that detailed study of the actual condition of the stairway was necessary before a final decision could be made.

As Joyce (n.d.) argues, these meetings reveal varying perspectives on the appropriate experience of the Copán site and on what makes it significant. These perspectives derive in part from the expertise of the individuals concerned and from their perception of what different publics should and do derive from the site. I would further argue that notions about an appropriate experience of the site and its monuments are rooted in differing senses of authenticity: specifically, the authenticity of stone.

The Site as Museum

I turn now to the second site museum at Copán, the archaeological park. Following Castañeda (1996) and his discussion of Chichén Itzá in Yucatán, I consider the Copán Archaeological Park, and probably all archaeological parks for that matter, to be museums in and of themselves. Copán, although an original place, has been deliberately and specifically crafted for public display. The symbiotic pursuits of archaeological research and tourism development have required clearing large sections of Copán's once overgrown public spaces, uncovering structures, reconfiguring fallen monuments, and adding modern amenities to facilitate both research and tourism activities. This physical and formal transformation of space is a common practice that configures ruins into places understood as "parks," and it is pursued everywhere that tourism intervenes. The result is a scripted combination of manicured lawns and uncultivated spaces, signed pathways and uncleared jungle, reconstructed buildings and unexcavated mounds, all of which are maintained on a daily basis by paid groundskeepers. Together, these modifications of Copán's landscape form a physical map that selectively guides tourists on routes through the Park and frames their vision of the ancient city in the present. As with all museums, the site follows a set of narratives of display, and as is the case with the sculpture museum, these narratives are based on the grammar of stone sculpture.

Unlike other archaeological parks and historical interpretive centers in various parts of the world that attempt to simulate past environments in the present, such as Colonial Williamsburg (Handler and Gable 1997), the Yorvik Viking Centre (Addyman 1990), and Plimoth Plantation (Kirshenblatt-Gimblett 1998), most Maya sites open to the public make little or no attempt to re-create the context in which the ancient Maya lived.[2] That is not to say that Maya sites are left, so to speak, untouched. Instead, Maya archaeological parks are specifically configured so as to retain a sense of mystery, which in the context of Maya archaeological tourism means creating an environment of individual discovery, delicately balanced by opportunity for intellectual revelation. In more concrete terms, this experience is accomplished in part by selective reconstruction and clearing at an archaeological site that allows some monuments to stand free for the camera and others to peek out from the underbrush. A crucial element in this formula is the tropical forest, which is deeply associated with Maya archaeology in the public imagination. Thus, in describing the development of Cahal Pech, a Maya archaeological park in Belize, archaeologist Joseph Ball is explicit about how designers sought to "represent a *ruined* site" by creating "the most attractive and yet natural blending of an ancient ruin and forest setting" and "avoiding the production of a barren and desolate effect" (Ball 1993: 53, emphasis in original). In the words of one seasoned archaeological tourist, "You can't separate the Maya from the jungle,"[3] and indeed the "jungle" at Copán is cultivated to provide the proper Maya archaeology experience.

When conducting tours of Copán, guides are obligated to point out which sculptures have been replaced by replicas (and also inform the tourists that the original is housed in the nearby sculpture museum). Tourists generally understand the need for conservation measures to protect Copán's sculpture, and they can see the damage that continued exposure causes. However, in my interviews with a variety of visitors, both local and international, many still expressed disappointment by what they characterize as a sense of loss. Of course, the original sculptures are not lost but merely moved. Nonetheless, the replacements on site create an entirely different experience for the visitor, most of whom mourn what they see as a modern alteration to the authenticity of the site. Other modern alterations do not seem to harm the visitor experience. In fact, bathrooms, fences, and road access are as much a naturalized and expected part of the tourism experience of an archaeological park as is a reconstructed building. But offering a replica in place of an original stone sculpture unsettles the public location of Copán's authenticity. Most tourists prefer the in situ situation.

Conversely, the singular replica housed in the sculpture museum is by far the most memorable element for many visitors. This replica (Figure 4.6) is a full-scale model of a temple, dubbed Rosalila by excavators, that was discovered buried intact under the tallest structure at Copán. The Rosalila replica is in fact the centerpiece around which the museum was constructed. Consequently, its image lingers long after others have faded. Ironically, in a museum devoted to original sculpture, it is this lone replica that attracts the most attention, so much so that the museum's director has lamented that many visitors come only to take its picture and neglect to visit the rest of the museum (Luis Reina, personal communication, 2001).

I suggest that there are several reasons for this popularity. The Rosalila temple replica, with its soaring stucco facades and blazing colors, offers the most evocative experience of the imposing artistry of the ancient Maya. It is nearly the only attempt anywhere at the site to re-create a structure that approximates the multisensory experience of the ancient Maya monumental environment. The rest of the sculpture museum, with its many individual pieces and the seven impressive reassembled building facades, pays remarkable homage to the craft

Figure 4.6. Two interior views of the Copán Sculpture Museum, showing the Rosalila replica. Photographs by Lena Mortensen.

Figure 4.7. Appropriate decay: Temple 11 at Copán. Photograph by Lena Mortensen.

and vision of the ancient Maya sculptors. But the museum's emphasis on stone is decontextualized from both the contemporary site and the ancient environment, which for many visitors results in a dead and mute experience. Reconstructed temple facades in the museum, despite the many hours of painstaking research invested to achieve best-guess accuracy, come across to some visitors as somehow less authentic.

I contend that some of the criticism of the sculpture museum derives from the same public sentiment that condemns some archaeological parks as "manicured." To some, a place that is supposed to manifest the past should not be too clean or risk the label of "Disneyfication"—a sanitized and ultimately fake version of the past. Keeping mounds uncleared and leaving sculptures on site surrounded by vegetation helps Copán and places like it maintain the authentic experience that tourists have come to expect. This sentiment most likely originates with the nineteenth-century development of a sense of the picturesque, which often incorporates elements of nostalgia (Lofgren 1999: 20–21). In short, for many, the authenticity of stone is about its enduring legacy in the midst of its decay (Figure 4.7).

But what kind of authenticity is this? I argue that this is the essence of the Maya *archaeology* experience—a particular image generated over time that reproduces the romantic tropes of nineteenth-century explorers, finding their way through the jungles of Central America to the overgrown stone cities, long abandoned. The most authentic Maya sites, from the tourist point of view, are inevitably those that best simulate the sense of discovery and decay of an idealized nineteenth-century environment, combined with enough reconstruction and clearing to permit visitors to appreciate the form and structure of the ancient cities (Figure 4.8). Recounting a visit to the site of Palenque in Mexico, Clifford reflects upon his search for "a 'pre-excavation' feeling: the tangled foliage and intense sounds that would have greeted early explorers like Del Rio Dupaix and Castañeda, Waldeck, Walker and Caddy, Stephens and Catherwood" (1997: 222). The Copán Park helps to re-create precisely this sense of discovery and mystery by providing almost no interpretive signs in the Park, a deliberate strategy to allow visitors a more emotional, even "spiritual" experience, unencumbered by contemporary rhetoric.

In effect, both of these Copán museums—the archaeological site-as-museum and the sculpture museum—are museums not of Maya culture but of Maya exploration and archaeology. This is especially evident in the site but also, in more subtle ways, in the sculpture museum. In the first place, the sculpture museum houses the products and results of many years of research at the site, not just artifacts and monuments. An exhibit plaque inside the sculpture museum reiterates the claim, "Copán is unique in the Maya world for its emphasis on sculpture." In effect, the re-created facades honor exactly who and what they are meant to: the sculptural genius of the ancient Maya. Whether or not the ancient Maya revered their sculptors and their products is unclear, but contemporary archaeologists, art historians, and epigraphers certainly do, and they have been in charge of the museum's design.

Another element of the museum's design reinforces this argument. The entrance to the museum, flanked by a large stucco serpent sculpture, is supposed to represent a sacred Maya cave, a portal to another time and place. But this cave quickly becomes a replica of an archaeological tunnel (a popular technique for exploring the layer-cake architecture at Copán), allowing visitors to be transported to the time of archaeological discovery, instead of the time of the ancient Maya. As journalist Jonathan Shaw notes, "If the dramatic entrance to Copán's new sculpture museum reveals anything it is this: the museum is the creation of archaeologists eager to share the mystery and excitement they experienced when monuments housed here were first excavated" (Shaw 1997).

Kirshenblatt-Gimblett describes all museums as representations of travel, in both space and time (1998: 139). Following routes through cleared forest paths

Figure 4.8. Copán's
West Acropolis
and Temple 11.
Photograph by
Lena Mortensen.

or tunneling through a serpent cave, visitors to the Copán site museum travel
more easily to the nineteenth- and twentieth-century places of archaeological exploration than they do to the Maya kingdoms of the eighth century AD.
While there are inherent pitfalls in re-creating "living history" and plentiful
criticism of simulated ancient environments (for example, Rowan and Baram
2004), privileging the romance of archaeological exploration over the subjects
of that exploration can also be problematic.

Authentic Maya Archaeology

The 1994 Nara Document on Authenticity (see ICOMOS 1994), which applies to
World Heritage Sites such as Copán, states that the source of a site's or object's
authenticity can include "form and design, materials and substance, use and
function, traditions and techniques, location and setting, and spirit and feeling,

and other internal and external factors." For most archaeologists, conservators, and other specialists, the authenticity of stone resides in its very originality, as well as the information that can be sourced from that original. Most tourists tend toward implicitly locating authenticity in the "spirit and feeling, location and setting" of the stone and its environment. Bruner (1994) notes that debates over authenticity are never binary, a matter of determining whether something is "authentic, or not"; instead, they are ultimately based in the power to authorize, to decide which kind of authenticity is legitimate in which context. Rather than worry about which kind of setting is more authentic for the stone sculpture of Copán, perhaps we should focus on the ramifications of placing an overwhelming emphasis on stone in the first place.

One of the stated goals of the sculpture museum is to give "Copán's modern inhabitants greater insight into the importance of the ancient sculpture" (Fash and Fash 1996b: 28). Today, local residents certainly recognize the importance of ancient sculpture, as do international tourists who flock to Copán to see it. But exalting the achievements of the past can diminish the potential for a dynamic present. This can be seen even in the small example of the tourism souvenir market. As mentioned, stone carving is perhaps the only craft for which Copánecos are known. Many contemporary sculptors have trained working on archaeological projects, and several with whom I have spoken claim that such work has given them a deep respect for the craft practiced by the ancient sculptors they mimic. But these contemporary artisans do not make a living by employing their own creativity. The most highly prized items are those that most closely resemble the original pieces on which they are modeled, and the most respected local sculptors are those who can best copy the style that has made ancient Copán famous.

Conclusion

Site museums offer extended opportunities to educate the public about a given archaeological site. They are the interpretive interface of archaeology, connecting the products of archaeological research to local, national, and international communities. If the authentic experience of a Maya site is one in which the ancient Maya are frozen in stone, waiting to be discovered, then this may serve to distance local communities from the past rather than engage them. Fash and Fash contend that the sculpture museum creates the potential for contemporary Maya and other indigenous peoples in Central America to be "strengthened by the attention and respect for the artistic achievements of their forebears" (1997: 51). Fash and Fash also note, "Increasingly the townspeople of Copán appreciate the cultural legacy of the ancient Maya and the need to not only conserve it but to understand it as part of their own cultural heritage" (1997: 50–51). However, the objects and architecture featured in the sculpture museum and throughout most of the site represent the ancient Maya elite, not the everyday people (see Pyburn 2004). These interpretive choices have been made by archaeologists, conservators, and government officials; it is possible that Maya descendants and local ladino residents might be interested in different stories about the past (Pyburn 1998). The impressive monuments may give local residents and other citizens of Honduras quite a bit to be proud of, but it may not allow them to feel truly connected to the ancient Maya past through a sense of personal heritage.

At Copán, varying perspectives on the authenticity of stone lead to very different kinds of visitor experiences that, in the end, usually have less to do with the authentic stone itself than with the context in which it is presented. Ultimately stone remains an expressive and malleable medium. Neither its meaning nor its authenticity is fixed. Perhaps there are ways to showcase this most famous of Copán's ancient products that privilege neither the ancient elite nor the nineteenth-century image of Maya exploration. If site museums focused on the everyday uses of stone, its fragility, its malleability, and its continual reinvention in both artistry and prosaic media, from the time of the ancient Maya through the present, then perhaps visitors could experience a different kind of authentic Copán. Although the history of Copán may be "carved in stone," it is by no means set in stone. Copán's history continues to change as we discover not only new data but also new ways of thinking about the past, relating to it, and most of all presenting it. As malleable as stone was once to the ancient Maya, it remains so for the many publics of the present. Ultimately this is a better metaphor for Honduras' past and the continuous process of Honduran nationalism, a project that shifts with the social context of the present and is negotiated by the power to authorize what is authentic and what is not.

Notes

1. This training program came under the subcomponent "Pre-Hispanic Heritage" of the Interactive Environmental Learning and Science Promotion Project, or PROFU-TURO (World Bank project number P057350). This project also funded the revision of the Copán Archaeological Park's Management Plan, among a host of other activities.

2. The site of Xcaret in Yucatán is an exception in the Maya world (Schuster 1999). There, too, the question of authenticity is contested on the basis of the perceived appropriate experience of a Maya archaeological site.

3. The statement comes from a survey conducted via e-mail in 2002 with clientele of Far Horizons, a well-known archaeological tour company.

5

The Kuntur Wasi Museum in Northern Peru

YOSHIO ONUKI

Introduction

Between 1988 and 2002, the University of Tokyo Archaeological Project (UTAP) conducted large-scale systematic excavations at Kuntur Wasi in the Cajamarca region of the northern highlands of Peru. Kuntur Wasi was already known as an important Formative period site with monumental architecture and important stone sculptures. One day in the first field season in 1988, the mayor of the nearby town of San Pablo came to the excavation with a group of people to voice objection to the transportation of the excavated materials to Cajamarca. They insisted that UTAP leave the materials in the municipal office. Until then, we had been taking them to the base camp at the city of Cajamarca, because there was no facility for laboratory work in the village of Kuntur Wasi or in the town of San Pablo. The situation between the townsfolk and the archaeologists was so tense as to threaten to physically block the excavation. So, UTAP agreed to deposit the materials in one room of the town office.

Then, in 1989, we made a great discovery. Three tombs, dating to about 800 B.C., were found under the floor of the central platform of the U-shaped temple located in the center of the summit area. Within the tombs were eight artistically elaborated gold objects (crowns, nose ornaments, ear ornaments). The discovery of these spectacular objects caused a sensation among the local people and a security problem for us. UTAP asked the local (Cajamarca) and national (Lima) offices of the Instituto Nacional de Cultura (INC, or National Institute of Culture) to send an official who would be empowered to take measures to solve the problem of safeguarding the objects. But neither office did anything. Reluctantly, we again left the objects in the town office.

At the end of 1989, the town mayor failed to be reelected. He suggested to the villagers that they remove the "treasure" from the town office and take it to the village because he feared that the newly elected mayor would not respect the promise of the former local government to cooperate with UTAP. The material was taken back to the village and secretly hidden in a private house.

In 1990, the fourth and fifth tombs were found at Kuntur Wasi. These contained more ornaments of gold, silver, copper, and precious stones as well as conch shell. By this time UTAP was confronting not only a locally unstable political and economic context but also real danger from Sendero Luminoso terrorists (Peru's Shining Path guerrillas). Therefore, in the middle of 1990, we decided to take those objects to Lima. This transfer was conditional upon the villagers' insistence that we would take the objects to Japan for temporary exhibition and there obtain the necessary funds to build a museum in the village so that the treasure of Kuntur Wasi might be kept and displayed there. This chapter discusses the Kuntur Wasi site museum that we were able to build, in fulfillment of the community's wishes, and its impact on the local community.

Creating a Site Museum at Kuntur Wasi

After the legal exportation procedure in Lima, we organized a Kuntur Wasi exhibition in ten cities of Japan. In Japan we were successful in raising about two hundred thousand dollars for the site museum project. In addition, the Embassy of Japan in Lima kindly added another fifty thousand dollars to our fund. With these monies the Kuntur Wasi Museum was built (Figure 5.1). It was inaugurated on October 15, 1994.

I thought that the Kuntur Wasi Museum should not be a national site museum under the control of the INC, because the museum would require two or three round-the-clock staff members and it seemed infeasible that the INC would or could pay this cost of maintenance and administration. Rather, I decided that the museum should be a kind of private museum with the active participation of the village people. Thus, the Kuntur Wasi Cultural Association

Figure 5.1. Kuntur Wasi Museum. Photograph by Yoshio Onuki.

Figure 5.2. Meeting of the Kuntur Wasi Cultural Association. Photograph by Yoshio Onuki.

was born (Figure 5.2). Once this group was legally recognized, the museum was donated to the association.

A general assembly of approximately one hundred members of the association was held. They chose me, Yoshio Onuki, as the director of the museum. Members of the University of Tokyo archaeological team together with the association officers made a manual and rules of administration. According to these guidelines, I nominated ten villagers as staff of the administrative committee.

In 1996 and 1997, as the UTAP excavations at Kuntur Wasi expanded, more tombs containing gold and other special objects were discovered on the summit area of the archaeological site (Figure 5.3). Those objects were registered and kept in the new site museum for temporary exhibition. Then all of these objects, together with the eight objects previously taken to the Museo de La Nación,[1] were sent to Japan again for exhibition. They returned to the community along with a special donation of fifty thousand dollars with which an expansion of the third floor of the site museum was built. Today the museum has a floor area of about 350 square meters in a fenced area of 800 square meters.

Happily, the INC gave the museum the permission to keep in custody all the objects, including the first eight pieces of gold. Today the museum exhibits all the original gold objects, about two hundred pieces in total, and other fine pieces of pottery as well as stone and bone objects from the excavations.

Figure 5.3. Assemblage of a Kuntur Wasi tomb with gold ornaments, found in 1997. Photograph by Yutaka Yoshii.

Several years after the inauguration of the Kuntur Wasi site museum, a police station was established, attached to the entrance gate. Then, three years ago, the association built a two-story building, the first floor being for storage and laboratory work and the second floor with three rooms for lodging. Another single-story building is under construction for storage of excavated materials.

Fortunately, the United Nations Educational, Scientific and Cultural Organization (UNESCO) agreed to carry out the restoration and preservation of the principal part of the site's ceremonial architecture (Figure 5.4), in cooperation with our Japan trust fund. The UNESCO team comprises almost the same members of the archaeological team of the universities of Tokyo and Saitama. UNESCO's restoration and preservation work was finished in 2003.

Figure 5.4. The restoration and preservation of Kuntur Wasi was finished in 2003. Photograph by Yoshio Onuki.

The Functioning Site Museum

The site museum has received between two thousand and three thousand visitors every year for these past ten years. With the entrance fee and other small incomes, the museum is able to pay its water and light bills, but it cannot afford other expenditures. It depends, therefore, on occasional donations by tourists and the Japanese archaeologists working at the site.

The museum staff is composed of peasant farmers from the small village of Kuntur Wasi. They are not paid regularly, but two or three times a year they receive a kind of "gratification" from the exterior donation fund, amounting to between one hundred and two hundred dollars each year.

Every day, except Monday, two or three staff members attend the visitors. Every Sunday, two staff members check the accounts. Every Monday, ten members of the association are rotationally called to clean the outside and inside of the museum. They are not paid. From time to time, the Ladies Committee is called to prepare a special lunch for a tourist group or for housekeeping at the lodge. The payment from the tourists for these services is saved in the committee deposit box. It is worth mentioning that these kinds of association activities were commended in 1997 by the Convenio Andrés Bello of Colombia and also

Figure 5.5. The restored temple above the Kuntur Wasi Museum. Photograph by Yoshio Onuki.

highly praised by the United Nations Development Plan as an excellent case of human development.

The Village and the Site

The village of Kuntur Wasi has only about one hundred houses with four hundred inhabitants, almost all of whom are humble peasants. It is to their credit that they have not looted the archaeological site for a long time, even after the gold objects were discovered in the archaeological excavation in which more than one hundred villagers worked as laborers and witnessed the discovery. The people of Kuntur Wasi are proud of the museum, because they are its owners and are entrusted with its administration and maintenance. The local people think that they have received the electricity, sewer system, better roads, public telephone service, and the police station because of the site museum. The sense of self-government has been remarkably elevated in comparison with its condition ten years ago. Now that the facade of the old pre-Hispanic temple is restored, the hill shines in the sun every morning. We can surely say that the site and the museum are the symbol of identity, pride, and hope for development of the village people (Figure 5.5).

Analysis

The Kuntur Wasi Museum seems to be a successful case of a site museum with active participation of the local people under a moderate guidance of Japanese archaeologists, but it must be looked at in a longer term, for there are many things to be done from now on. The Japanese archaeologists recognize that the seeming success of the Kuntur Wasi site museum has been supported by several favorable factors, which were not intentionally prepared for. On the basis of our experience, I would like to present some points that this site museum (and others discussed in this volume) has to handle.

First, there is the issue of participation of the local people. Kuntur Wasi is only one small village of peasant farmers, and the nearest small town is two kilometers away. For the local people to get to a modern city such as Cajamarca, Trujillo, or Chiclayo takes more than five hours. This means that the Kuntur Wasi village is isolated. This factor favored the definition of who the local participating people were to be. Had the community of Kuntur Wasi been a large city or even a small town, local intervention would have had to have taken some form of indirect participation through local government or perhaps an organization with a kind of exclusive membership. Even at Kuntur Wasi, we have a problem of membership in the Cultural Association. Today, after fifteen years since the foundation of the association, many young inhabitants are excluded from membership. Fifteen years ago, they were young children, but now they are young adults who are qualified to be full members in regular village activities. Some of them are already married with children. As full members of their community, they want to be members of the association. An increase in the number of members will inevitably affect not only the management of the association but also the curatorial work in the museum. Thus, participation of the local people is not as easy to define and accomplish as one might think. Clearly, it entails such questions as inclusion of all inhabitants or exclusion of some, which causes discontent among the excluded. There is also the issue of how particular museum tasks (such as reception and orientation of visitors, archiving materials, cleaning toilets, and so forth) should be divided among the participants, by whom, and how payment or recognition for the tasks is to be decided.

Given that even national museums are under financial pressure in many countries, a site museum in a remote province in Peru or any other Latin American country will suffer from financial difficulty for maintenance and activities. The production of archaeological replicas and contemporary folkcrafts is frequently mentioned as a source of revenue, but precise economic studies are lacking.

Tourism is a useful source of income, but in many cases local people do not understand tourism, especially as it concerns foreign tourists. Local people tend to expect too much from the tourists and do not offer sufficient services. At Kuntur Wasi, as in other remote archaeological sites (or those off the usual tourist circuit, such as the case discussed by Paredes and coauthors in this volume), more tourists are arriving and income from tourism is growing—but the tourists, in general, are demanding about what they expect to see and how they expect to be treated. The promotion of tourism is important, but the training of local people to receive these tourists, support for museum activities, and financial aid for infrastructural maintenance (that is, the infrastructure for the museum and tourism) are among the most urgent necessities for a site museum.

Conclusion

Site preservation, creation of local pride, and the generation of income are three of the key goals of the Kuntur Wasi site museum and, I think, any site museum. Although many problems and issues remain to be resolved at the Kuntur Wasi site museum and the restored site, we, as archaeologists, are willing and keen to collaborate. We also hope that the INC and other organizations, both governmental and nongovernmental, will help the people of Kuntur Wasi to manage by themselves, since one day UTAP will leave Kuntur Wasi. To accomplish this future goal of self-reliance, everyone from the outside must first listen to the local people and talk with them, standing on the same level with them, living in the village for some period, and being patient. This is the only way to establish the mutual understanding and trust necessary to achieve the successful participation of local people in the preservation of cultural heritage.

Notes

1. Prior to the inauguration of the site museum, we had several meetings with the village people to convince them to exhibit in the new museum not the original gold objects but excellent replicas that had already been made in Japan with the same quantity of mixture of gold and silver. We showed the villagers two sets of gold objects: the original and the replica. Finally the conclusion was reached among the people that the museum would exhibit the replicas. The eight original pieces of gold were transported from Kuntur Wasi to Lima to be stored in the Museo de la Nación.

6

The Tourist Circuit Project at Pukara, Peru

Perspectives from a Local Site Museum

G. ROLANDO PAREDES EYZAGUIRRE, GRACIELA FATTORINI MURILLO,
AND ELIZABETH KLARICH

Introduction

The Museo Lítico Pukara is the site museum for the archaeological ruins of Pukara,[1] a prehistoric regional population center dated to the Late Formative period (200 B.C.–A.D. 200) in the northwestern Lake Titicaca basin of Peru. The museum and site are in the modern town of Pucará (again, see note 1), located along the Puno-Cusco highway in the province of Lampa, department of Puno, at an elevation of 3,860 meters above sea level (Figure 6.1). The contemporary town is known throughout the Peruvian Andes as the home of the *toritos de Pucará,* the clay bull figurines (signs of prosperity and fertility) adorning rooftops from the rural highlands to the suburbs of Lima.[2] In general, the town exhibits an interesting and complicated mesh of pre-Hispanic and colonial influences on every corner.

The Museo Lítico Pukara is administered by the Puno regional office of the Instituto Nacional de Cultura (INC, or National Institute of Culture). The museum is located on the edge of the Plaza de Armas, just south of Santa Isabel, an impressive colonial church dating to the seventeenth century. Because of Inca and colonial population relocation policies, the central area of the archaeological site of Pukara is southwest of the Plaza de Armas, peripheral to the daily workings of the town, and accessed by a one-kilometer-long road past the site museum.

At the site, the monumental stone-lined terraces and sunken courts of the Qalasaya architectural complex sit at the base of the Peñon, an impressive pinkish sandstone outcrop visible across the region (Figure 6.2). This rock formation clearly influenced the location of the prehistoric center of Pukara, and its influence continues to this day, as it is a local pilgrimage destination during Fiesta de las Cruces (Festival of the Crosses) on May 3 of every year. Well above the Qalasaya platforms, there is a series of crosses that line the summit of the Peñon,

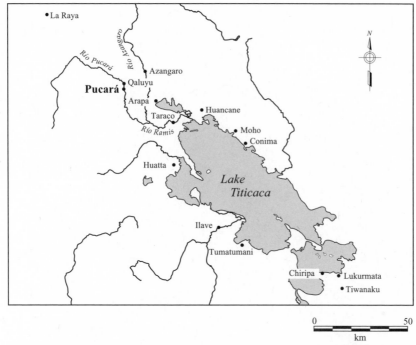

Figure 6.1. Location of the town of Pucará and the archaeological site of Pukara. Adapted from Stanish 2003. Map by Steven J. Holland.

while on the adjoining hill of Puca Orqo, a Late Formative period monolith continues to be the location of burned offerings. Given that the prehistoric site covers at least one square kilometer, it is impossible to walk through the town of Pucará or along the nearby riverbank without encountering evidence of three thousand years of dense occupation.

The first major excavation project at the archaeological site of Pukara was conducted in 1939; it was directed by Alfred Kidder Jr. of Harvard University's Peabody Museum (Kidder 1940). This project established the monumental nature of the terraced architectural complex and fully exposed the famous central sunken court and surrounding structures. None of the excavated materials remained in Pucará. Rather, the materials were sent to the Peabody Museum and to museums in Lima. There then ensued a hiatus in research at the site of more than thirty years. In spite of this break in active field projects, the collections from the Kidder excavations have been analyzed and published in a number of articles and theses (see Carlevato 1988; Chávez 1992; Franquemont 1986).

Beginning in 1975, a series of "Methods and Techniques in Andean Archaeology" courses were conducted in the central ceremonial complex of Pukara with

Figure 6.2. The Peñon and the upper platforms of the Qalasaya architectural complex at Pukara. Photograph courtesy of Nathan Craig and Nico Tripcevich.

the participation of archaeologists from across the Andes. This fieldwork-and-classroom project was sponsored by the United Nations Educational, Scientific and Cultural Organization (UNESCO), the Organization of American States (OAS), and the INC. Plan COPESCO (the Special Commission for the Coordination and Supervision of the Tourist and Cultural Plan of Peru-UNESCO) intervened for over four years at Pukara, with its efforts including both the archaeological investigation and restoration of the monumental stone architecture.[3] In addition to clarifying the Classic Pukara architectural elements, the project encountered a pre-Pukara occupation and also excavated areas of late pre-Hispanic Collao and Inca influence at the site (Wheeler and Mujica 1981).

Today, visitors can easily access the reconstructed platforms and restored central sunken court of the site's monumental architecture. Unfortunately, as will be discussed further below, major areas of the Qalasaya complex were damaged through removal and breakage of the cut-stone blocks and other areas of architecture exposed during the restoration project.

Due to the presence of Sendero Luminoso (the Shining Path terrorist movement) in the northern Lake Titicaca basin in the early 1980s, the COPESCO project was hastily concluded before many of its goals could be met. During the restoration project, the space presently housing the site museum was built as laboratories and storage rooms (architect Freddy Escobar of INC-Puno, personal communication, 2004). At the time, it was assumed that a formal site museum would be constructed at the conclusion of the field project. Years passed, and owing to a lack of funds and other limitations this was never accomplished; many of the collections were left uncatalogued, uncurated, and in a general state of disarray. This included a large collection of monoliths (many acquired from throughout the region before Plan COPESCO) and thousands of bags of ceramics, bones, and other excavated materials.

In 1999, the INC-Puno, with the support of the University of California at Los Angeles (UCLA) and the University of California at Santa Barbara (UCSB), began a multiyear project to refurbish the museum facilities and initiate new archaeological research at the site. This has been an extremely fruitful collaboration, but one not without its challenges at a variety of levels. In this chapter the goals, challenges, and progress of the project are outlined in the context of four major themes: facility improvements, community involvement, cultural resource management, and development for tourism.

Facility Development: Continuing Research and Museum Improvements

In 1999, after a twenty-year hiatus, the buildings and grounds of the museum were reopened. They were in a state of complete disrepair—the ceilings leaked, the floors were rotting, there was no plumbing, and every window was broken or missing. The task seemed daunting, but a multiyear, cooperative project was initiated between the INC-Puno, under the directorship of archaeologist Rolando Paredes, and Dr. Charles Stanish of UCLA. The project involved a number of graduate students who were planning on conducting research projects in the northern Lake Titicaca basin. A *convenio* (memorandum of agreement) was outlined in which all research projects using the facilities of the museum would contribute to infrastructure development. Since the beginning of this *convenio*, two exhibition rooms, two temporary exhibition spaces, an artifact display area, several storage areas, laboratory and work space, a patio area, and a residence for visiting scholars have been completed and are in regular use. The museum complex has housed two major excavation projects, a geological project, and a number of smaller-scale regional surveys and visiting researchers. Peruvian students from the Universidad Nacional del Altiplano (National University of the Altiplano in Puno or UNAP), Universidad Nacional Mayor de San Marcos (San

Marcos University or UNMSM), and the Pontificia Universidad Católica del Perú (the Catholic University, or PUCP) in Lima and the Universidad Católica Santa María (Catholic University in Arequipa, or UCSM), as well as a number of students from the United States, Canada, and Britain, have participated in projects housed in the research facilities. The recently recovered collections are stored in these facilities and will be incorporated into the exhibition spaces in the near future.

Collections storage is a constant struggle for space, resources, and conservation materials. A major goal of this aspect of the project, directed by Graciela Fattorini, is to complete the inventory, organization, and cleaning of materials stored in the facilities by Plan COPESCO. The reorganization of the artifact storage rooms began in August 1999 and has continued steadily in periods of two and three months. The project has various phases: emergency conservation, preventative conservation, and then selection, ordering, and organization of archaeological materials. Since participating in a course entitled "Preventative Conservation in Museums" sponsored by the U.S. Embassy in 2002, Ms. Fattorini has been applying techniques to monitor humidity, light, and insects in the museum. Presently, she is focusing on the conservation of the monoliths displayed in the open-air patio of the museum. To promote collaboration with researchers working throughout the south-central Andes, Ms. Fattorini has participated in a number of workshops and conferences in the fields of conservation and museum studies in both Lima and Arequipa.

In May 2000, the main exhibition room of the museum that features a number of monoliths and textual guides was inaugurated with the support of the INC-Lima. The patio of the museum was also remodeled to serve as a public space for visitors and community events and for the display of Pukara monoliths. The layout features a *chakana* (Andean cross) in the center of the patio with two circular areas of monoliths on each side. In the center of the patio, an altiplano *queñua* seedling was planted at the reopening of the museum.[4] Overall, the facilities are quite adequate for housing research projects; the exhibition spaces provide basic information and display materials for visitors; and in the near future, the complex will include spaces for local artisans. The goal is to have a combination of a workshop-exhibition space in which a rotation of potters from the community will demonstrate the process of pottery production and have a facility in which to sell their wares and meet with other craftspeople.

Community Involvement: From Site Museum to Local Museum

Challenges at the community level are varied and can be difficult to navigate for any newcomer, whether from as close as the nearby city of Juliaca or as far away as California. There are issues of local politics and also resource control—who "owns" the past, and who decides how it is represented? How can the popular conception of a space be transformed from one seen as catering to tourists to one utilized by the community? Integrating the museum into community life is challenging. Members of the community have commented that it is a place for tourists and removed from their daily lives. Many children and adults had never entered the museum even though it is located in the center of their town, nor did they have a sense of what "Cultura Pukara" was, beyond the monumental architecture, pieces of carved stone encountered during construction, and pottery fragments scattered throughout the adobe of their homes. A major goal of the museum has been to make it a more dynamic, educational, and accessible space. This effort is in its initial stages and has been approached through a process of experimentation and a constant dialogue between researchers and the townspeople.

In the town of Pucará, the museum is in a unique position to serve as a bridge between the local residents and the prehistoric Pukara culture through a very tangible material practice—the production of ceramics. The *toros* of Pucará are the most recognized of local wares: they are present throughout Peru and are also exported. Also, the community is known regionally for its reliable ollas (ceramic cooking pots), decorative wares, and clay stoves (Litto 1976; Sillar 2000; Spurling 1992). The modern relevance of ancient Pukara culture is materialized through this three-thousand-year-old tradition. While major elements of ceramic production have, of course, changed through time—for example, the incorporation of the potter's wheel, lead-based glazes, and, most recently, the electric kiln—many of the fundamental elements remain the same. The clay is still mined from the nearby riverbanks, then processed in household patios using similar technologies, and ultimately the finished products serve many of the same economic and social functions as they did in prehistory, such as facilitating interregional interaction (Karen Chávez 1992; Sillar 2000).

Craft-related activities are so central to daily life in Pucará that it is impossible to talk about the sexual division of labor, seasonal rounds, and local economics without considering the organization of ceramic production and exchange. In 2001, this connection was further developed through the participation of community members in a six-month field research project directed by Elizabeth Klarich. Through a work rotation, a number of families from the community participated as members of the excavation team and contributed to the interpretation of prehistoric activity areas, including a ceramic workshop area.

Figure 6.3. Examples of prehistoric and modern Pukara pottery: *top*, prehistoric *incensario* from Museo Pukara collections; *bottom*, modern vessel produced in Pucará in 1999. Photograph courtesy of Cecilia Chávez Justo.

As the field season progressed, several potters invited the research team to their homes to view production areas, observe the process of production and division of tasks within families, learn about local systems of exchange, and discuss the differences between prehistoric remains from the field project and those encountered in modern household workshop areas. As in all small towns, word spread quickly, and numerous potters expressed interest in participating in future ethnoarchaeological research on local pottery production. The ultimate goal is to create a museum exhibition space that illustrates the entire process of ceramic production—presented in Spanish, Quechua, and English—that simultaneously emphasizes the antiquity and the dynamic nature of this tradition (Figure 6.3).[5]

Local authorities, including the district mayor of Pucará, the president of the Tourism Bureau of Puno, and many members of the community, have given their support and provided suggestions about strategies for increasing community participation. For the past three years, there have been events at the museum in May for the International Day of Museums and in August for the anniversary of the Pukara museum directed at different groups of participants. In May 2003, the INC-Puno and local authorities sponsored a drawing and painting competition for students ages seven to fourteen on the theme of the museum, archaeological complex, and monoliths (Figure 6.4). There were a number of student participants, the mayor donated and presented the prizes, and the work of the finalists was displayed at the INC-Puno gallery. In August 2003, a competition of Pucareño artisans was sponsored, in which local potters were judged on their productions of clay replicas of the Pukara monoliths on display in the museum patio. Also during the anniversary, a temporary photography exhibition was opened: "Life and Textile Arts of Taquile: Weaving Life." Two weavers from the island of Taquile in Lake Titicaca attended the anniversary event to demonstrate weaving techniques and to promote cooperative projects among artisans throughout the region.

Cultural Resource Management

The issues of community involvement, public education about cultural resources, and site protection are inextricably linked. The Pukara archaeological site has been extensively damaged and defaced by graffiti over the years, in addition to the mining of pottery-tempering materials from the worked stone blocks of the sunken court. While the monumental architecture is technically a protected area, in daily practice the platforms of the Qalasaya are used for grazing livestock, growing crops, and gathering building materials from collapsing prehistoric walls.

Figure 6.4. Drawing and painting competition for Pucará students, ages 7–14, held in May 2003 at the site museum. Photographs courtesy of Graciela Fattorini.

Figure 6.5. Festival of the Decapitator held in 2000 on the terraces of the Qalasaya complex. Photograph by Elizabeth Klarich.

The first step in attempting to reduce this damage was to develop and implement programs that would take place at the archaeological site. Over the past few years, the central sunken court area, representing the earliest large-scale public architecture constructed in the Lake Titicaca basin, has been the location of a number of festivals and smaller-scale local events, such as Catholic masses. The Fiesta del Hatun Ñaqaq (Festival of the Decapitator), based on modern interpretations of a common theme in Pukara iconography, has been sponsored by the INC and local authorities on the platforms and courts of the Qalasaya. Hundreds of school children participate in dramatic reenactments using locally produced Classic Pukara period ceramic replicas (Figure 6.5). Dance groups from across the northern Lake Titicaca basin perform at the festival, and it has also included a cooking contest of local dishes. Overall, these events have been quite successful; there has been high attendance, and responses by the participants and attendees are generally positive. However, there also have been some critical comments about the focus on violence in the staging of the festival. Why does it focus on the Decapitator versus other images from Pukara iconography (see Sergio Chávez 1992 for a detailed discussion of Pukara ceramic iconography)? This is an issue that needs to be further explored and considered by the organizers when modifying the script for subsequent festivals.

In relationship to site preservation, the most critical elements of the event are the setting and intended audience. If the archaeological site is to be viewed as relevant, as a resource to be used and an area to be protected, events such as these seem to be a productive first step in that direction. The audience at the Fiesta de Hatun Ñaqaq is almost completely comprised of local residents from the town and surrounding region. This contrasts markedly with the audiences of foreign tourists that predominate larger festivals such as Inti Raymi in Cusco and the solstice celebration at Tiwanaku in Bolivia.[6] Whether or not the audience changes and/or expands will be influenced by a number of factors, including the outside role of tourism companies in Puno and Cusco and, ideally, the desires and goals of community members.

School-age children in Pucará and surrounding communities comprise a major audience for educational programs targeting site preservation. The local grade school is located at the eastern edge of the archaeological site, and this facilitated guided visits by students during the 2001 fieldwork season. The INC, in conjunction with local teachers, is in the process of developing a formal unit in the curriculum about Cultura Pukara, to be incorporated into the study of Peruvian history. Many children also have independently visited the site to ask questions and see the excavations on their walk home from school. These interactions, however informal, are an integral element of building stronger, long-term relationships between the INC, researchers, and local community members.

Tourism

The town of Pucará, located on the asphalted route of Cusco-Puno-La Paz, seems like the ideal stopping point for tourists en route. For several years tourist buses have stopped in Pucará, but only long enough to buy the famous *toritos* from the few families that monopolize the ceramics trade on the highway. In spite of the museum, the monumentality of the Pukara site, and the presence of an impressive colonial church in Pucará, attracting attention from local tourist companies has been a struggle. Visiting researchers and museum staff have utilized a number of techniques, including talking to the tour companies stopped on the highway, visiting tour-company offices in Puno, and giving guided tours to groups that visit the site during field projects. Over the last few years, the number of visitors has increased substantially through the support of a few tourist companies in Puno, but because it is a six-hour trip from Cusco to Puno, the groups are often rushed and do not visit both the museum and the archaeological site.

The most productive method we have found for increasing site visits is to work directly with the tourism students and guides from companies in nearby Puno. For example, after completion of excavations in 2001, Elizabeth Klarich had the opportunity to give a public lecture to several hundred students and tour operators at the university in Puno through the sponsorship of the local tourism bureau. The talk was followed up by visiting the site with interested tourism students, one of whom was developing a thesis project for a tourist circuit incorporating Pucará, Lampa, and the church of Tintiri in the northern Lake Titicaca basin. Another positive result of coordinating with various authorities, specifically the vice president of the Region of Puno, has been the proposal of a regional by-law that requires regional tourist companies to promote the museum and site within the tourist circuit of Lampa-Pukara-Ayaviri. Developing interest in the archaeological site, museum, and town is a slow process, but significant progress has been made toward putting Pucará/Pukara on the tourist map along with Sillustani, Raqchi, and other nearby archaeological sites over the past few years.

Discussion

Many years of work remain to be conducted in the town of Pucará and at the Pukara Archaeological Complex. Future plans include continued excavations at the site, museum development, and sponsorship of activities that promote community participation. Funding for museum development is being pursued from outside sources, both public and private. One of the goals is to sponsor interdisciplinary internships and cultural exchanges at the facilities. It is the vision of the INC-Puno to treat the Pukara museum as a pilot project for how to develop local and site museums throughout the region. By moving beyond the national borders of Peru and the geographical boundaries of the high Andes, important insights have been shared by a range of parties, and new ideas have been sparked for paths to pursue in Pucará. We look forward to continued dialogue with the community of Pucará, fellow researchers in the Andes, and museum specialists confronting similar issues across Latin America.

Acknowledgments

We thank Helaine Silverman for organizing the SAA symposium and recognizing both the relevance and the challenges of developing local and site museums. The feedback we received from other participants and the discussants at that symposium gave us a number of ideas for future directions to explore at the museum and in the town. We also thank Charles Stanish of UCLA, graduate students Amanda Cohen and Elizabeth Arkush of UCLA, Dr. Luis Repetto Málaga (International Council of Museums), the INC-Peru, Elizabeth Cornu, Puno tourism bureau, Edwin Castillo from the Pukara museum, regional and local authorities, a number of students, and the community members who have shared their time, advice, and support of this monumental project. Mil gracias!

Notes

1. As preferred by local people, the name of the modern town is Pucará (with a *c* and the accent on the final *a*), while the name of the archaeological site and ancient culture is Pukara (with a *k* and no accent on the final *a*), meaning "fortress" in Quechua and Aymara. Both spellings for both the ancient and the modern settlement appear throughout the literature; we are attempting to standardize usage.

2. There is some debate about the actual origins of the famous *toros de Pucará*. It has been argued that beliefs surrounding the *toritos* represent the transfer of Inca ritual practices involving llamas to the Spanish bull (Litto 1976). General consensus is that the *toritos* were originally produced in the village of Checca Pupuja, about five kilometers from Pucará, but the location of the latter on the Cusco-Puno train line and near the main highway led to the spread of the misconception that the bulls were actually produced in Pucará (Litto 1976: 32).

3. Results of the archaeological excavations are published in two *licenciatura* theses (Rolando Paredes and Ernesto Nakandakari) and a report to the National Science Foundation of the United States (Wheeler and Mujica 1981).

4. The hills behind Pukara are one of the few areas in the Lake Titicaca basin with stands of native trees. Their preservation is a goal of environmentalists working in the region, but it is a struggle because of a lack of fuel for firing pottery and other daily household tasks.

5. In Nazca, located on the south coast of Peru, community potters are an integral element of the local tourist industry through the production of archaeological replicas.

6. Helaine Silverman (2002) provides a detailed and thoughtful discussion of historical reenactments in the cities of Cusco and Nazca, in addition to plans for future events in other regions.

7

Building the Community Museum at Chiripa, Bolivia

CHRISTINE A. HASTORF

Introduction

That people's identities are created relationally is still true today as it was in the past. Individuals are woven into cultural groups by their shared histories, daily practices, and communicated beliefs. Groups also find identity through their constructed differences with their neighbors. From a larger vantage point, self-identifying similarities exist across regions and in transnational groups, as people find their identities formed within the context of national ethnicities (Appadurai and Breckenridge 1992). Such an active construction of group and self has always occurred, but recently, new entities are being initiated to actively promote a sense of "groupness." One avenue that is active is the local museum. Given that museums have been born out of the European colonial epoch to preserve non-Western curiosities, it is intriguing that these small-scale entities are now being harnessed by the "other" to promote themselves. Is this promotion for themselves or to create a face for the outside world that the outside world can understand?

Nested scales of identity interactions are the cultural trajectories that we study about the past in archaeology, but they also have come into our practice today through the material we excavate, present, and curate. Archaeologists have begun to realize that the curation of their material life's work is a large and looming problem, part of the larger curation of collected objects in general. The artifact and its documentation are databases for future analysis and hold an innate value. We all know that one person's or one team's analysis would not be replicated by another group, as different questions would be asked of the same material data set. Furthermore, the destruction of sites through excavation makes such curation crucial to every field project. Storage and curation of archaeological collections are a logistical problem within the discipline (Childs 1995; Davis 1998; Nelson and Shears 1996). Field archaeologists have begun to include curation as part of a planned field project in planning and proposals. When this occurs in rural settings, what does this mean for the local inhabitants? Buildings, depositories, and museums have been initiated across the globe for such purposes, based on archaeologists entering the regions. But also there is a new local interest to curate what has been found in the nearby fields. What do the residents see in these Western-derived museums? How do they feel about their world being treated like the "other"? Why are they usually happy to see a museum built in their community? What advantages are there for the local residents?

In the issue of the place of self-identity and reclaiming one's past, I join other scholars to ask: Why have museums become part of indigenous groups' identities, given the place of the museum in colonial and Western history? Are museums now becoming more multivocal and shifting from this past purpose to other purposes? More specifically, why are subaltern, indigenous peoples linking their claims to their histories, identities, and differences from the West through the Western concept of a museum? Such a question is especially relevant as I write this chapter, given the recent opening of the National Museum of the American Indian in Washington, D.C., which hosted over twenty thousand Native Americans to celebrate their history through a museum. This is a public display of heritage, curation, and self-determination on the national stage. It also is providing a place for people to gather with their heritage.

Some scholars have pointed out that our archaeological work joins the public culture in museums and outreach through curation and presentation (Karp et al. 1992). Museums have been used for the old colonialist purpose of documenting fading peoples and activities, but they are now also becoming a place for education, social development, and self-identification for groups around the globe. What are the new additional meanings of such places and institutions, and how can they be re-formed for local people?

To begin to approach these questions, I present one example from my personal history with the Aymara community of Chiripa in Bolivia. I examine the recent building of an Aymara community museum to look at why indigenous Aymara communities are interested in using a Western institution to maintain and solidify their identities. For that is what they seem to be doing across Andean South America. Are they mimicking what they have learned is important to the "Western other" in the cities? Do they see these spaces very differently from Western eyes, as places of ancestral storage, as the Incas did (Doyle 1988: 111; Moore 1996: 125)? Are these just new versions of the old caves that curated their ancestors and were places of power consolidation? Or do they gain identity and local social capital from such institutions in the modern regional political scene?

Background: Aymara Politics at Tiwanaku

My first archaeological fieldwork in Bolivia was in 1989, when I was honored to participate on the Wila Jawira project directed by Alan Kolata, who was at that time excavating at Tiwanaku, the Middle Horizon imperial city whose influence was felt across the south-central Andes (see Kolata 1993). As I moved around this great site and the community, I realized that the current inhabitants of Tiwanaku had a strong and engaged interest in the site and its interaction with the wider world, specifically with the state and the tourist trade at the site. Parts of the site are fenced in, with admission charged to these areas. Two museums also are placed at the heart of the site. Tourist buses and vans arrive at the museum entrances in the middle of the Tiwanaku River valley, returning to La Paz at the end of the day. Financially, the state seemed to be the taker gaining the ticket sales, and the tourists the givers spending money at the site, with the community diversely in the middle, perhaps selling handicrafts or meals to the visitors.

These Aymara speakers have been especially concerned about the transfer (and, therefore, loss) of many historical items to La Paz and beyond. Over the past five centuries (and probably before with the Inca), they had watched as both foreigners and urban Bolivians shifted the monumental stone carvings and artifacts out of the site and the region. For instance, beautiful stone stelae such as the Bennett Stela (Figure 7.1) have been housed in traffic roundabouts in La Paz. The Aymaras' only political wedge was the control of access to the site and its museum, since they are the people who live at the site. Periodically over the past seven years, the local syndicates have taken over the site, closing it to tourists and demanding that they be in charge of access to the site. This has had an impact on tourism and also on the policies of the Ministry of Culture, because Tiwanaku was the touristic jewel in the country's archaeological crown—made so especially as it was used strongly in Bolivia's nation building during the 1970s and 1980s. Part of the demands of the Aymara has been to have more control over the site and its contents. They wanted control over the entrance, the museum, and the placement of Tiwanaku's objects. They wanted the objects back at the site.

During the 1990s, two new museums were built with foreign money (from the Banco Interamericano de Desarrollo [BID] and InterAmerican Development Bank, along with the Spanish government) to house and curate the artifacts. These facilities created plenty of space for the objects.

The local Aymara political voice crescendoed in 2002 when the Bennett Stela (Figure 7.1) was moved out of La Paz and into the new museum, where it is the centerpiece of the museum, displayed to visitors as well as being protected from the elements. A six-member committee oversees the site, with three local

Figure 7.1. Tiwanaku's Bennett stone stela. Photograph by Christine A. Hastorf.

Tiwanaku organizations, including the mayor's office (*alcaldía*), the Ministry of Culture, the Ministry of Tourism, and the regional government (*prefectura*) of La Paz. As Clare Sammells, an ethnographer currently working in the community, noted when she wrote to me in April 2004, "effectively, the *Alcaldía* and the *Central Agraria* [agrarian community group] run the site." Now the Tiwanaku Aymara residents manage the site and its new museums in conjunction with the Directorate of Archaeology.

The cultural power among these stakeholders has shifted over the past twenty years. The Bolivian altiplano region has seen the Aymara nation gain power over their heritage as well as gain access to the associated money-making potential of this heritage. The clashes that led up to this shift in power reverberate throughout the region as acts of Aymara identity versus the still largely Hispanic

Bolivian state. Even as recently as June 2004, the Aymara closed Tiwanaku to all visitors over national political issues, curbing tourism as well as local economic trade.

Fieldwork at Chiripa

I began my own research project in Bolivia in 1992, focusing on the earlier phases that led up to Tiwanaku influence in the southern Titicaca basin. The Ministry of Culture was interested in my returning to Chiripa on the nearby Taraco Peninsula (Figure 7.2), a site that had been studied in the past by Wendell Bennett (1936), Alfred V. Kidder III (1956), David Browman (1978), and Gregorio Cordero Miranda (1978). These archaeologists all excavated on the mound. They took their artifacts to La Paz and the United States. Bennett's material is at the American Museum of Natural History in New York City; Alfred Kidder's material is curated in the University of Pennsylvania Museum. Since their work, artifacts have filtered into the Archaeological Museum housed at the Directorate of Archaeology in La Paz.

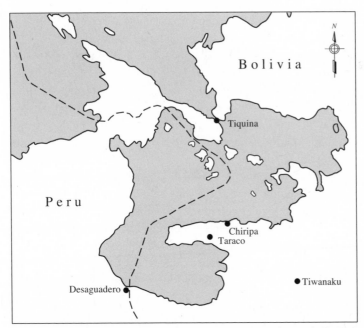

Figure 7.2. Regional map showing location of Tiwanaku and Chiripa. Map by Steven J. Holland.

Figure 7.3. A community meeting at Chiripa. Photograph by Christine A. Hastorf.

Beginning in 1992 I directed the Taraco Archaeological Project (TAP). The project has spent six field seasons (the last being June and July of 2004) at Chiripa studying the Formative, pre-Tiwanaku manifestations of early settled life. We have focused on the site as a whole, mapping and surface collecting its extent and dating its initial occupation and growth, as well as testing the three cultural terraces that form the site. We have found the best-preserved remains to be ceremonial architecture, with domestic middens surrounding these structures. In the Formative period, Chiripa was one of only four sites with elaborate sunken courts and a large population.

As we have lived and worked in two-*ayllu* Chiripa, we have gotten to know the people of this community. Most arable land is privately owned, while grazing land is communal. In regular community meetings (Figure 7.3), we have received permission to excavate, live, and work in the community. In return, all landholding families rotate through a work rotation with us. We rent community buildings to live in, and we hold open days for the school and community. As in all small communities, there are always different stakeholders, trying to pursue their desires.

While in general the community has been supportive and encouraging of our work and time there, some of the family leaders have wanted to have Chiripa's heritage remain and not go to La Paz or Tiwanaku. The idea that has been operative in Tiwanaku also became part of the discussion when we met with the community about our research. They wanted their own museum, and they wanted the Chiripa material brought back to it. There are other community museums around the region—Tiwanaku is not alone. Taraco has a museum, as does Lukurmata. This museum would change Chiripa's position in the region. The museum had somehow become an icon of identity and value within local politics in addition to housing artifacts of the residents' past.

During our first three field seasons, we boxed up our excavated artifacts from Chiripa and transported them to the Tiwanaku storage depot some fifteen kilometers away, under the jurisdiction of the Directorate of Archaeology and the Wila Jawira project. While there was always a debate about this removal of artifacts, the explanation that the community received from the Ministry of Culture as well as from ourselves was that the artifacts needed to be securely curated. This was always a sticking point with the community, as residents wanted to retain the artifacts from the excavations. The core of the Chiripa community land is the modern school, built on land that had been the hacienda's. Next to the school was a slowly collapsing hacienda structure, also located next to the Formative mound. The rooms were not safe, but there was much potential; some of the schoolteachers lived in the back. There was talk about fixing up the hacienda for a museum, but that would require money. The idea was that if the historic building of the hacienda was renovated, it could hold the material on community land. This was when I began to ask myself why this Western concept of curation, renovation, and construction was valued here, given that these same communities throughout the region had killed the *haciendados* some years earlier. Was not this structure something to tear down?

I appreciated the community's concerns for an artifactual residence and held out hope that the large, slowly deteriorating hacienda building that sits at the edge of the mound might be renovated into a visitors center and museum of the Formative period. Over the years of negotiation with ministries in La Paz, architectural visits, and much discussion, it became clear to me that the hacienda renovation was not moving forward at all quickly, although all agreed that this was a terrific idea. The architects that came out from La Paz provided a costly estimate that had no chance of being funded by Bolivian institutions. Nevertheless, clearly a museum was important to all involved. I decided that even without a building, we should at least provide a display for the community and for visitors to this early iconic site in the *sede*, the community's meeting house (which we rented when we resided in the community during the field seasons). I measured the walls of the building's communal room.

Upon returning from the field in 1998, I approached Dr. Rosemary Joyce, director of the Hearst Museum of Anthropology at the University of California at Berkeley at that time, to see whether she and her museum class could help organize wall posters. She agreed to do this, and so over the spring term, she worked with the students to design five display placards about the site and our research results. Building upon the students' core ideas, Charles Wade, a graduate student, joined the team and, working with Dr. Joyce and myself, created a layout and produced the display placards on the computer. Dr. Joyce knew of a way to make them large and laminated, making them transportable yet durable. The layout was designed to be readily comprehensible through photographs and diagrams; brief verbal descriptions were added but were not required.

The five panels included the time line of the settlement and region with its major artifact types, maps of the excavation units holding evidence for the ceremonial structures, and photographs of the residents participating in the fieldwork. I enlisted a noted Aymara linguist, Juan de Dios Yapita, to translate our brief English descriptions into Aymara and Spanish, so that Bolivian visitors, as well as any foreign visitors who came to the site, could read the placards. The idea was to be able to see photos of the excavations, as well as the artifacts, even if there was no secure place to view the objects after they had been excavated. Juan de Dios Yapita noted that the statements he translated had a very Western slant to them, making them harder to translate into Aymara, as he had to translate not only the words but also the concepts.

Thus, when we arrived to excavate in June 1999, we carried the placards that had been measured and planned to be mounted in Chiripa's sede. Both the Directorate of Archaeology and the community were pleased with the displays. During the negotiations of our stay and work, however, the community again brought up the desire for its own museum. Residents did not want to wait for some unknown date after the major renovation of the hacienda to have a museum; they wanted one in this field season. I met again with the Directorate of Archaeology to more concretely find a workable plan. Along with the community leaders, we decided to build a small structure that would house both a display room and a storage room for TAP's artifacts. The public room had to be big enough to hold the five placards.

It came to be, between June and August of the 1999 field season, that TAP, the community of Chiripa, and the Ministry of Culture (specifically, the Directorate of Archaeology, or DINAR), agreed to construct a local museum to have a place to present the Formative culture of Chiripa, the type site of early settled life in the Titicaca basin. After several meetings between the representatives of these three institutions, concerning the security of the community curation and the costs of the construction, each participating group agreed to contribute a part to build a small museum that would also hold TAP's excavated collections. The archaeologists wanted to curate their artifacts there. The Directorate of Archae-

Figure 7.4. Construction of the Chiripa museum. Photograph by Christine A. Hastorf.

ology wanted to promote tourism and make a circular route for day-trippers, and members of the community wanted their patrimony to remain in their community.

The three institutions shared in the construction of the building. The community contributed labor and the mud bricks for the walls. The Directorate of Archaeology contributed the windows, doors, and display cases. TAP contributed the other building materials for the roof, the cement, and the paint as well as paying the salary for two master builders to orchestrate the construction (Figure 7.4).

The work began simultaneously with the excavations. A place was agreed upon between the Formative mound and the hacienda, next to the road. The door opened onto the area in front of the mound, where visitors entered the mound. Local workers rotated between the excavation teams and the construction. I spent much of my time counting bricks, organizing supplies, and encouraging the master builders. The team used traditional construction methods for the foundation, the mud-brick walls, and the roof, with truckloads of river cobbles for the foundation (Figure 7.5). The structure looked similar to the community buildings that communities built throughout the Taraco Peninsula. By the end of the field season, the structure had been completed (Figure 7.6), and the opening was inaugurated in October 1999. The panels were mounted on the walls by the directorate, with plastic coverings for protection (Figure 7.7). Residents of the community gained a museum to mark their place within

Figure 7.5. The construction of the Chiripa museum progresses. Photograph by Christine A. Hastorf.

Figure 7.6. The completed Chiripa museum. Photograph by Christine A. Hastorf.

Figure 7.7. Inside the Chiripa museum. Photograph by Christine A. Hastorf.

the rich historical heritage of the southern Titicaca basin, separate from Tiwanaku.

The following year, TAP negotiated for and transported the project's artifacts from Tiwanaku storage rooms to the museum storage room (Figure 7.8). Later, Matt Bandy wrote a short history of the site in Spanish and English to be given to visitors by the guard of the museum. We gave periodic talks to the community about the material and the settlement's history. Local leaders gathered to discuss the running of the museum (Figure 7.9). I gave presentations about the archaeological history in the museum to the leaders. Over the years, visitors have begun to visit the site and its museum, though the tourist route has not really expanded, owing to the woeful condition of the circumpeninsular road.

Issues surrounding Chiripa artifacts held in the Tiwanaku museum continued, however. While we could transfer the boxed, excavated material to the new museum out of the Tiwanaku deposit, the special finds—the whole pots and the metal—had not been released but were displayed in the new museum in Tiwanaku. In 2001, I went with the local community leaders of Chiripa in their official regalia to a meeting with the head of the Tiwanaku Museum and the mayor of Tiwanaku to officially request the material. We specifically requested the pieces that were on display in their museum. We presented our request, noting that the community was upholding its end of the bargain by building a safe location for such displays and storage. The Chiripa community was taking care of the museum and opening it to tourists when requested. The Tiwanaku representa-

Figure 7.8. The storage room in the Chiripa museum. Photograph by Christine A. Hastorf.

Figure 7.9. Chiripa officials meet in the museum. Photograph by Christine A. Hastorf.

tives assured us that they were in the middle of an inventory and that as soon as it was done, they would be able to send these items back. In 2003 money came from the regional government to actually renovate the Chiripa hacienda. Two ideas were linked to this grant to Chiripa: one was to make the rooms an elegant museum; the other was to have it be a hotel for visitors. In 2004 these two ideas were still being debated, as the rooms, while in much better shape and contained in an entirely repainted building, still needed more work before either plan could occur. Each stakeholder has a different story about this situation. But the situation is such that now the Directorate of Archaeology is saying that until the new hacienda museum is completed and safe, the complete set of artifacts on display elsewhere will not be released to the Chiripa community. The community residents are still waiting for their patrimony, which sits in the Tiwanaku and the La Paz museums. Meanwhile, the caretaker's key annually rotates between the two *ayllus,* as they wait for visitors to come to the mound and the museum.

Contemplation

What does this museum and its ownership really mean to the local residents? Is this the new strategy for the creation of community identity being made manifest in Aymara communities, or does this perhaps represent a dialogue between national and regional identity being played out on the ground? Is the site museum a place of local debate or merely a place to gain some of the touristic funding and development funds, as seen in the renovation of the hacienda? Or is it just a status symbol to place the community on par with or above its neighbors? Is this the new form of monumentality? Is this a foreign status symbol or the remaking of an earlier tradition of guarding and curating the dead within the rooms on top of the mound?

I do not know whether this museum has generated more sensitivity about the site among the residents who live there. Are they more concerned with preserving the material within their fields? Are more schoolchildren learning about the site and their ancestors through the placards? Alternatively, the local actors might be charting out the possibility of an even grander reconstruction of their past, harnessing the artifacts and their descriptions to gain a stronger local and regional voice. Interestingly, Tiwanaku residents, who for years had actively struggled to gain possession of their own artifacts, now find that they are being petitioned by the residents of Chiripa, who want Tiwanaku to give back Chiripa's artifacts so that these may be curated and used in the original home of those objects. The neighbors of Chiripa are jealous and keen to have their own museums. The intercommunity tensions continue—now on the cultural stage of archaeological heritage and the world's view of their archaeological past. We archaeologists surely fit into the negotiated equation.

Still the question lingers in my mind as to why this form of self-identity, this Western strategy, has become part of the indigenous strategy. Is it the impact of global heritage and tourism entering the community? Is it seeing Tiwanaku gain prestige and funding through that community's museums? Is it "globalizing" education that supports heritage and history? Is it that a museum is much like the old ways of marking history on the landscape? Whatever it is, I hope that the future hacienda museum will include more of the Chiripa residents' own exhibits and stories about the past, which they can create without us Western archaeologists. I hope that through viewing these histories of cultural change, archaeologists can learn more about the place of the local museum in the maintenance and creation of the group for the subaltern as it is playing out today across the altiplano and all of Latin America, providing us with an understanding of how heritage and memory are re-formed in the twenty-first century.

Acknowledgments

All TAP members have helped in this project, especially Matt Bandy, Bill Whitehead, Lee Steadman, José Luis Paz Soria, and Kate Moore. Many residents of Chiripa were active in their museum creation, most intensively Emeterio Choquehuanca and Marca, the master builders of the building, and Silverio Choquehuanca, who helped with other aspects of the organization of construction, including purchasing of supplies. Eduardo Pareja and Javier Escalante of the Directorate of Archaeology in La Paz were always enthusiastically supportive of this project. Juan de Dios Yapita and Denise Arnold were gracious in helping with the translations. Rosemary Joyce was extremely generous with her time and resources, covering the cost of the placards as well as offering her museum class to work on the Chiripa material. I have learned a lot about life through working with the community on this endeavor; I am very grateful to all who are Aymara for being strong and sure about the quality and worth of their lives and ways of being.

PART 3

Site Museums at Nonmonumental Sites

8

Community Involvement in the Development of the Museum of the Lovers of Sumpa in Coastal Ecuador

KAREN E. STOTHERT

Introduction

The Museo Los Amantes de Sumpa (Museum of the Lovers of Sumpa, or MLS) was made possible by an archaeological find that, while not precisely monumental, has become an icon of national significance in contemporary Ecuador. This find, which sparked community interest, facilitated the development of an ambitious site museum and cultural center. The most challenging aspect of the development process has been creating a community-based institution in the midst of a rapidly urbanizing region where the indigenous population and the traditional community are being transformed by the forces of modernization.

In this chapter I describe the site museum (see also Stothert 1998, 2000) and discuss how individuals from local communities have been involved in its inception and management in a burgeoning urban environment. I argue that the museum and cultural center is a community-based museum because it is a venue for innovative cultural programming related to the celebration of the ethnic identity of the indigenous people of the region and also because it disseminates knowledge concerning putative community ancestors or, perhaps more accurately, the people who inhabited the locality in the past. The MLS is understood as community based because the indigenous community of the Santa Elena Peninsula is its principal referent, because members of the indigenous community have participated both in designing exhibits and in living-history performances on campus, and because the institution was designed and continues to be administered by the Foundation of the Museum of the Lovers of Sumpa (FMLS), composed of individuals drawn from the contemporary urban community. I conclude with a brief account of another newly created small museum, which demonstrates that the community museum is an idea whose time has come.

Community Interest and the Inception of the MLS

In 1978, while excavating the type site of the Las Vegas culture, my team and I uncovered the double burial that became known as the "Lovers of Sumpa" ("Los Amantes de Sumpa"). The find consists of two embracing skeletons (Figure 8.1), the remains of a woman and a man who died seven to eight thousand years ago (Stothert 1998: 24). The find instantly attracted media attention and presented an opportunity to disseminate interpretations of the Las Vegas preceramic peo-

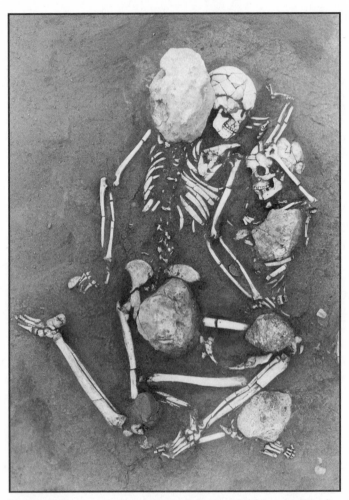

Figure 8.1. These skeletons, known as the Lovers of Sumpa, have been popularized as an emblem of the origin of the indigenous people of Ecuador. Visitors to the museum in Santa Elena are attracted by this grave, dated to 7,000–8,000 years ago, and others assigned to the Las Vegas cultural phase. Photograph by Karen E. Stothert.

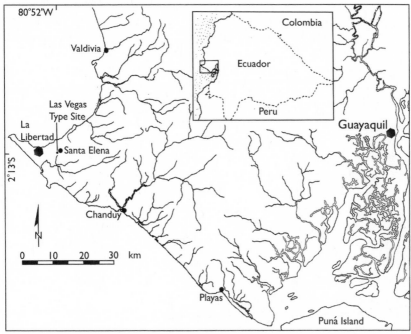

Figure 8.2. Location of the Lovers of Sumpa site museum and cultural center. Map by Karen E. Stothert.

ple who occupied the semiarid Santa Elena Peninsula in southwestern Ecuador between 8000 and 4600 B.C. (Figure 8.2).

Inasmuch as cultural values in Ecuador do not impede the public display of human remains, the find was conserved for exhibition in situ. The burial has acquired the status of "shrine" for Ecuadorians—especially children—who return frequently to marvel at the millennial embrace of the skeletons of the Lovers of Sumpa. This pattern of visiting reminds me of Andean pilgrimages to the tombs of sacred ancestors. Since the discovery of this grave, Ecuadorian poets have written odes to the Lovers; sculptors and painters have interpreted them; choreographers have composed ballets about them; and because of the attention of the popular press, people all over the country know about this prehistoric landmark.

Since 1978 I have worked with Ecuadorian collaborators to promote the Lovers as an emblem of cultural identity. The grave, professionally conserved and protected in a transparent case, is today part of our mission to inform Ecuadorians, especially schoolchildren, about the value and richness of their cultural patrimony and to foster the protection and study of heritage resources. Curiously, the term *Sumpa* (alleged to be an ancient name for the Santa Elena

Peninsula) has also experienced a contemporary revival. It names streets and restaurants and is being used by people who feel that they have roots in the peninsula and who admire the indigenous peoples and cultures of the region. Use of the word *Sumpa* is helping to create a community that is aware of its history.

The location of the MLS is an archaeological site with both national and international scientific importance (Appenzeller et. al. 1998; Stothert 1985, 1988, 1992). It is the type site of the Las Vegas preceramic culture, which is characterized by a sedentary settlement pattern supported by broad-spectrum exploitation of animal species in a rich environment as well as wild-plant harvesting and the cultivation of early domesticated species (Stothert 1992). The earliest paleobotanical evidence for the domestication of squash in the Americas was recovered from the site (Piperno, Andres, and Stothert 2000; Piperno and Stothert 2003; Stothert, Piperno, and Andres 2003). The Las Vegas type site also is the location of a Middle Holocene Las Vegas cemetery—still one of the earliest large populations of human skeletons excavated and reported in the New World (Stothert 1985, 1988; Ubelaker 1980, 1988). An especially moving experience transpires when docents at the museum describe the achievements of the preceramic people while standing on the hill where the ancient Las Vegas people once gathered to perform mortuary rituals—ceremonies of memory and intensification.

The Lovers of Sumpa are not only visually alluring but also symbolize the origin of the indigenous peoples of Ecuador, whose creativity and achievements are now being brought to light and celebrated in that modern nation. Because of the popular appeal of the Lovers, the site museum functions to protect the unexcavated portion of the archaeological site and to carry out several related missions, including the dissemination of knowledge about the earliest, well-described human occupation of Ecuador and the celebration of the endangered indigenous community. The MLS is the chief eco-cultural tourist attraction of the burgeoning urban center of Santa Elena/La Libertad/Salinas, and it also functions as a community cultural center and educational resource.

The Museum

Today the MLS is a significant tourist destination, promoted by Ecuadorian tourism institutions as part of the new "Ruta del Sol." Ecuadorian military and political authorities frequently invite visiting dignitaries to the museum campus, and the MLS is counted among the best national museums in government publications; it is mentioned in international guidebooks. While the MLS caters to international and eco-cultural tourists and vacationers from the highlands of Ecuador, it is perennially popular with local people, especially students, who

Figure 8.3. Entrance to the main exhibition hall on the campus of the Lovers of Sumpa site museum and cultural center, where visitors enjoy archaeological, ethnographic, and historic displays. Photograph by Karen E. Stothert.

arrive in class groups. The MLS is widely recognized as a major educational resource in an educationally impoverished provincial city. Now that numerous Ecuadorian universities have programs to train tour guides, college-level student visitors and interns frequent the museum. The public in general is aware of the historical importance of the site, and the MLS campus presents a positive pedagogic environment. So far the archaeological resource has been adequately protected for future scientific research.

The lack of a great "monument" in Santa Elena never seemed important. From the beginning we knew that there was more than enough material to make a museum. Today, when you visit the museum campus, you probably will walk up the hill to the cemetery, where a building, constructed over an excavated portion of the archaeological site, protects several 7,000–8,000-year-old graves and presents photographs and interpretive materials (Figure 8.3). After enjoying the main attraction of the grave of the Lovers of Sumpa, visitors usually walk with their guide to the main building, which contains an interpretive display on the Las Vegas culture, thematic exhibits, and eight large-scale dioramas and walk-in environments. These explain how history is written in the ground, the value of archaeology as compared to *huaquerismo* (looting), what archaeological analysis reveals, and the nature of the environment and environmental problems, and then a series of substantial displays explore selected aspects of the prehistoric cultures of the region, which show mostly excavated artifacts and place emphasis on the accomplishments of ancient people.

The archaeological exhibits are followed by ethnographic and historic displays including an installation concerning Colonial period tar boiling; photographs documenting the petroleum industry in Santa Elena between 1910 and 1920; rural bronze casting and blacksmithing in the twentieth century; traditional spinning, weaving, and dyeing activities; and the beautiful tables of food offered on the Day of the Dead. Visitors may peer through the windows of a mid-twentieth-century house to see a mannequin laid out in an old-fashioned coffin and wearing both handmade white clothing and a *cordón,* a kind of belt traditionally fabricated during wakes for the protection of the dead individuals. This custom has roots in the prehistoric and Colonial periods but today is part of the unique ethnic identity of the indigenous people of Santa Elena.

Outside the main building there are open-air exhibit areas spotlighting navigation and traditional foods, but people enjoy best their visit to the old-style house, furnished as it might have been in 1935. Here, elderly workers perform traditional activities and converse with the public, but living-history exhibits are possible only on special occasions when the MLS has money to pay the artisans and to buy the raw materials necessary for fabricating wooden washtubs, palm-fiber hats, and woven tablecloths and saddlebags, or for baking tortillas in an indigenous oven. Our museum guides report that several visitors, with tears in their eyes, have exclaimed that this is just like his or her grandmother's house. Sometimes elderly visitors spontaneously expound on food and other details of life in the early twentieth century, when hat weaving was the principal cottage industry in Santa Elena.

The museum is full of intriguing things to look at, and visitors are given opportunities to converse with guides (Figure 8.4), participate in activities, and enjoy live performances on special days (Figures 8.5, 8.6, 8.7). The guides are paid employees or trained volunteers, including young people who feel enthusiastic about the historical narrative and the social mission. Cultural celebration is the mission made manifest throughout the museum and in the publications sold there. Didactic texts are presented in colorful panels on the walls of the museum. These also have been gathered into a short book that may be purchased (Stothert and Freire 1997).

The contents of the museum reflect what I learned from archaeological and ethnographic research in the 1970s and 1980s. In creating the museum exhibits, I worked with indigenous people, especially the men, all natives of the peninsula, who excavated the Las Vegas type site with me (Lindao and Stothert 1994, 1995). I learned about traditional culture in the region during projects that brought me into contact with men and women who identified themselves as bronze casters (Figures 8.6, 8.7), spinners and weavers (Figure 8.5), carpenters, fishermen, cooks (Figure 8.5), housewives, bakers, tortilla makers, farmers, and petroleum

Left: Figure 8.4. A group of tourists is guided through the cemetery of the ancient Las Vegas site. Several 7,000-year-old burials have been left in situ and are displayed with interpretive materials in a special building erected on an excavated portion of the archaeological site. Photograph by Karen E. Stothert.

Below: Figure 8.5. Visitors converse with Ulberta Filomena Soriano Laínez and her sister, two of the artisans who weave and cook in the old-time house as part of the living history exhibit on the campus of the museum. Photograph by Karen E. Stothert.

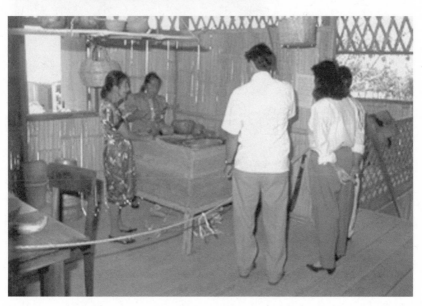

Figure 8.6. Adela Borbor works the bellows and tends the forge during a public demonstration of traditional bronze casting in the workshop located under the old-time house at the Lovers of Sumpa Museum. Photograph by Karen E. Stothert.

Figure 8.7. Bronze casters Adela Borbor and Rosa Camatón work together to pour molten metal from a small crucible into hot molds during a public demonstration of the art of making stirrups, spurs, and bridle elements, artifacts that used to be important in rural life in coastal Ecuador. Photograph by Karen E. Stothert.

workers. I played a pivotal role in the creation of the museum, accompanied perpetually by Roberto Lindao Quimí, who, until his death in 2002, guided me through rural and urban Santa Elena and verified my perceptions and interpretations. I edited his memoir (Lindao and Stothert 1995), and he nurtured me with information. Through him I learned about being a native of the Parish of Chanduy, about bearing the traditional culture of the peninsula, and about his experience as an economic refugee in La Libertad. By talking to don Roberto, his relatives, and a host of artisans and loquacious friends (called "informants" by anthropologists), I began to translate the traditional culture into a narrative suitable for public consumption. Influenced by the politics and philosophy of teachers and development workers, and encouraged by many people in Ecuador, I adopted for myself the role of storyteller for the indigenous community and for their ancient ancestors.

Of course, the exhibit design and educational materials used in the MLS ultimately were the products of a broader collaboration among museum professionals from the Anthropology Museum in Guayaquil, teachers from the Santa Elena community, and myself. We worked together to forge a narrative based on the archaeological and anthropological information that was also tailored for the diverse populations of visitors we expected and reflective of the social mission articulated by educators, spokesmen from rural communities, cultural promoters, activists, and development specialists operating in local contexts (Stothert and Freire 1997). A theme that unites the entire museum is the celebration of putative cultural ancestors. This is integrative, especially in Santa Elena, where today the bones of ancestors are believed to function as protective charms and where the dead are feted at least once a year by many indigenous families.

Today the museum speaks for the site and for the ancestors who occupied the Santa Elena Peninsula "once upon a time." Visitors enjoy the expressions of appreciation of the indigenous culture of rural coastal Ecuador that are embedded in the museum's portrayals of skillful and environmentally knowledgeable artisans, fishermen, and farmers. People associated with the MLS and who articulate its narrative are proud of the long history and prehistory of the peninsula, filled with achievements comparable to those of other ancient peoples. The MLS presents new information about the distant past while expressing appreciation for aspects of the disappearing traditions of the nineteenth and twentieth centuries that are not usually valued positively in public discourse. People in the urban community who were searching for ways to be proud of their unique identity and heritage have been supported and inspired by the creation of the museum. In other words, the MLS has adopted a rhetoric that expresses community pride. We museographers did not invent this way of speaking, but I confess that during my fieldwork in Santa Elena (spanning thirty-odd years), I have appropriated it from local teachers, community development workers, and community promoters.

Creating the Museum and Cultural Center

The MLS grew out of my long-term archaeological investigation of the Las Vegas site, which began in 1977 under the auspices of the recently established Anthropology Museum of the Central Bank of Ecuador (located in Guayaquil). In collaboration with the founding director of that museum, the late Dr. Olaf Holm, I carried out a large number of ethnographic research projects focused on the Santa Elena Peninsula and became committed to sharing the fruits of our research with Ecuadorian students and the public in general.

In the early 1980s, Dr. Holm and I wanted to give the region a museum, and at the same time we hoped to protect the archaeological site for future research. Because petroleum revenues had been flowing into the Central Bank since the 1970s, Dr. Holm thought that the government would build the Las Vegas site museum, and in fact the project was approved, but the price of oil fell and the project was never effectively funded.

Our urge to make a museum was also supported by other developments in the 1990s, as people in both rural villages and big towns began to hear the voices of political activists from indigenous organizations in Ecuador and elsewhere in Latin America. Community development organizations (these were nongovernmental organizations, or NGOs) and some schools promoted cultural and heritage education and encouraged visits to museums where people could celebrate aspects of their culture that many had learned to be embarrassed about. At this time indigenous people became more familiar with publications and television programs about themselves and their traditions, and in coastal Ecuador there were several successful small museums at Real Alto (El Mogote museum and cultural complex), Agua Blanca, and Salango, which served as models for my thinking (see chapters by Weinstein and by McEwan, Silva, and Hudson in this volume).

The idea of creating a community-based museum on the Las Vegas archaeological site matured in the 1990s as we continued to successfully disseminate archaeological and anthropological interpretations. Encouraged by teachers and students who visited the dormant archaeological site and by politicians and businessmen and -women who wanted to promote tourism and educational opportunities for the growing population, I began to think that the disparate elements of the Santa Elena Peninsula community could be mobilized to make a permanent museum and culture center.

Early in our project I worried about making a museum when only socio-economically privileged people knew what a museum was. But people in the indigenous villages repeatedly said to me, "Write this down, señorita, because when I die nobody will pay any attention to my craft." Similarly, when I gave so-called motivational lectures to social promoters and other participants in community development projects sponsored by NGOs, I frequently heard eloquent expressions of people's desire to help their families and communities remember disappearing customs and crafts. I also noted that the people of Santa Elena were familiar with ritual places where they remembered what was valuable to them, and they celebrated annually the Day of the Dead—as they still do. Some individuals seemed ready for a museum to celebrate their distinct identity—as a kind of balance to the painful knowledge that modernization was transforming their traditional way of life.

In the late 1970s, when Santa Elena and La Libertad had a population of perhaps 20,000 and most of the people were recent migrants from the rural towns of the peninsula, the newly settled urban neighborhoods were relatively traditional and homogeneous. But by 1997 La Libertad had grown into a regional commercial center of almost 200,000 people. The increase resulted from the flood of economic refugees from all over Ecuador and beyond that inundated provincial commercial centers in every Latin American country in the late twentieth century. The museum today is embedded in a continuous urban agglomeration of immigrants unfamiliar with the indigenous traditions of the previous century.

The MLS has no natural local community. When the Las Vegas archeological site was being excavated, and even when the construction of the museum building began, the campus lay beyond the inhabited area of the town of Santa Elena, but now the museum occupies a square block in the middle of a residential neighborhood, with a Mormon temple and a small hotel nearby. The first houses in the neighborhood were built by the families of the men who excavated the archaeological site, and who served as watchmen during the museum's fourteen-year gestation period, but today the neighborhood is full of ethnically heterogeneous immigrants.

I hope that with time and effort this aggregation of neighbors may be converted into a support community for the MLS, but at present there is mostly mutual ignorance between the MLS and its potential local community, although some small businesses have benefited from the presence of the museum. Currently museum programming does not cater to that diverse group of neighbors, and the exhibits celebrate the ethnic group that dominated the peninsula in the earlier part of the twentieth century. That culture is not the principal glue that binds the newborn urban society together. The people who value that culture are mostly aged, living poor in dispersed and depopulated rural towns, or scattered throughout various neighborhoods within the Santa Elena/La Libertad/Salinas urban sprawl.

The MLS is very different from the other museums of the Ecuadorian coast: it originated in a complex urban context, whereas site museums at Agua Blanca and Real Alto were developed in the context of relatively small and homogeneous local communities. In all cases, however, the museums resulted from the collaboration of members of surrounding communities and outsiders. Nevertheless, I contend that there has been significant community involvement in the MLS project. Community may be understood as a work in progress, and the museum is part of the struggle of members of the urban aggregation to create a community organization and develop community resources in the midst of a perfect storm of modernization.

I saw community commitment in the ceremony, held in the mid-1990s in Santa Elena, when (with the president of Ecuador presiding) five signatories agreed to execute the project that created the MLS. In the swirl of tremendous urban growth, the museum was inaugurated in 1997 with great fanfare and kudos for the five contributing entities. In the same period of the opening of the MLS, the peninsula obtained its first shopping mall and Chevrolet agency and, shortly thereafter, its own state university.

The first party to sign the agreement that made the museum possible was the mayor of Santa Elena. He supported the MLS project as one of his development initiatives and community projects; he threw his personal support behind the prospective museum and cultural center because he perceived it as a popular thing to do.

The second signatory was the president of the newly created FMLS. Because the Anthropology Museum in Guayaquil could not, according to its regulations, own or directly administer the prospective museum, we created an independent foundation. In developing the FMLS, I solicited participation from people whom I knew to be community minded and interested in education. Beginning with several teachers who identified with the indigenous culture of Santa Elena, we recruited more teachers and school administrators born and raised on the peninsula, some businesspeople (including both Ecuadorians and foreigners who were long-time residents of the peninsula), a city council member, and some younger people who expressed the multicultural perspective. The founding board of voluntary directors worked with a volunteer lawyer to set up a nonprofit organization designed to administer and oversee the financial wellbeing of the future museum (then under construction). The charter members of the foundation, including myself, sought a retired medical doctor (enamored of the history of the region) as our first president, thinking that his experience in community organizations and his prestige as the founder of the first public high school on the peninsula would bring honor to the board and facilitate fund-raising. Polling these people, I found that they participated in all sorts of civic and charitable organizations. Together they seemed to be broadly connected in the urban community.

I continue to think of the MLS as a "community" museum because it is governed by this board made up of individuals drawn widely from Santa Elena, La Libertad, and Salinas, and many of the directors eloquently express the values that underpin the institution: they stress the importance of knowledge of the past and pride in the cultural heritage of the peninsula. As the initial twenty members of the board of directors (including myself) labored over a charter for our nonprofit organization, we honed our goals and designed the foundation's structure. This was a great experiment in creating community.

For the past eight years, the daily functioning of the MLS has been managed by three or four employees under the supervision of the FMLS. The employees consisted of several younger relatives of the men who originally excavated the archaeological site, as well as some newcomers who identify with the indigenous tradition of the peninsula. These people, together with student volunteers, make the museum seem like a community effort. Over the years, however, conflict has developed between the FMLS and the employees, who now seem physically present but marginalized in terms of the decision-making process. The FMLS has generated a stratified situation and has also become handicapped by internal factional conflict. The foundation may have successfully created a museum community, but like many other communities it is characterized by disagreements and political struggles.

The agreement that created the museum project was signed by three other participants from beyond Santa Elena—all of which supported grassroots cultural initiatives. In the 1990s the National Cement Company, which built the museum and generously paid its operating expenses for three years, was committed to investing in community development projects in southwestern Ecuador. My participation in the design and installation of the MLS was made possible by the Fulbright Commission of Ecuador, which apparently believed that the project was good for Ecuador and that my participation reflected well on the United States government. The final signatory of the agreement that made the MLS possible was the director of the Anthropology Museum in Guayaquil, who supported the project because the development of a popular regional museum was part of the cultural mission of his institution.

This brief summary of the inception of the MLS shows how an idea developed slowly over many years, and how in the 1990s several groups of people and institutions rallied to create a community-based museum.

The Uncertain Future of the Museum

The creation of the community-based MLS may have been easier than providing for its long-term well-being. In the following analysis I describe three interrelated challenges that need to be addressed if the MLS is to thrive. These involve the financial and administrative problems of the museum, leadership and governance issues, and the development of deeper relationships between the museum and the wider urban community.

Eight years after the inauguration of the MLS, the archaeological site is protected and the campus looks clean, but budget limitations have caused maintenance problems, and the exhibits have begun to look faded. Furthermore, the exhibits that were unfinished in 1997 remain so, and there have been no new exhibits. I worry because any museum that is not changing is surely in decline.

The future well-being of the museum depends upon the successful development of an endowment or the acquisition of a generous patron to promote the growth of the institution and to provide a safety net when attendance is curtailed, such as during El Niño events or because of global economic downturns. The prospects for the MLS seemed good during the first few years of its operation, when it was receiving a monthly infusion of money from the National Cement Company, as well as support from the Anthropology Museum in Guayaquil, but now, in a time of economic stress throughout Ecuador, the MLS, which keeps its admission fee low to encourage attendance, can not maintain itself from its ticket window alone.

Although the members of the FMLS, who constitute the voluntary board of directors, knew that the museum would lose its high level of initial support, they were unprepared for that event. Furthermore, during the period of support there was a notable lack of transparency in accounting, a fact that caused serious conflicts among the members. The FMLS developed no successful strategies for fund-raising in these early years, and because of the lack of adequate financial records, the foundation was in a poor position to seek private or public funds when the institution became more needy. Although the FMLS values its status as a private, nonprofit corporation, and although it considers itself independent, the organization continues to depend upon help from the Central Bank of Ecuador to pay its employees. This situation will persist until the board finds some way to gain economic strength. Some members of the FMLS are fearful of being taken over by another institution, in which case they will lose their authority and prestige. Others wish that some outside institution would intervene to give the museum an opportunity to grow.

The FMLS is several years in arrears in making its mandatory contributions to the national social security fund on behalf of three employees (who currently are being denied access to health-care benefits because of this illegal nonpayment). This debt could result in the closure of the museum.

This apparent financial crisis is closely related to a crisis in leadership. The officers and the board of directors are divided into factions and in mid-2004 were not meeting together to discuss this or any other issue. The clash of personalities and accusations of irregularities in administrative practices have poisoned the waters. Privately members accuse other members of being egotistical and of not working cooperatively in the group. Some whom I interviewed complain that the FMLS has been exploited by its officers for personal aggrandizement or gain: they say that some individuals have found ways to employ their relatives in the museum and that this has resulted in the marginalization of some employees, a reduction in the size of the group of institutional decision makers, and the development of a kind of class warfare in the MLS. In this context, it has been impossible for the presidents of the FMLS to be effective, and the board has failed to undertake any kind of strategic planning. Some observers point to the lack of institutional continuity as a problem in Latin American organizations in general. This experiment in creating an organization managed by a community-based volunteer organization may be failing. Or this community organization may be normal and subject to conflicts the way many communities are.

Although I invested a great deal of time and energy in the creation of both the museum and the FMLS, I cannot be responsible for solving its problems, because I am a North American academic who normally spends only three months a year in Ecuador. I am honorary lifetime president of the foundation, but I have no power or authority. I no longer understand the factional conflicts that go on. At this time I actively avoid participating in the FMLS, although I am forced annually to listen to the litany of woes, which often boils down to struggles over money. For better or worse, the FMLS is the organization responsible for the management of the museum. While economic troubles that afflict Ecuador have impaired the job performance of the FMLS, I think there is a fundamental problem of leadership within this community-based organization. This seems to be an issue in other site museums as well.

It is good that the volunteer board of the MLS is composed of educators who have directed the educational mission well, but these people, who earn their livings as teachers, are overworked and underpaid. In addition, they lack experience in small-business management, they are not connected to well-to-do potential donors who might be expected or induced to support a public institution such as a museum, and they are hamstrung by a culture in which people do not make charitable donations to museums, especially not in times of economic stress. They have not been able to build an adequate community of support for the MLS. Although there is much talk in Ecuador about the efficacy of local initiative (*gestión local*), grassroots organizations require persistent and intense charismatic leadership, which has been missing from the FMLS, especially after the loss of its first two presidents because of poor health.

The lack of full-time professional leadership in the MLS has meant that problems have not been identified and solved in a timely manner, strategic planning has not been undertaken, there is no discussion of improving the exhibits (which constitute one important aspect of the educational resource), and the stewardship of the archeological site is discussed only when there is an emergency. Currently the museum has several employees who earn minimum wage and who act as guides, ticket takers, and custodians, and a security guard is paid by the city of Santa Elena, but there is no budget for a full-time director or curator. A few years ago the national Ministry of Education agreed to assign a half- or full-time teacher to the MLS, but that project was lost in the wake of a change of government.

If the museum possessed a professional director, more attention might be paid to fund-raising, public outreach, development of educational resources and maintenance, and development of exhibits and programs. A full-time director might be expected to develop craft production and marketing on the museum campus. Whereas originally it was thought that the artisans who worked in the living-history exhibits would sell their products in the museum shop (and through the web site of one of the collaborating NGOs), there was never adequate organization or leadership in this area, never adequate production, and very little attention to marketing. When the level of support for the museum was reduced, the craft activities virtually stopped. The museum shop, which has the potential to contribute to the operating fund of the MLS, has not been well managed.

Everyone agrees that the MLS is at its best when artisans and elderly people appear in the living-history exhibits and talk to the public about the good old days. At these times the museum is truly a community museum, but this part of the activity is rare—apparently because of financial constraints. The artisans and community docents have not organized themselves, because they are elderly and programmed by their culture to be passive when interacting with better-educated people in urban contexts. Leadership is absent here also.

To be fair I will state that the voluntary board has been successful in the educational and cultural programming that attracted crowds to the museum. There have been creative children's programs and special workshops for young and volunteer docents. But the several training sessions for teachers have been inadequate to meet the needs of the hundreds of teachers who bring their classes to the museum. These teachers are inadequately prepared to talk to their students about the prehistory of Ecuador, archaeology, local history, ethnic identity, environmental issues, or the disappearing traditional culture of the Santa Elena Peninsula. Professional leadership and a higher level of funding are necessary prerequisites for designing and executing the programs that are critical in accomplishing the museum's mission.

The current problems of the FMLS reflect a larger challenge facing Latin American countries and institutions. Juan Felipe Yriart has pointed out that "privatization policies and the reduction in the scope of the state, of government action, has made it of critical importance that Latin American civil societies be ready to take on new responsibilities. This is new for us [Latin Americans]. We have had a tradition of state dependency whereby the state plays an interventionist role in our economies. Thus, our civilian sector has not yet acquired the experience and vitality that exist in other . . . countries where civil societies have a tradition of participation" (1996: 145). Furthermore, Yriart points out that "the economic and monetary policies, which had to be implemented in order to reduce the public debt and control inflation, had an initial recessive impact, which increased and broadened the level of poverty," but Yriart is optimistic that "[n]ew opportunities for action have been created by the crisis we are now facing. The growing democratization in the region and the slow retreat of the public sector from many areas has provided new space for civil society, especially increased opportunity for independent action in the area of development" (1996: 145). Yriart explains that there is "no 'self-help' culture" and "no real philanthropic culture in Latin American countries": indeed, he notes, "the idea that citizens will be called upon to make large contributions to civic organizations beyond those they are compelled to make to the state is a totally new concept; it has neither tradition nor roots" (1996: 146–48). For Yriart the challenge is to "establish private institutions that will have the capacity to mobilize civic action to benefit lower income sectors, stimulate collaboration and cooperation between public and private institutions so that new and effective initiatives to improve the standard of living can be implemented" (1996: 146).

There is speculation about the future of the MLS. Some people think that it is so important locally that the City of Santa Elena will not allow it to perish. Others believe that the museum is vital for tourism and therefore that the new State University of Santa Elena (with its training program for tourist guides) will not let it disintegrate. However, in terrible economic times, these entities are unlikely to want to accept responsibility for a museum. There is no clear community coalesced around the museum that has the wherewithal to protect the institution. While the museum continues to exist thanks to entrance fees and the financial support from the Central Bank of Ecuador, the bank—under pressure from international financial organizations to curtail spending and pay down the national debt—is unlikely to be able to solve the long-term problems of regional institutions such as the MLS. It does not bode well that in Guayaquil two important archaeological museums disappeared in the wake of the collapse of private banks, and at present there is no functioning archaeology museum in that great port city.

In conclusion, my recommendation is that the FMLS focus on the financial well-being of the museum by negotiating relationships with other institutions or some aggressive form of fund-raising. The latter seems impossible because of the poor track record of the foundation in managing funds. My second recommendation is that the FMLS seek some way to hire a full-time professional manager, capable of overseeing and developing the exhibits, the cultural and educational programming, and the business aspects of the MLS. This, of course, would be very expensive or require signing an agreement with another institution.

When there is a strong hand on the tiller of the MLS, then the board of directors and the professional director of the museum might be able to address issues such as creating new exhibits and programs, training teachers, and building more dynamic relationships with the school system and with the neighboring community, which is struggling to develop itself.

The Site Museum: An Idea Whose Time Has Come

I conclude by telling the story of how one rural community created the newest community museum in Santa Elena. The MLS is an example of a site museum that was developed in an urban context but with many features of a community-based museum. Another museum has recently appeared in the rural town of San Marcos (located in the Colonche Valley, forty-five minutes by bus from Santa Elena), which is an example of a site museum that developed entirely in the minds of the local community.

In 1997 the elected authorities of the *comuna* (corporate community) called San Marcos approached me to ask for help in conserving their cultural heritage and stopping the looting that had erupted when El Niño rains ravaged their community. These gentlemen were already familiar with the MLS and other site museums of the coast, and they wanted to take control of their own cultural and environmental resources.

As a first step I sought an emergency grant from the Anthropology Museum in Guayaquil, and my colleague Ana Maritza Freire and I undertook a project of excavation in San Marcos with the explicit goal of introducing ideas about stewardship, scientific archaeology, and local history to the residents of the town, including schoolchildren and teachers as well as the community authorities. Thirteen looters and several community officials were hired to excavate with us for about three weeks, during which time we removed ten intact burials (whereas the looters had destroyed several hundred). At the same time, the authorities prohibited unauthorized digging. I analyzed the excavated materials and within a year returned them to the community. Meanwhile, at the suggestion of the comuna, Ms. Freire and I designed a small but effective exhibit, which was then mounted in space provided by the regional high school located in San Marcos. Labor was donated by members of the San Marcos community, volunteers from the staff of the Anthropology Museum in Guayaquil, and other friends of the project. Some materials and services were provided by the Anthropology Museum, and critical financial support arrived in the form of a check from the mayor of Santa Elena. The exhibit has been very popular because it makes archaeological materials from the town available to the citizens and because everyone is now more familiar with two historic caciques of Colonche who were described by an eyewitness in the sixteenth century (Benzoni 1985). The correspondence between the archaeological evidence and the written account has stimulated enthusiasm for local history.

The story does not end there. I have been impressed by how the community of San Marcos maintained and valued its small exhibit for several years. Then, in 2003, because of conflicts with the high school over the continuing use of the exhibit space, the authorities of San Marcos again moved assertively and received a major grant from the City of Santa Elena to build its own freestanding community museum in the middle of their archaeological site. This grassroots effort resulted in the inauguration of the Museum of Cacique Baltacho in August 2004. The people of San Marcos de Colonche have clear cultural goals and aspirations toward developing heritage resources for themselves as a source of local pride and to attract tourists.

Now "museum" in coastal Ecuador is not just of and for the people, but also by the people. Even without money from the central government of Ecuador, grassroots efforts are successfully creating community museums. I am sanguine about the future of site museums because they are part of the thinking of communities, politicians, activists, promoters of eco-cultural tourism, and people concerned with stewardship of archaeological, cultural, and historical resources. In coastal Ecuador, the site museum is an idea whose time has come.

9

Proyecto Las Costeñas

A Program for Training Tour Guides in the Cultural Heritage and Ecology of Coastal Ecuador

ELKA WEINSTEIN

Introduction

The culture of contemporary coastal Ecuador is an admixture of various and different groups of European settlers, African slaves, and indigenous peoples. The population is a patchwork of peoples who share nationhood but who have effectively different ideas about traditions, commerce, and selfhood. Ecuadorians mainly define themselves by where they live—coast, mountains, jungle—and many of the problematic aspects of the country's political and economic strategies are based on these strongly felt localizations. Guayaquil (the main port city) and Quito (the capital, located in the mountains) are essentially rivals, and although many of the country's elite make their homes in both cities, the majority of the population identifies with one or the other.

The coast (and Guayaquil) seems always to have been underprivileged and overlooked, perhaps because the first Spanish settlers to the area preferred the more salubrious climate of the mountains to the wet, steamy coast. The Spanish chroniclers of first contacts with the natives on the coast describe them as plying their trade in large balsa rafts from northern Peru to Colombia, but this trade was not considered valuable enough for the Spanish to concern themselves by interfering with it. There must have been a fairly large pre-Hispanic population of indigenous groups on the coast—as evidenced by the abundant remains of large communities (pertaining to archaeological cultures called Manteño or Huancavilca) throughout the low range of coastal hills and valleys—but with the Spanish conquest, much of this population probably simply died out. The people who live on the coast today self-identify as "mestizo," not as natives or indigenous, although as Karen E. Stothert indicates (chapter 8), there are surviving traditions from the earlier periods.

Proyecto Las Costeñas

Proyecto Las Costeñas was created at the Cultural Complex of Real Alto (CCRA), which is a small site museum and recreational center on the Santa Elena Peninsula on the southwest coast of Ecuador (Figure 9.1). The CCRA is located about twelve kilometers from the entrance to Kilometer 115 on the Guayaquil-Salinas highway. The complex is actually next to the community of El Pechiche, but also nearby are two other communities—El Real and Chanduy, which are both fishing ports.

The Museo El Mogote was inaugurated in 1988 as part of the CCRA. It was built beside the archaeological site of Real Alto, which was discovered in 1971 by Dr. Jorge Marcos, an Ecuadorian archaeologist. Real Alto has seen an intensive excavation program resulting in the identification of an important Valdivia or Early Formative occupation (circa 4400–1700 B.C., replete with pottery, agriculture, and ceremonialism (for a summary, see Lathrap et al. 1977). Real Alto is one of many Valdivia sites now known (see Figure 9.1), and it is one of the most important in terms of archaeological understanding of cultural developments in the Formative period in the coastal region of Ecuador (again, see Figure 9.1; see also Lathrap 1980).

Proyecto Las Costeñas was a short course, the practical objective of which was to train local women as museum docents and tour guides to the cultural and natural heritage of the coast of Ecuador. An embedded goal was to sensitize them to issues involving their national heritage and the natural environment in which archaeological sites and other examples of national heritage occur. The ongoing project is important because it is directed toward the preservation and promotion of Ecuadorian national heritage sites by making local people aware of their heritage resources, including prehistoric, historic, and ecological resources; by empowering local people to preserve and protect their own heritage resources; and by providing local women with a possible source of income.

During 2000 the course was hosted at Real Alto by Mariella García, the director of the Archaeology Museum of the Central Bank of Ecuador, and César Veintimilla, a paleobotanist who has planted many native species at Real Alto as a reforestation project. At that time the two of them were running the museum and site as members of an organization called the Asociación de Graduados en Arqueología y Antropología del Litoral (AGAAL, or Association of Students

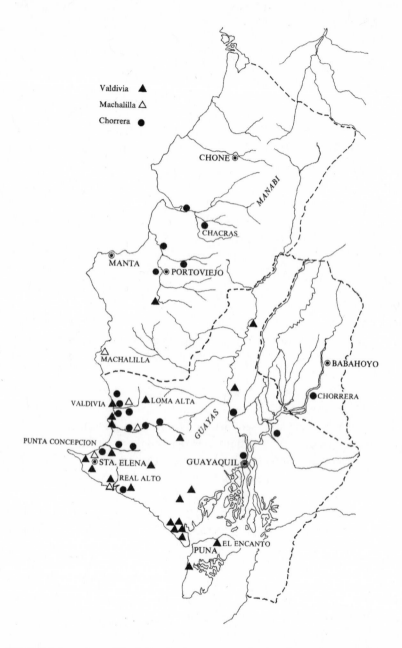

Figure 9.1. Location of Real Alto in the context of other Formative period sites of coastal Ecuador. *Source:* Lathrap 1980: map 2. Used with permission of the Field Museum of Natural History, Chicago.

Graduated in Archaeology and Anthropology) from the Escuela Superior Politécnica del Litoral (ESPOL).

The Course

The course at the Museo El Mogote was based fundamentally on group learning techniques, also sometimes called cooperative learning methods. Cooperative learning methods "strive to create a setting responsive to students' questions and productions and offer a variety of ways of increasing active student participation in the learning process. . . . when students study together in small groups, they help each other and, at the same time, develop self-direction and responsibility for their learning" (Sharan and Sharan 1994). This method of teaching is especially effective for heterogeneous groups and helps to integrate the various levels of skills and knowledge that individual members of the groups possess.

The course was a five-day set of seminars or lectures and interactive group workshops. The seminars/lectures were conducted by me in Spanish during the mornings, often with slides to illustrate points. The seminars were intended to give the participants background knowledge, which they would then use in the workshops. The course was designed to proceed in a stepwise fashion, so that the information and knowledge gained by the participants during each day would build on the information given the day before.

The first half of this course (general museology/basic museum theory and practice/exhibit design) was originally designed by me as a series of training workshops for a group of new museum employees at the Museo de Los Niños in Sucre, Bolivia, in 1994. That series was created for a rather disparate group of adult professionals who had no previous training as museum workers. Some of those workshops were modified for this course. The first day of this part of the course was devoted to giving the participants some basic knowledge of museum theory and practice, followed by an emphasis on exhibit design during the second day (see appendix for the course schedule as it was presented to the participants).

On Day 1 the assigned task for the workshops was to create an outline of an exhibit based on a theme, which had been given to each group. The outline was to include a theme, several objectives, subthemes, and content, based on a simple template, which likewise had been given to each group. Group A was assigned a theme of "Ositos" (teddy bears), Group B was assigned a theme of "Cactus," and Group C was assigned a theme of "Pescado" (fish). None of the participants was expected to necessarily have any specific knowledge of any of these themes—the object of the exercise was to focus the group's topic enough to create a coherent, workable, and presentable exhibit theme.

During the afternoon of Day 2 and part of the afternoon of Day 3 (the participants asked for extra time to work on this project), the participants worked on a design and some drawings of their exhibits, as well as on some text, which they could include as part of the exhibits. Designs were drawn on graph paper provided for this purpose.

The second half of the course (guided/walking tours) was based on similar principles but focused on teaching the participants how to adapt their knowledge from the objectives learned in the first half of the course so as to create guided walking tours suited to particular groups and audiences, including various types of presentation. Teaching was accomplished by means of lectures that presented information about how to design guided tours for different levels of audiences. The lecture for this part of the course included a tour of the museum and its resources. There was a presentation by Mr. Veintimilla on the ecology of the coast and native plants as well as a tour of the site's ecological resources.

The groups were given their assigned topics for the guided tours that they were to present; during the afternoon of Day 4, the participants worked on creating walking tours of the museum and the archaeological site. All of the assigned topics were based on the resources and information presented in the museum, so that Group A was given the topic of "Daily Life in Valdivia Times," Group B had "The Ritual Life of the Valdivia People," and Group C had "The Daily Life of Our Grandparents." On Day 5 the participants were given part of the morning to continue working on their walking tours. Work by the participants on the walking tours was slightly delayed because the participants wanted to work on their exhibit presentations during part of the afternoon on Day 3.

Final Presentations

The fifth (last) day was devoted to presentation of the tours and exhibits. First, each of the three exhibits designed by the groups was presented to the other two groups and evaluated orally by myself and by those other two groups. The second half of the day consisted of the presentation of the walking tours that each group had created, and these were evaluated orally by myself and by the other two groups.

All of the participants in the course were assembled into three working groups, and this division was intended to distribute their various areas of knowledge, skills, and expertise as equally as possible. There was some disparity in the general level of knowledge about museums and design, given that some of the participants were either at university or were university graduates and some had not finished high school. However, local knowledge of ecological conditions and customs were as important to the participants' success in this course as were their academic skills (see discussion below). The members of the three working groups were as follows:

Group A: Juan Carlos (graphic design, ESPOL), Karol (graphic design, ESPOL), Mónica (Comunidad El Real), Nora (Museo del Banco Central, Guayaquil), Vicky (Comunidad El Real), Cesibel (graphic design, ESPOL)

Group B: Yvette (graphic design, ESPOL), Margarita (Universidad Estatal, Sta. Elena), Mónica (Comunidad El Real), Maritza (Museo del Banco Central, Guayaquil), Byron (Comunidad El Real)

Group C: Yaniré (graphic design, ESPOL), Sury (Comunidad Pechiche), Roy (Comunidad El Real, guardián del Museo El Mogote), María Fernanda (tourist agency, Quito), Wendy (graphic design, ESPOL)

During the seminars/lectures, the participants were expected to listen, to take notes, and to ask questions if the explanations were not clear. Lectures were supplemented by slide shows giving examples of exhibits and signage from various international museums. Two hour-long lectures were presented by the members of AGAAL. On Day 2, Mariella García presented a lecture on Ecuador's national patrimony; on Day 3 César Veintimilla presented a guided tour of the native plants and trees, which he has been planting systematically at the museum for several years.

During the afternoons, the participants were expected to work together in their groups on the tasks that had been assigned to them. All of the participants were presented with diplomas for taking part in the course. These were signed by myself and by Mariella García in her role as the director of AGAAL.

Analysis

Although I had some initial doubts about the combination of the different characteristics and skills of the participants in the course, all of these individuals were expected to contribute to the workshops equally. On the second day of the course, Sury Cruz, a local schoolgirl from Pechiche who had been looking a bit discouraged, expressed her feelings about her academic inadequacy. I encouraged her and the other non-university-educated participants to contribute their own knowledge about the local coastal environments and their villages' traditional technologies and customs to the discussions. After this discussion and during the course of the workshops, the *comuneros'* additions to group work contributed greatly to the final exhibit demonstrations and tours.

Similarly, I also had initial doubts about communicating some fairly sophisticated theoretical ideas about museology and museum practices to many of the participants who lacked prior training in this area. Somewhat surprisingly (to me), although a few of the participants seemed to have a bit of trouble following the explanations, their verbal contributions to the subsequent discussions showed a good understanding of the main points of the lectures. Their motivation to contribute to group discussions about their projects seemed to be a prime factor in their grasp of the subject matter. I found this to be particularly true of the young women from Pechiche and Real who participated in the course. Once they had overcome their initial shyness and intimidation about their co-participants, they contributed equally to discussions and presentations and felt confident that they were making a real contribution.

Finally, in retrospect, I think the course should have been held over three weekends, rather than as a single intensive five-day course. Some of the participants from the city had trouble getting time off from their regular schedules to attend the course and would have preferred weekends, and more people might have attended the course if they had been able to attend on weekends. I also believe that the participants might have retained more of the seminar material if they had been given a chance to assimilate it over more time. The material was quite concentrated, and by the third or fourth day, everyone's attention span (including mine) was visibly lagging.

The course did train sixteen people in general museum theory and practice and in methods for giving guided tours to different types of audiences. All of the course participants now have the basic skills for planning and implementing museum exhibits and teaching others how to do this. The course participants also enhanced their presentation skills through participating in exhibits and tours developed during the workshops.

Results

Several archaeological museums on the coast (at Real Alto, Salango, Museo Los Amantes de Sumpa, and the Central Bank Museum of Ecuador) have benefited directly from the professional training that their employees received through this course.

Three local women (Sury, Mónica, and Mónica Villón) are being included in the exhibit upgrading projects, which have been undertaken by Yaniré and her students at Real Alto and Salango. Sury also has been employed as a walking tour guide at Real Alto. Margarita is currently employed at the Museo Los Amantes de Sumpa and will be using her expertise to create new programming at that museum. Maritza and Nora are currently employed at the Museo Arqueológico del Banco Central in Guayaquil, where they are working on a series of new archaeology and art exhibits for the new Museo Malecón 2000 and the Museo del Banco Central in Manta. Their enthusiastic participation in the course has been translated into an equally enthusiastic and expert contribution to the new museum exhibits at both locations. Finally, María Fernanda is a tour agent in Quito who now knows much more about her country's coastal heritage and is able to send tourists to some of the less visited locations on the coast.

Tourism in Ecuador

The principal problem with courses such as this one is, of course, continuity. Although the Museo El Mogote is used as a center for archaeological and ecological projects and is currently being served by various ongoing workshops out of ESPOL in Guayaquil, there are no trained professionals (except for the two members of AGAAL, who have other priorities) with a long-term interest in the surrounding communities' links with the museum or in educational programming. The caretakers and guardians of the site know a considerable amount about the area and are adequate guides but cannot extend the museum's current programming (such as it is). For museums and heritage sites on the Ecuadorian coast to be made into viable community-run institutions and a paying proposition, they need to offer educational programming. This is the sort of programming routinely undertaken by most museums in the United States and Canada, such as programs especially geared to school groups and foreign tour groups. The expertise to create this programming does not really exist in Ecuador.

Tourism projects in locations other than Real Alto on the coast are scattered and isolated, and each individual project jealously guards what little progress has been made with regard to successfully attracting the lucrative foreign tourist market. The Ministry of Tourism of Ecuador does not seem to recognize the possibilities of a coastal tourism circuit, apart from the well-established zones of the Galápagos Island (hundreds of miles offshore) and Salinas. Unfortunately, the beautiful Ecuadorian coast has the potential to become like Mexico's resort-dense Pacific coast, with its concomitant destruction of the environment, overcrowding, commercialism, and other undesirable effects. It also has the potential to be well managed in a similar manner to tourism in Costa Rica, for example, with much better results. Not much capital investment is necessary to achieve this potential. However, training of personnel and an overall plan are vital. Meanwhile, precious archaeological resources (such as ancient Manteño villages), ecological resources (such as mangrove swamps), and ethnographic resources (such as the aging artisans) are disappearing, being replaced or dying. Unless Ecuador does something about this dissipation of resources soon, they will simply vanish.

So far, large commercial projects aimed at partially revitalizing the economy through tourism have not succeeded in Ecuador, perhaps because most Ecuadorians do not understand why tourists might want to come to their country except to see the animals on the Galápagos Islands. However, projects such as Proyecto Las Costeñas are steps, albeit small ones, toward creating a consciousness of the resources that do exist on the coast, and how to utilize these resources to their best advantage.

Acknowledgments

Funding for the course and my stay in Ecuador was provided by the Canadian Bureau for International Education, part of the Canadian International Development Agency.

Appendix: Curso de Capacitación for the Museo El Mogote, 2000

The books used in the course were *The Good Guide: A Sourcebook for Interpreters, Docents, and Tour Guides,* by Alison L. Grinder and E. Sue McCoy; and *Interpretación Ambiental: Una Guía Práctica para Gente con Grandes Ideas y Presupuestos Pequeños,* by Sam H. Ham.
   The schedule was as follows:

Día 1. Mañana

¿Qué es un museo? Un ejercicio en posibilidades por servicios y usos y experiencia de espacio en museos; una breve historia de museos; una introducción básica a los conceptos antropológicos; la sensibilidad antropológica. ¿Quién está servido por los museos?

Día 1. Tarde

Preparación de las ideas para las exhibiciones. Objetivos, ideas centrales, importancia.

Día 2. Mañana

¿Qué es el patrimonio cultural? ¿Qué es el patrimonio natural? (César) La arqueología en el Ecuador. Huaquerismo.

Día 2. Tarde

Preparación de los textos para las exhibiciones.

Día 3. Mañana

Formación de las exhibiciones: acceso y interpretación, educación, interpretación de las colecciones, etiquetación, iluminación, orientación espacial y seguridad.

Día 3. Tarde

Preparación de las exhibiciones.

Día 4. Mañana

Paseos del sitio. ¿Dar paseos del sitio, por qué? Cómo presentar su museo o sitio para los grupos diferentes (turistas, estudiantes, niños).

Día 4. Tarde

Preparación de paseos del sitio por el Museo El Mogote.

Día 5

Presentaciones de las exhibiciones y evaluaciones. Presentaciones de los paseos y evaluaciones. Fiesta final.

10

Modular Site Museums and Sustainable Community Development at San José de Moro, Peru

LUIS JAIME CASTILLO BUTTERS AND ULLA SARELA HOLMQUIST PACHAS

Introduction

Museums are social institutions that should be studied to assess the importance of recognizing and understanding the variety and complexity of local dynamics that shape "national archaeological heritage" management (Kaplan 1994). Among museums, archaeological site museums probably offer the widest possibilities for assessing in a more comprehensive way the expectations that exploitation of given cultural resources raise in a local community. Site museums function as spaces that, if integrated into the local social landscape, may benefit the local people most directly by bringing about tourism, added income, educational facilities, and special projects such as roads, electricity, and potable water (Trotzig 1989). This, of course, depends on how much the community and/or community leaders are involved in the management of the site, which in turn is determined by the degree of collaboration between the archaeological teams and the community.

From both archaeological and museographic points of view, site museums allow for contextual presentation of collections. In site museums, objects are not radically detached from their spatial context. Therefore they simplify the problem of what to keep and what to leave out in an installation or museographic presentation, since there are no major transportation problems. On site, facilities for storage and analysis can be set up, as they are in San José de Moro, Túcume, and other archaeological projects along the north coast of Peru. There are also spaces that may be used as "work-in-progress" exhibitions to be viewed by the public. From a museological point of view, site museums make access to contextual and ethnographic information easier, which enhances interpretation of the findings and increases local community participation in the interpretive process. In addition, museums contribute to the social construction of a "national cultural heritage." The significance and connotation of this "heritage" shift in accordance with their inscription in past and present social practice and also vary according to the agenda within which they are used by the agents in charge of the management of "heritage," as well as by the social actors who appropriate the images, symbols, and objects that constitute this "heritage" and use them differently (Molyneaux 1994; Shanks and Tilley 1992).

Site museums have created expectations in the local communities because of their potential for economic, educational, and local development (Stone and Molyneaux 1994). However, community expectations have been assessed differently by the teams in charge of the managing of sites, depending on such factors as the relationship between the communities and the archaeological projects; the socioeconomic conditions in each community and the different values imposed on the archaeological collections obtained at the sites; and the role that these collections are playing in the promotion of local, regional, national, and international tourism. The demands presented by tourism entail the "commodification" of the archaeological past (Kaplan 1993), thus increasing the "economic value" of the potential tourist resources: the sites and "antiquities" that constitute part of the "national cultural heritage." In this context, sensitive management of archaeological resources related to tourism development and sustainable development come to the fore of the discussion.

Since 1987, the archaeology of the north coast of Peru has seen its most remarkable period of development, starting with the discovery of the royal tombs of Sipán (Alva and Donnan 1993). Dozens of projects have been digging into the cultural development of ancient societies in this area, which witnessed the development of some of the first complex civilizations of the Central Andes. In contrast to what was the usual practice, most of the research efforts in the past decade have been sustained, long-term programs that have involved several institutions (both national and foreign), multidisciplinary approaches, and large quantities of resources (Quilter 2002). The intellectual quality of these projects is outstanding, as evidenced by the high number of publications and scholarly meetings organized around them and the many archaeologists, including graduate and undergraduate students, who are involved in the research. One unusual aspect of many of these programs, and the central theme of this chapter, is the emphasis given by many of these projects to the conservation of their findings (both artifactual and contextual), the development of these sites into touristic resources, and the implementation of research centers, site museums, or full-blown regional museums. Archaeologists, conservators, museums, and tourism experts have started to work together to develop the sites and their surroundings. These developments, owing to their origin in the efforts and interests of the researchers and of the research programs from which they sprung, are quite distinct among themselves, reflecting the multiplicity of motivations and resources as well as the complexity of the archaeological data.

In the first part of this chapter we will focus on the development, motivations, and tendencies of this new scenario for Peruvian archaeology and cultural patrimony. We try to determine what have been the motivations and trends behind these efforts and to explain the different approaches to the issues at hand. We attempt to understand why some researchers and institutions involved themselves in the efforts, and why others, particularly non-Peruvian archaeologists, have shied away from these kinds of endeavors. The second part of the chapter is devoted to the San José de Moro Modular Museum Program (Figure 10.1).

Archaeology and Museums on the North Coast of Peru

Starting with Max Uhle in 1899 (Uhle 1913), the north coast of Peru has been one of the most privileged regions for archaeological exploration in the New World. Projects of different size and configuration have focused on the Salinar, Virú, Moche (Mochica), Transitional, Lambayeque, Chimú, and Chimú-Inca periods and on research subjects such as domestic household, monumental architecture, funerary practices, paleoethnobotany, paleozoology, diet, ceramic sequencing, craft production, social organization, military resources and infrastructure, political and ideological power, religion, iconography, ritual life, and the origin, apogee, and collapse of societies (Quilter 2002). Pioneered in a first phase by work done by Max Uhle (1913), Rafael Larco Hoyle (2001), and the Virú Valley Project (Strong and Evans 1952; Willey 1953), ancient Moche culture is conspicuously one of the most attractive areas of research in the region.

In the second phase of Moche research—the approximately forty years between the Virú Valley Project and the discoveries at Sipán—Moche archaeology was practiced almost exclusively by foreigners, under a scheme of low-profile, limited-impact, and short-term explorations, with little involvement in community development programs (Bawden 1996). The very few archaeological projects in those days were seasonal engagements carried out by North American researchers or longer programs conducted by doctoral candidates. The only exception to this rule was the Chan Chan–Moche Valley Project (CCMVP; see Moseley and Day 1982), directed by Michael E. Moseley and Carol J. Mackey, which undertook the exploration of the entire Moche Valley, including its two largest sites, Chan Chan (capital of the Chimú state) and the Huacas de Moche (the largest and most complex Moche ceremonial center). Under the umbrella of several CCMVP doctoral candidates, there were explorations of previously unknown sites, the study of settlement patterns in the valley, and research on previously unconsidered subjects such as diet and urban planning (for example, Bawden 1977; Pozorski 1976; Topic 1977). Overall, Peruvian archaeologists participated in these explorations as assistants or collaborators, not having the

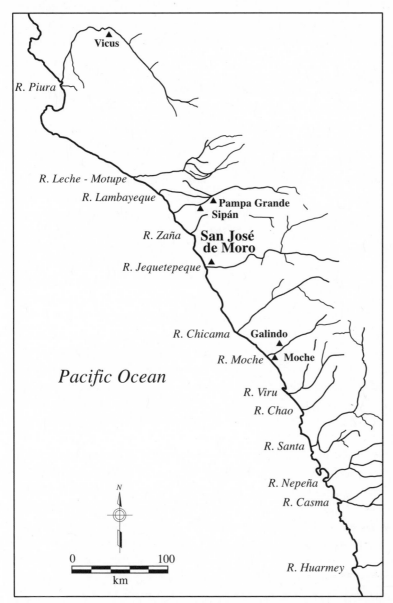

Figure 10.1. Location of San José de Moro site museum and other principal Moche sites (adapted from Garth Bawden's Figure 1 in "The Symbols of Late Moche Social Transformation" in *Moche Art and Archaeology in Ancient Peru,* National Gallery of Art, Washington, D.C., 2001). Map by Steven J. Holland.

capacity to determine research agendas or to participate in budgetary decisions. Regulation by national (Peruvian) agencies in those days, although strict, was aimed at preventing mishaps during excavations and material handling, not at building local capacities.

Up to this point the museum situation on the north coast of Peru was quite weak, with only two exceptions: the Larco Museum (originally located in Chiclín, a little town fifty kilometers north of Trujillo that was moved in the mid-1950s to Lima; see Larco 1939), and Lambayeque's Brüning Museum (focused mainly on the rich material culture of its region). Trujillo had a small and deficient university museum and a private collection exhibited in the basement of a gas station (still functioning today). Archaeological projects made no effort to include activities that would raise the awareness of the local population about their cultural heritage. For instance, CCMVP, the largest single effort to study the north coast, contributed little to the local people in terms of archaeological sites that could be visited. Furthermore, less than 20 percent of the project participants' writings were published in Spanish, whether as original material or in translation from English-language sources, making it difficult for the local archaeologists and population to appreciate the large amount of information that CCMVP had recovered through several years of work.

But we should mention that no legal requirement made it necessary to include community outreach programs in any archaeological exploration, something that is still the case today. Foreign archaeologists argue that they already had a difficult enough time raising funds for research and having to deal with the complicated and sometimes obstructionist bureaucracy of the National Institute of Culture (Instituto Nacional de Cultura, or INC) without seeking to engage in community extension programs.

In 1987, following the discovery of the Sipán tombs (Alva and Donnan 1993), Moche archaeology made a sudden and unexpected turn, starting its third phase. Since 1987 the number of archaeological projects focused on Moche, researchers, students, publications, and scholarly meetings has multiplied. At the same time, a diversity of subjects is now under investigation, often with the use of sophisticated, state-of-the-art techniques for remote sensing, computer management of databases, biological analysis, and materials analysis. Regional approaches are now common, and most of the north coast valleys have already been surveyed, some more than once.

From our standpoint, the two most important transformations occurring after 1987 have been the extension and complexity of the research program conducted on Moche sites and the fact that the leading research programs are conducted by Peruvian archaeologists, often working in collaboration among themselves and with foreign researchers. Four of the largest projects—those centered at Sipán, Huaca de la Luna, Huaca el Brujo, and San José de Moro—have conducted continuous excavations since 1987 (in the case of Sipán) or 1991 (the other three). As these projects have reached a level of maturation—through a better understanding of the sites and their surrounding regions—the extension of the excavation areas has shown a steady increase, allowing them to address issues of a larger scale. Larger projects have included the participation of specialists in physical anthropology, paleoethnobotany, ceramic analysis, and so forth. In many instances the larger programs have included subprojects conducted by specialists or doctoral students. The second characteristic—the fact that most of the larger research programs have been conducted by national archaeologists—is in part attributable to the facts that year-round permanence at the sites is required to conduct these programs and that only national archaeologists would attempt research strategies that include, for example, dismantling part of a large *huaca* (pyramid mound) to expose previous occupations. Even though it is true that Peruvian archaeologists would have had a better chance to succeed in this kind of situations, several other considerations have to be pointed out.

In the 1980s and 1990s, for the first time, large numbers of Peruvian archaeologists began to study in graduate programs in North America and Europe. Better trained, these Peruvian graduate students have added a new dimension in the way archaeology is done on the north coast, contributing new interests and concerns and becoming, for the first time, real counterparts to the foreign archaeologists, both for research design and for regulation of research activities. At the same time, although for different reasons, Peruvian corporations, such as Backus and Wiese Bank, were convinced of the promotional opportunities that funding large archaeology programs would give them. As major discoveries were being made, the public became increasingly interested in what was going on at the archaeological sites. It was evident in regions such as Chiclayo that archaeology could provide new income opportunities for the local population, generating revenues in previously unforeseen sectors because of the increasing number of visitors. Soon after, municipal and regional governments and, to a lesser degree, national agencies started to sponsor excavations aimed at the presentation of archaeological sites to the public. Likewise, foreign funding agencies and private foundations—such as the World Monuments Fund, Bruno Foundation of Fresno, Kon Tiki Museum, and the United Nations Educational, Scientific and Cultural Organization (UNESCO)—contributed funds for archaeological research and habilitation of sites for tourist purposes. Partly because of the nature of the funds and partly because of the motivations of the archaeologists and their interactions with their communities, a new kind of archaeology emerged. This process has resulted in a multitude of strategies to increase interaction with local communities (Holmquist 1997), as well as in the implementation of tourist circuits, site museums, and regional museums at most of the sites under investigation. In synthesis, changes in the way archaeology is practiced on the north coast of Peru are a combination of better-trained researchers, availability of funds, and changes in the conception of the role of archaeology in the development of the region. Ultimately, and under the leadership and patronage of the Backus Foundation, these efforts and motivations have coalesced in the integration of archaeological sites and museums as a "Ruta Moche."

Table 10.1 suggests that only archaeological research programs conducted by Peruvian nationals engage in museum creation and community-related activities. This, of course, is not true in every case. Many Peruvian programs have had no impact on their surroundings, and many foreign programs, such as Izumi Shimada's development of the Sicán Museum, are examples of foreign archaeologists who are deeply involved in the development of the communities where they carry out their work. What Table 10.1 shows, however, is a trend: the tendency is that it is more natural for nationals to engage in museum implementation and community development activities, while it is rare for foreigners to do so. The fact that outreach activities contribute little to academic advancement in the careers of North American professors and the fact that funding agencies will fund only scientific activities and not community development programs are reasons often cited to explain the sharp national division in terms of the subject discussed here. In addition, keeping a low profile to prevent harassment from the community, or even from the INC, is also cited as a reason not to engage in active community programming. The INC requires a compulsory national academic codirectorship in foreign-run projects. Regrettably, in practice and in general, most Peruvian codirectors become paid field archaeologists working for the project. However, a possibly unintended benefit of the codirectorship requirement is that the national counterpart also may be able to handle more efficiently the interactions with communities and become a readily available reference for the work done during the project.

It is now time to put into perspective the development of the new condition of archaeology on the north coast of Peru, an archaeology that is integrated with community development. In spite of the vast archaeological resources of this region, until recently tourism was not considered an important source of sustainable development on the north coast. Traditionally, Chan Chan and, to a lesser degree, the Brüning Museum were the only archaeological points of interest in the region, adding very little to local economies and providing very limited indirect employment. This situation changed dramatically after 1987 and the opening for tourism of the sites of Sipán, Túcume, Batán Grande, Zaña, San José de Moro, Huaca el Brujo, Huaca de la Luna, and Castillo de Tomoval,

Table 10.1. The Fourteen Largest or Most Conspicuous Moche Research Programs Conducted since 1899

Project Name/Site and Date	Principal Investigator(s)	Investigator Nationality	Museum Built?
Excavations (1899)	Max Uhle	Germany	No
Excavations (1930s)	Rafael Larco Hoyle	Peru	Yes
Virú Project (late 1940s)	G. Willey, W. Strong, & others	U.S.	No
CCMVP (1970s)	M. Moseley & C. Mackey	U.S.	No
Galindo (1970s)	G. Bawden	U.S.	No
Pampa Grande (late 1970s)	K. Day, I. Shimada	U.S.	No
Chavimochic (late 1980s–early 1990s)	INC–Trujillo	Peru	Yes
Sipán (1987–present)	W. & S. Alva, L. Chero	Peru	Yes
Huaca de la Luna (1991–present)	S. Uceda & R. Morales	Peru	Yes
San José de Moro (1991–present)	L. J. Castillo	Peru	Yes
Huaca el Brujo (1992–today)	R. Franco, C. Galvez, S. Vasquez	Peru	Yes
Dos Cabezas (1990s)	C. Donnan	U.S.	No
Huancaco (late 1990s–2002)	S. Bourget	Canada	No
Valle de Santa (2000–present)	C. Chapdelaine	Canada	No

Note: Reading down the table, the first three entries correspond to the first phase of Moche research, the next four to the second phase, and the last seven to the third phase. Next to the program the table lists the principal investigators and their nationalities, followed by an indication of whether or not a site museum or community outreach program was created as part of the archaeological program.

as well as the University Museum in Trujillo, the Chan Chan site museum, and the Royal Tombs of Sipán Museum and the Sicán Museum in the Lambayeque region. Other smaller or less-known—but important—sites such as Pampa Grande, Cerro Chepén, Pacatnamú, Dos Cabezas, Cañoncillo, Ascope, Galindo, and Huancaco can add new points of interest in the region.

In this process the state, paradoxically, has played a very limited role. Instead, the project directors (PIs) are the ones responsible for obtaining funding for research and habilitation of sites for tourism. For the PIs of most large projects, it is clear today that conducting scholarly investigations is not enough: sites need to be prepared for visitors and artifacts require preservation to be exhibited. Under the new scheme of corporate sponsorship, there has developed a pressure to make visible that which corporate investment has, in essence, revealed and to give it a social repercussion. At this point we reach the first in a set of problematic situations. Archaeologists are not trained to accomplish the tasks at hand. Implementing sites for visitors, building and furnishing site museums, developing conservation facilities, and engaging in multimillion-dollar projects to erect regional museums are not part of the traditional training of archaeologists. An association with museologists, conservators, architects, urban planners, and a large array of experts and technicians is necessary. Depending on the scale and complexity of the findings, different magnitudes of operations have been developed. For instance, the Sipán royal tombs and their treasure clearly deserved a large, regional museum that can raise public interest in the whole north coast. Huaca de la Luna and its impressive murals have an equally monumental character. Smaller and more localized or isolated sites and findings, such as San José de Moro and Huaca el Brujo, can have impact only in a localized area. But their impact in the development of their regions is certainly increased if these smaller sites are inscribed in larger regional tourist routes.

A Brief History of the Town of San José de Moro and Archaeology at the Site

San José de Moro is located 701 kilometers north of Lima and 4 kilometers north of Chepén, the largest city in the Jequetepeque Valley (Figure 10.1). Migrants started settling around the *huacas* of San José de Moro in the 1950s. The very few families who originally settled in San José de Moro grew in size, adding new generations to the occupation of the site. In the 1990s the contemporary settlement expanded over the archaeological site because of demographic pressure by the traditional inhabitants as well as actions of corrupt authorities who assigned lots to migrants. Today, the entire contemporary settlement rests on top of the archaeological remains of a vast Moche occupation area that features a stratigraphy more than 3 meters in depth and corresponds to 1,500 years of continuous occupation. For most of its history, the archaeological site of San José de Moro was a regional ceremonial center, with outstanding burials belonging to the elites of the societies living at the site, particularly the Late Moche. Excavations conducted throughout the area of the contemporary town have revealed that the ancient occupation is continuous; thus the entire archaeological site is overlain by the modern settlement.

Regrettably, local looters understood this stratification as well. They destroyed most of the site, including contexts within private houses, before the archaeologists arrived. Although the community is aware of its underground wealth, little interest and respect has been paid to these resources, maybe because today the inhabitants of San José de Moro are migrants to the site, many from the adjacent highlands of Cajamarca. This lack of continuity from the archaeological past to the present is in part responsible for the depredation of the site.[1] Nevertheless, the site is rich enough to still contain unspoiled sections that—properly studied and displayed—can portray its long and complex cultural history (Castillo 2001, 2003; Castillo and Donnan 1994b). San José de

Figure 10.2. The Tomb of the Priestess, San José de Moro, 1991. Photograph by Luis Jaime Castillo.

Moro offers one of the most complex and best-documented stratigraphic occupations of a ceremonial site on the north coast of Peru.

Our excavations at San José de Moro started in 1991, first as a codirected project with Christopher Donnan (1991 and 1992), then as a collaborative project with Carol Mackey and Andrew Nelson (1995 to 1997), and since 1997, directed by Luis Jaime Castillo. Spectacular findings have resulted in almost every year of excavations, bringing a high profile to the site, particularly in academic circles and the international media. Some of the most complex contexts excavated since 1991 are large chamber burials containing the tombs of Late Moche priestesses (Figure 10.2), elite chamber burials corresponding to the Transitional period. Associated with the burials we found outstanding ceramics (Figure 10.3), particularly Late Moche Fine Line bottles, stone and shell beads, metal objects (Figure 10.4), and ceramic artifacts pertaining to the Cajamarca Traditions and to Middle Horizon Wari and Wari-related styles.

During the first years of excavations, our attention focused on understanding the basic occupational history of the site, particularly in relation to its funerary and ceremonial function. Our strategy at that time involved small and restricted excavation areas aimed at finding burials. As we became more acquainted with the site, and as funding and excavation areas grew, our research strategies changed. First of all, not all elite burials were very rich, nor were

Left: Figure 10.3. Fine-line ceramic vessel found at San José de Moro. Photograph by Luis Jaime Castillo.

Below: Figure 10.4. Copper face mask found at San José de Moro. Photograph by Luis Jaime Castillo.

they necessarily Moche. A complex representation of Moche society—the rich and the poor, young and old, males and females—was present in our funerary sample. At the site we found funerary contexts pertaining to the Moche in at least five chronological phases classified as Transitional (Rucabado and Castillo 2003), Lambayeque, and Chimú, showing the same high degree of variability in gender and wealth-status. But the site was a cemetery only when someone deserving burial there died; for most of its history, the site had been a vast ceremonial center, serving the entire Jequetepeque Valley. Thus, burials were punctual events in a long-standing tradition of ceremonial feasting. Next to the burials we found a wealth of information about *chicha* (maize beer) production and consumption and other related ceremonial activities, all included in a long continuous occupational history. San José de Moro, like many other specialized ceremonial centers, provided cohesion for communities otherwise disconnected and also served as a seat of power for elites who controlled and manipulated the rituals performed there.

Excavations have continued without interruption on a seasonal basis, but with activities occurring almost year-round. Our research questions have taken us outside the site and into the immediate Jequetepeque Valley region. For the past several years, members of the project have been conducting surveys of specific areas in the valley, as well as limited excavations in key sites such Pampa Grande in the Lambayeque Valley.

One unexpected aspect of our first years of work at the site was the interest that the research provoked in people who visited us, particularly the local residents. People in town as well as many educated visitors had never seen an archaeological excavation or funerary and ceremonial contexts as they were uncovered. Almost immediately after we began working at San José de Moro, we started to hear from the locals that they were interested in being able to see the findings and showing them to other people. These first experiences were an educational process. Locals, many of whom had been looters at some point, had never seen funerary contexts fully exposed. They all knew that there were rich tombs below their feet, and they even knew what materials these burials could contain, but they had never seen a real burial with real dead people. Suddenly, a sense of attachment grew in the community. When the Priestess burials were found in Moro in 1991 and 1992, we were surprised by the sudden identification of the locals, particularly women, with the hypothetical characters that were produced by the archaeologists. The local residents wanted something left behind to show to visitors and to their own children. Several years into the project, the mayor of Chepén, Lorenzo Sánchez, embraced the idea of using the preliminary results of the excavations to launch a cultural program in town. A public park in Chepén was decorated with Moche iconographic motives, and a

Figure 10.5. Statue of the Priestess of San José de Moro at the entrance of Chepén. Photograph by Luis Jaime Castillo.

five-meter-tall statue of the Priestess was erected at the intersection of the main road in town with the Pan-American Highway. Now, a larger-than-life female, goblet in hand, greets the visitors who come into town and anyone traveling through this region of the north coast of Peru (Figure 10.5).

The Modular Museum System at San José de Moro: Things Done and Lessons Learned

In 1998 we finally felt confident enough of our understanding of the site, and of the support of the community and its authorities, to develop an exhibition strategy. Our original idea was to build a small module directly on top of the spot where the burial of the Priestess was found. This was not feasible, because the spot had since been somewhat damaged. Alternative sites for the module were discussed with the community, and finally it was decided that the best spot was a vacant area where the community had long wanted a plaza. As the module was being built with resources from the project, the Bruno Foundation, and the Municipality of Chepén, the community organized itself and the plaza was finally put together. The inauguration of the first exhibition module (Figure 10.6) thus coincided with the inauguration of the main plaza of San José de Moro. As we were dealing with the issue of how to build the module, how large to make it, what services to include, and where to place it, several concepts came to mind that ended up shaping the way the project has developed since. Clearly, although a big effort had to be made to put together the module, long-term maintenance would not be easy to address. The module had to be built of materials that could withstand time and weather, and it could not include services that would require paying monthly bills. We therefore decided to build the module using only local expertise, materials, and construction techniques, so that any required maintenance could be done locally; maintenance of the modules would require very little work by the project guard on site. No services (running water and electricity) were required, because we did not expect nightly visitors, and these services, anyway, were not available in town. What to exhibit was another issue to deal with. We decided that the first module had to feature the Tomb of the Priestess because every visitor who comes to San José de Moro wants to see the "real" Priestess as she was found (Figure 10.7). In the implementation of the tomb, no "originals" could be used; thus, replicas were made and set in the tomb in such way that removal is almost impossible.

Our discussion of form, content, location, and purpose led us to the development of the idea that whatever we did had to be self-supporting in the long run

Figure 10.6. Module Number 1: The Tomb of the Priestess. Photograph by Luis Jaime Castillo.

Figure 10.7. Inside Module Number 1: reconstruction of the Tomb of the Priestess. Photograph by Luis Jaime Castillo.

and had to contribute to a larger scheme of community development. The idea to develop a number of modules came to mind. We had no funds and also, to avoid alienating the local residents, no intention of building a museum larger than any structure in town. Rather, we wanted to start and complete one fully furnished module each season, so that at the end of the process there would be a sequence of modules telling the story of San José de Moro in the past and in the present.

On the basis of these ideas, we developed a plan for nine modules that would be built throughout town over the course of several years (Figure 10.8). Although each module would be different, adapting to the kind of context exhibited, all would be small and sturdy.

Our second module was built next to the primary school in town. We managed to get a donation of a prefabricated structure from the local Eternit (water tanks and toilets) firm, which constructed to our specification a single-room structure measuring fifty square meters (Figure 10.9). Our idea was to locate a children's museum inside. Although the idea is still in play, we have not been successful in finding a museum professional interested in implementing a children's museum. Instead, we lent the second module to the elementary school

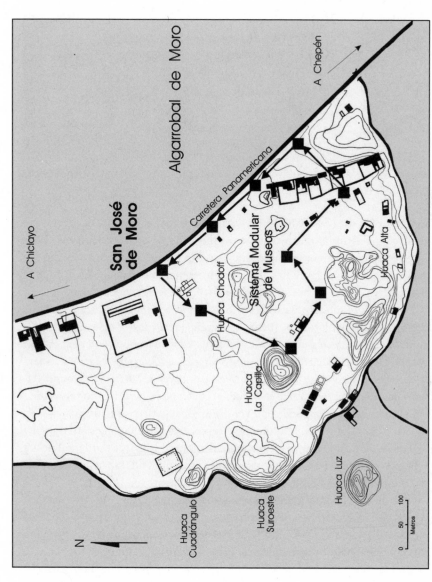

Figure 10.8. Location of the nine projected modules at San José de Moro. Map by Luis Jaime Castillo.

Figure 10.9. Children's Module Number 2, next to the town's elementary school. Photograph by Luis Jaime Castillo.

for classroom use (Figure 10.10). At least the children in San José de Moro have received a classroom much better than the others they have. Lately we have invested resources in basic bathrooms for both the local kindergarten and the elementary school (Figure 10.11). It is our intention to pursue the furnishing of the children's museum but sharing its use with the local school.

For the third module, we decided to use an idea from the Huaca de la Luna and Huaca el Brujo projects, that is, to exhibit a real excavation area with relevant findings protected under a roof constructed with bamboo and reed. At San José de Moro we selected and prepared a large, 144-square-meter area, 3 meters deep, where Late Moche, Transitional, and Lambayeque burials were found. After excavation and removal of the original contexts, each burial was reprepared with imitation skeletons and copies of the original pottery. A stairway was built so that visitors can walk into the area, experiencing the complex stratigraphy and the superpositioning of archaeological findings. Thus, the third module is a visit to a real archaeological unit, where the contextual and associative character of burials of different periods can be inspected (Figure 10.12).

The fourth module is the guardhouse, storehouse, and research facility, where we also receive visitors (Figure 10.13). For the development of the third and fourth modules, the Bruno Foundation, the Municipality of Chepén, and the San José de Moro Archaeological Project contributed funds.

Finally, the fifth module is a project developed in conjunction with the Backus Foundation and the "Ruta Moche" Program. This module is a children's archaeological activity area. Using an old excavation area (Figure 10.14), we have implemented areas where groups of children can dig and find an ancient cooking and storage facility, including large vessels, hearths, grinding stones,

Figure 10.10. Classroom use inside Module Number 2. Photograph by Luis Jaime Castillo.

Figure 10.11. Next to Module Number 2 are new toilets (left side of photograph) for the schoolchildren. Photograph by Luis Jaime Castillo.

Figure 10.12. Module Number 3, where a real archaeological unit with the contextual and associative character of burials of different periods can be inspected. Photograph by Luis Jaime Castillo.

and refuse areas; an ancient tomb, including its matrix and associated ceramic and metal findings; and a little shrine decorated with complex mural paintings. Groups of children, ages ten to thirteen, come to the site twice a week to dig the units and "discover" artifacts and contexts (Figure 10.15). Their activities consist of the excavation and interpretation of the findings. Since we have two settings of each kind, two groups can contrast their interpretations and reach a better

Figure 10.13. Module Number 4 is the guardhouse, storehouse, and research facility at San José de Moro, shown here with project participants from the 2001 field season. Photograph by Luis Jaime Castillo.

Figure 10.14. An old excavation area of the site becomes an activity area for children in Module Number 5. Photograph by Luis Jaime Castillo.

Figure 10.15. Inauguration of Module Number 5. Photograph by Luis Jaime Castillo.

understanding of the type of settings they are studying. This activity module is aimed at schoolchildren from San José de Moro and from the larger Chepén School District.

Thus far, and with a lot of help from friends and patrons, we have implemented five modules at San José de Moro. We have plans to roof a very interesting area next to Module 2, where we found outstanding Transitional burials, and to start excavations inside town to localize future modules next to the actual houses. But our plans have run into two unexpected problems. First, it would be better to place modules evenly throughout town so that the attractiveness of the site is raised and to create contact points between visitors and the community—however, it is actually more interesting for visitors to see real settings, where the matrixes are original. This would not be a problem in San José de Moro, where in almost any spot there are real and interesting settings. The problem is that the need to place the modules evenly has collided with local interests. The second problem is that some locals resist placement of modules inside town, next to dwellings. Some residents fear that finding archaeological contexts and artifacts next to their houses could lead to an expropriation of their property by the INC. The ownership of land here is rather unstable because of the archaeological nature of the whole area; thus, residents have what is technically a possession of their lots rather than real property ownership. Regrettably, then, long-term development plans are confounded by understandable resistance from a poor community because of the needs to satisfy short-term necessities, by a long history of unfulfilled promises and exploitation by unscrupulous individuals and politicians, and particularly by endemic local factionalism. Last but not least, one of the worst problems we have encountered in organizing the community around a development program is, contradictorily, the assistance of social programs run by the government and nongovernmental organizations (NGOs). Poor communities such as San José de Moro can find assistance, generally food, for free from the hands of NGOs, particularly confessional ones. Why would local people work or plan ahead under those conditions?

Final Remarks: From Cultural Patrimony to Cultural Resources

Our interest in this chapter has been centered not on the development of large museums at monumental sites that require multimillion-dollar investments in order to be set up and maintained, but in small site museums. Although we recognize the invaluable contribution of large regional museums such as the Royal Tombs of Sipán Museum and the Sicán Museum, including their importance for the development of regional identities and for the increase of regional attractiveness, our efforts have been centered in local, community-based efforts. We think that next to the monumental museums there is still a role for small site museums, which accomplish different objectives, focusing on local histories, benefiting the local communities, and making them part of larger programs or tourism circuits. In contrast to large museums, local museums should aim at presenting specific sites and items and should integrate the local populations. Furthermore, site museums can become, in archaeologically rich areas, key elements in sustainable community development, contributing to the task of generating opportunities to diversify income through the provision and offering of services and products. To illustrate our points we presented a specific case, the development of the modular museum system at the site of San José de Moro.

Throughout fourteen years of archaeological work at the site, we have been implementing small-size exhibition modules featuring some of the most important findings at the site. Small, modular museums have the advantages of requiring smaller investments for building and maintenance, permitting "completion" of yearly programs with evident results, and focusing on the integration of the community and the archaeological site, thus increasing awareness about preservation and conservation of cultural resources. In our experience, to have an impact in community development, archaeological patrimony has to be transformed into archaeological resources (Pearce 1990). An open-air modular museum system can be an important aid in the development of income based on a rational exploitation of these resources. In a modular system, visitors are forced to walk form one module to the next, creating a circuit within the site that increases the opportunities for contact between visitors and community-run businesses.

During the past six years, the San José de Moro Archaeological Project has worked in a community development program centered in the modular museum system (MMS) concept. This MMS concept has been the product of a pragmatic interaction with the community, a limited resource base, and the need to make all efforts self-sustainable. Instead of building one large museum in the middle of town or in the archaeological area, we opted for the implementation of a series of small modular units, none more conspicuous than any local house. In this way, during every field season we have been able to complete at least one new module, adding step-by-step to a larger project. The reason why we chose the modular system is also based in the idea that closely localized modules will invite visitors to walk from one to the next, thus through town, exposing them to what the locals have to offer in terms of products and services.

In addition to the construction of the modules, we have emphasized two parallel programs, one aimed at raising awareness of the archaeological patrimony in the site (in which the target population is basically schoolchildren), and another aimed at improving skills for the development of products based on the local cultural heritage.

Parallel to the creation of the modules at San José de Moro, it has become apparent that research programs have to be integrated with local and regional communities and that they must pursue every possible effort to make available to these communities the information produced through research. This information will be the base upon which any development effort will be built. In our experience, the most fruitful opportunities are working with children in school settings through the creation of learning and activity programs. But integration with the community implies more than learning programs and inevitably leads to interaction with community organizations. This seems to be the most difficult aspect of any program, since fragmentation and factionalism are common features of small communities' interactions, accentuated by partisan political leadership. In this scenario, it is imperative to work with local leadership that has long-term vision as well as creativity, enthusiasm, altruism, and solidarity. Likewise, archaeologists need to become agents in the development of local capacities aimed at the production of goods, mostly handicrafts, based in local natural resources and at the provision of services demanded by visitors.

The bottom line of this chapter is that if cultural patrimony is transformed into cultural resources, then schemes for sustainable community development are possible. Actors in this process include both the archaeologists and the communities, at the local and regional level alike (in Peru this means working with local, municipal, and provincial governments). But we need to recognize that not all archaeologists are trained to pursue successfully these kinds of programs, and communities might lack the vision and the leadership to embark on their own development. For archaeologists this means that we may need to outsource programs to experts in development, health, education, material culture, tourism, technology, and social organization. Additionally, it might be interesting to consider the rationale of including some elements of developmental theory in the basic training of archaeologists. On the side of the communities, it might be important to recognize the pivotal role of local leaders sensitive to cultural resources. In many cases municipal governments have hired archaeologists for their stable staff to oversee the tasks of monitoring and devising programming based on their cultural resources. Archaeological patrimony, because of its peculiar conditions and needs, requires properly trained people—otherwise, actions undertaken in its management become detrimental.

In our understanding, real development happens only if there is a tangible benefit for the local people. From this standpoint, all activities should be aimed at contributing to personal development in terms of identity, pride, and identification. Equally important aims are the development of self-respect and community respect, insertion in the civil society, and adherence to fundamental social values. But if the activities do not aim at the same time at the development of income, based in a rational exploitation of cultural resources, then it will be doomed to fail. Activities must include an aspect of income generation through the creation of services and products that take advantage of the competitive opportunities of each community, such as local natural resources and traditional technologies. This kind of development should be sustainable and self-supporting and should not contribute to the degradation of the environment or the archaeological resources; it should not contribute to economic dependency, and it should combat labor exploitation. Some successful examples of this kind of development are already in progress. In Túcume, for example, the archaeological excavations were followed by the construction of a local museum and a resource center. Lately a group of designers and artists, the Grupo Axius from the Pontificia Universidad Católica del Perú, has been helping the community develop a line of attractive reproduction artifacts for sale—basically silver jewelry decorated with the iconography and designs recovered from the excavations. Archaeological research also has to be conducted parallel to the developmental programming, to give all the activities a sense of legitimacy based on the real research. Furthermore, it is a known fact in archaeology that visitors to archaeological sites are as interested in the work done by archaeologists as in the site itself (see discussion about Copán in chapter 4). In the Huaca de la Luna Project, for example, archaeological findings are publicized gradually, to meet the demands of the visitors and the interest of the media and also to coincide with the high tourism seasons. This has resulted in much larger crowds visiting the site and much more public exposure of the archaeologists' work.

Figure 10.16. Replicas of fine-line ceramic vessels, produced by San José de Moro craftsmen. Photograph by Luis Jaime Castillo.

Arguing that cultural patrimony has to be transformed into cultural resources does not mean that we think that the "use" of the archaeological remains (that is, visiting the site) will be a source of important income—with very rare exceptions, this will not happen, neither for the community nor for the state agency in charge of the custody of these archaeological resources. The "pay for view" choice of exploitation of an archaeological site is an absurdity. We are talking about national goods. Thus, archaeology is revealing only the appealing qualities of the site, and if it is well presented, its attractiveness will account for the desire to visit it and, therefore, provide a chance for local people to produce local goods and services for the newly generated demands of the visiting public (Figure 10.16). These goods and services should nevertheless achieve an adequate standard of quality and be offered in a safe and appealing environment. Needless to say, goods and services ought to be of local production so that they have a larger impact in the local community, through both production and commercialization.

One final thought has to be given to the operating agents. As we said above, it is quite complicated to engage with the internal politics of communities. Factionalism is the rule rather than the exception. A desire for immediate satisfaction of immediate needs is the outcome of years of neglect by the state, a terrible education system, and, ironically, the assistance policies implemented by NGOs. To engage in the kind of activities described here, it will be necessary to find special individuals who either will lead the community or can recognize and take advantage of opportunities. Leaders with sensibility and a capacity for commitment to long-term programs are rare, but they do exist. We have found them in the community among schoolteachers, artisans, and even some of the same people who work in our archaeological programs. These individuals should pursue their own improvement and through it that of their communities; as such, they become role models for their communities. Initiative must shift from the archaeologists to these local leaders once the process has started.

Notes

1. Of course, this is not to say that communities that recognize a direct link with their archaeological past do not engage in looting. Susan Ramírez (2002) has suggested that since the sixteenth century, traditional north coast communities have transformed their perception of the past from one populated by ancestors to one that could provide riches through looting. If native communities engaged in looting, even shortly after the arrival of the Spanish settlers, it was because they feared that not doing so would leave all their ancestral wealth in the hands of greedy Spaniards. The ancestors had accumulated a rich patrimony, a kind of social capital that could be used, then, to solve pressing economic needs. Looting is not seen traditionally as an illegal activity; quite the contrary, successful looters are praised in local folklore (Holmquist 1996).

PART 4

The City as Site Museum

11

The Historic District of Cusco as an Open-Air Site Museum

HELAINE SILVERMAN

Introduction

Cusco is a provincial city of some 350,000 inhabitants in the southern highlands of Peru (Figure 11.1). It is also the former capital of the ancient Inca empire. I consider Cusco's historic district to be an open-air site museum because, at the most basic level, in it are *displayed, interpreted,* and *managed* material remains of ancient societies. Most notable among these remains are the still-standing walls of Inca and Colonial buildings. These constitute the urban fabric of the historic district. Moreover, various of these buildings are themselves museums displaying prehistoric and historic materials—museums within a museum. Also contributing to the identification of Cusco's historic district as an open-air site museum are the plethora of tour guides and tour books that interpret the remains in the historic center in multiple languages. The municipal government and local branch of the National Institute of Culture (Instituto Nacional de Cultura, or INC) are active in the management of Cusco's cultural patrimony (although the quality of that management is debatable; see below).

In addition to being a provincial city and capital of the department of Cusco, the city of Cusco is a World Heritage Site and a World Heritage City. Cusco was inscribed in the coveted World Heritage List of the United Nations Educational, Scientific and Cultural Organization (UNESCO) under criteria Ciii and Civ, meaning that it is a "[c]ultural property . . . [that] bear[s] a unique or at least exceptional testimony to a cultural tradition or to a civilization which is living or which has disappeared; or [is] an outstanding example of a type of building or architectural or technological ensemble or landscape which illustrates (a) significant stage(s) in human history."[1] Cusco merits inclusion on any "A-list" of cultural heritage. But Cusco is also a living city, and therein originates the problem I discuss in this chapter: museumification, and whether Cusco's 170-hectare historic center (or, indeed, the whole city) would benefit from the museumification of that remarkable zone.

Figure 11.1. Location of Cusco, Peru. Map by Steven J. Holland.

Museumification

By museumification I mean those processes by which the municipal government, the tourism industry and the visitors it generates, and city residents cease to regard and claim the historic district as an organic living center, scripting it, instead, as an inert, consumable resource. In this regard we may recall Barbara Bender's (1998: 26) assessment of heritage making as the freezing of time and space so that the landscape, including its monuments, is packaged, presented, and turned into passive, nostalgic museum exhibits. Such a landscape is normative, and its managers attempt to impose only one story and produce only one kind of experience.

Mgomezulu (2004) speaks of museumification in neutral terms, observing that "the site and the museum each designate a space of heritage whose limits adapt and transform themselves, occasionally overlapping when a heritage space takes on the characteristics of a museum. This is often the case in 'museified' urban historic centres." However, I regard museumification as a pathology of many historic cities around the world. Its attendant symptoms include loss and displacement of residential population; loss of traditional lifeways, including associated economic patterns; conflicting demands of different groups for space; drastic changes in architectural integrity, scale, and character that damage the "authenticity" of the setting; and conversion of the historic city into a "theme park" environment.

These pathologies exist worldwide and have been repeatedly acknowledged by various international heritage organizations. Thus, at the 1972 meeting of its general assembly, the International Council on Monuments and Sites (ICO-MOS) expressed concern with the introduction of contemporary architecture into ancient groups of buildings. It advocated harmonious interventions where additional construction is necessary. In 1975 the ICOMOS General Assembly worried about property speculation and economic policies leading to dereliction in the historic fabric. ICOMOS argued that regional authorities must become involved in urban conservation in smaller historic towns so that property prices remain stable, historic buildings are not permitted to deteriorate, and pride in the historic environment is encouraged among residents. In 1987 the ICOMOS General Assembly argued that the social value of historic centers must take precedence over economic value. It encouraged the continuation of traditional residence and work in the historic built environment.

The condition of many historic cities on the World Heritage List deteriorated in the late twentieth century at the same time that awareness and proactive policies about cultural heritage were on the rise. This situation led to the creation of the Organization of World Heritage Cities (OWHC) in 1991. OWHC is a branch of UNESCO's World Heritage Convention. World Heritage Cities are named from the World Heritage List. OWHC promotes preservation and conservation of historic cities by means of charters and protocols, which participating states sign.

The Fez Charter was drafted at the first OWHC General Assembly in 1993. It "recognizes the important role that cities play as cultural centers and exemplars of human achievement" and argues that these fragile environments must be protected by means of cooperation on the part of residents, modern and efficient management techniques, and adequate financial resources.

The Bergen Protocol of 1995 was created at OWHC's Second General Assembly. It reiterates the goals of the Fez Charter and provides resources for accomplishing them through cooperative projects with UNESCO, ICCROM (International Center for the Study of the Preservation and Restoration of Cultural Property), ICOMOS, and other entities.

The goals of OWHC are supported by the World Conference on Sustainable Tourism. Its 1995 Charter for Sustainable Tourism clearly acknowledged that while tourism can be a positive force for socioeconomic development and cultural interchange, it can also have negative consequences for communities in both environmental and cultural terms.

Concern about the threats of cultural tourism in historic areas was the theme of OWHC's 1997 meeting. OWHC advocated protection for the quality of life of residents in historic cities and respect for their cultural identity. It encouraged multiple administrative levels of authority to develop legislation and policies that will make tourism a positive force in the affected community. It also encouraged the tourism industry to contribute financially to studies that analyze the impact of tourism on the actual monuments in World Heritage Cities.

In Cusco, as in many other living historic cities, there is an ongoing struggle between residents, municipal authorities, the private sector, and the global tourism industry over the problems recognized by ICOMOS and OWHC. The need for implementation of their policies is urgent if the museumification of the historic center is to be ameliorated.

Experiencing Cusco, Sharing Cusco

Seen from above, Cusco's historic district is charming, with narrow streets and red tile roofs (Figure 11.2). Seen from a tour bus, the historic center is even more impressive, with its Inca walls, even entire Inca streets, and beautiful Colonial churches (Figure 11.3). But from the sidewalk, much of the historic district is dirty; uncollected garbage, human waste, roaming dogs, and air-polluting vehicular traffic intrude on the picturesque architectural composition. And if the large wooden doors to the many grand colonial mansions (*casonas*) are open, and if these have not been converted to tourist hotels, then one sees an interior courtyard of urban squalor surrounded by dangerously deteriorated habitations (Figure 11.4).

Figure 11.2. Seen from above, Cusco's historic district is charming, with narrow streets and red tile roofs. Photograph by Helaine Silverman.

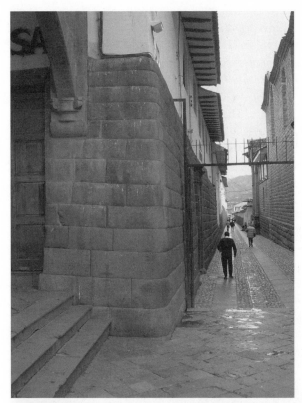

Left: Figure 11.3. Calle Loreto, Cusco: major Inca walls. Photograph by Helaine Silverman.

Below: Figure 11.4. The open massive wood doors of a *casona* reveal a slummified interior courtyard. Photograph by Helaine Silverman.

The traditional residential population of the historic district is increasingly impoverished. Moreover, this population is steadily declining. In 1987 there were approximately 27,000 inhabitants (Estrada Iberico and Nieto Degregori 1998: 9). In 1993 there were approximately 25,000 inhabitants (Estrada Iberico and Nieto Degregori 1998: 9). In 1997 there were no more than 16,000 inhabitants (Estrada Iberico and Nieto Degregori 1998: 10). Today there are fewer still. Peralta (1998: 54) laments, "The Cusqueño, who constitutes the spiritual wealth of the city, no longer lives in the center of Cusco, which is abandoned, and is dedicated to tertiary services, fundamentally tourism and its collateral services."

Hudson (1987) has stated that site museums "have a life and a reality about them which other types of museum cannot hope to approach." But what is that life and reality when applied to Cusco? Should the museum triumph over life and reality in the city? The municipality and other governmental offices of Cusco have a decision to make. Do they want to tolerate and even encourage

Figure 11.5. The tourist service sector dominates the four sides of the Plaza de Armas. Photograph by Helaine Silverman.

by deliberate apathy the existing situation in which the residential population is being expelled from the historic center at an increasing rate? This process will result in a true museum (even a theme park)—a historic district devoid of residents other than hotel guests and a very small elite class of gentrifiers. Or will the historic center be renovated for habitation, with an economy that permits local residents to benefit from tourism and survive without it?

Today the historic center is used largely by tourists and the service sector that supports tourism. The Plaza de Armas gives dramatic testimony to this. Mestizo Catholicism, a European-style garden, tourist restaurants, tourist shops, travel agencies, money exchange booths, and internet cafés dominate Cusco's greatest public space (Figure 11.5). With the exception of the traditional Café El Ayllu, none of the resident-oriented businesses of just thirty years ago exists here. And the seating area of the plaza is a kaleidoscope of negotiated social space as locals and foreigners occupy it differentially throughout the day (Figure 11.6). Indeed, one informant told me that the current mayor has floated the idea of permitting only tourists in the Plaza de Armas.

a

b

Figure 11.6. The seating area of the Plaza de Armas is a kaleidoscope of negotiated social space as locals and foreigners occupy it differentially throughout the day: *a*, local Cusqueño "old timers," who regularly meet in the plaza; *b*, tourists. Photograph by Helaine Silverman.

I agree with Cusco architect Lorgio Villena (cited in Mesa Redonda 1998: 55), who argues that "a city is more than physical structure. It is also an assemblage of the human beings who inhabit it, which implies *use* of the city" (emphasis added). Cusco's future hangs in the balance, both as a provincial metropolis and as a small historic district of incalculable interest to more than half a million tourists who visit the city yearly. Can the cultural patrimony of Cusco be preserved and deployed in a dynamic, modernizing context for the material and intangible benefit of all Cusqueños? This kind of question is rarely faced by archaeologists, yet it raises important ethical issues in terms of awareness of the larger social and political context in which we work, which in Cusco has the added dimension of international oversight by UNESCO and OWHC.

Reclaiming the Historic Center

Kirshenblatt-Gimblett (1998: 151) has observed, "Heritage and tourism are collaborative industries, heritage converting locations into destinations and tourism making them economically viable as exhibits of themselves. Locations become museums of themselves within a tourism economy." I am arguing that Cusco has become a museum of itself in a tourism economy. However, Cusco is not economically viable for all of its residents. Similarly, worldwide, international organizations and heritage professionals have expressed concern that the disproportionate massive presence of tourists in towns and small cities may act to expel residents as tourism prices them out of the housing market (see general discussion in Orbasli 2000). This problem is further exacerbated by the deteriorated condition of large numbers of residences in historic cities that have turned them into inner-city slums, as well as—in Cusco, specifically—a lack of municipal services, such as efficient garbage disposal and pickup, which are a normal aspect of urban life in developed countries.

Studies by a group of socially minded architects working in the Centro Guaman Poma de Ayala (CGPA; a nongovernmental organization, or NGO) and its professional partners are addressing these problems in Cusco (Mesa Redonda 1998; Estrada Iberico and Nieto Degregori 1998). CGPA is attempting to mitigate these defects on the micro-level by means of a remarkable urban redevelopment project, not as typically undertaken by the heritage and tourism industry (see Kirshenblatt-Gimblett 1998: 155), but in opposition to it. CGPA's rationale is that the historic district must be a living, sustainable center or it will turn into a theme park and true museum of no benefit to ordinary Cusqueños. For Cusco to be a city with life, "we must rescue our built patrimonial values, the culture, but also we must rescue our identity and our civic awareness. Only when we have quality citizens—citizens with civic awareness—will we achieve a city with better living conditions. The cultural patrimony, among other things, must be a means to achieve that quality of life, and not vice versa" (Estrada 1998: 62).

In 2002 CGPA began a pilot project in a city block near the San Pedro Market in the historic center. The objectives of this project were to (1) repair the physical structure of fourteen atrociously and dangerously deteriorated casonas in which sixty impoverished families were living in inner-city slum conditions; (2) rehabilitate the small apartments to decent standards by providing each with a bathroom, a kitchen, and running water as well as defined living room and bedroom areas; (3) assist residents to create their own small businesses serving residential rather than tourist needs, such as restaurants and traditional religious embroidery shops; (4) generate in the benefited population a desire to keep living in the historic center; (5) teach the residents how to use the bathrooms, keep the apartments clean, and live harmoniously as neighbors (civic education); (6) inculcate in them an affection for the casonas not just as their lovely new homes but also as cultural patrimony and pride in themselves as residents of the historic center: help them feel like stakeholders.

Goals 1 and 2 of the pilot project have been met with funding that CGPA obtained from foreign sources and a very small contribution from the owner of each casona. The INC and municipality had to be convinced, through arduous effort, to give their permission for the renovation and contributed little of what they promised materially to the project. The beautiful, renovated loft apartments (Figure 11.7) were inaugurated in June 2004. The agreement is that the owners of the casonas (who no longer live in them) will not sell these now-valuable properties for a period of ten years, nor will they evict their tenants. Also, in an organizational device similar to that created by Yoshio Onuki (chapter 5, this volume) for the local community at Kuntur Wasi, CGPA helped the block residents form a legally constituted residents association. Observations and interviews with the residents, to be conducted over coming years, will reveal whether the other worthy goals of CGPA are met.

The CGPA project is especially important because it explicitly eschews tourism as the basis of income for the casona residents. Cusco has lacked a stable, diversified economic base other than tourism for the past fifty years. The drastic decline in tourism during Peru's ten-year civil war (1983–93) showed just how economically devastating reliance on that single industry can be. Not having learned from this recent lesson, powerful interest groups continue to promote a mono-product tourism economy in Cusco. But CGPA is trying to create a living historic district that can withstand crashes in the tourism industry—whatever the cause.

Figure 11.7. Interior of one of Centro Guaman Poma de Ayala's new loft apartments, created within a deteriorated *casona* in the San Pedro market area of the historic district of Cusco. Photograph by Helaine Silverman.

Do You Identify with the Incas?

Enrique Estrada, a principal architect at CGPA, has repeatedly criticized the deterioration of the social conditions of the decreasing number of people residing in the historic district (what he calls a "belt of misery") and its accompanying deterioration of awareness and identity (see, for example, Estrada 1998: 60). Above, I explain how CGPA is brilliantly mitigating urban blight in the historic center and greatly improving the lives of one group of its inhabitants. Here I examine the relationship drawn by the CGPA urban planners between cultural patrimony and identity.

Because Cusco's prehistoric and historic architecture is still overwhelmingly visible, urban redevelopment necessarily is concerned with preservation. What makes the CGPA argument interesting is the expectation and desire that beyond conservation of the architecture within which they live, impoverished residents will come to feel an attachment to it as the symbol and facilitator of their identity. Perplexed, Estrada ponders how it is "that in spite of the fact that the discourses say we are a World Heritage City, that we're a city that's unique in the world, etc., etc., this hasn't translated into a practice of conservation on the part of that specific population inhabiting the city, who is using this patrimony. It's a problem, I believe, of a lack of awareness, of the loss of identity" (Estrada 1998: 60). Roberto Samanez Argumedo, a distinguished Cusco architect with an international profile, has collaborated with CGPA. He states,

> These traces from the past animate a conscious sense of continuity of one's own existence in time by permitting the human being to identify with the material world of his ancestors. This sense of continuity from the past towards the future is . . . the awareness of identity, the fundamental factor with which to look for common ideals, senses of nationality and belonging to a determined place. Thus, the cultural-historical patrimony, composed of representative monuments of the past and the urban framework around them, constitutes a symbol of identity and nationality. These are indispensable elements, tightly linked to a historical message that we need to conserve because they identify and differentiate us. In the case of Cusco, to permit that the ancient monumental historical zone be destroyed and that its traditional buildings be replaced is to attack our own identity and transform us into anonymous beings on whom any foreign cultural pattern at all can be imposed. (Samanez Argumedo 1998: 98)

The position of CGPA and its professional partners cannot be understood without reference to an important philosophical current, pervasive in Cusco from at least the end of the nineteenth century (and arguably earlier) and throughout the twentieth century and into today, that is known as *incanismo*: a proud feeling of identification with the glories of the Inca empire in an evocative, timeless sense of continuity with the Incas and resistance to outside influences (Flores Ochoa 1990: 11–12). But incanismo was, and still is, very much a middle-class movement. Nieto Degregori (1994: 446) is even more restrictive, identifying it with Cusco's political elite and intellectuals. I believed it to be important in my study to ascertain how ordinary Cusqueños across the social strata feel about themselves in terms of incanismo. I repeatedly found that, with few exceptions, Cusco's poorest inhabitants were unwilling to be interviewed, unable to understand various of my questions if they agreed to be interviewed, unknowledgeable about the world of tourism surrounding them (for example, unaware of the *Boleto Turístico* and the INC), uninformed about the Inca empire other than that the Incas had been the great rulers of Cusco and Peru, and unable to articulate ideas about themselves; in addition, because of their lack of education and imminent concerns about survival, they were unconcerned about Cusco's cultural patrimony. Because the CGPA project involves education, I will be interested to see in the future whether this particular group of urban poor, currently living in pleasant circumstances and (one hopes) employed, will acquire the luxury of a taught sense of identification with Inca and/or Colonial Cusco.

That said, the following is a representative sample of positive replies that I received from among thirty Cusqueños, arbitrarily approached in the Plaza de Armas, in response to these two interview questions: Do you identify with the Incas? Do you feel descended from the Incas?

> We are all descended from the ancient ones [he means racially]. We identify with our roots. (Sr. Hector, 21 years old, lower middle class, university student)

> Yes, we all feel it. Because as Incas the Spanish came to kill us, as if they were killing any animal. We know this. We feel badly about how the Inca empire disappeared. Maybe if the Spanish hadn't come there wouldn't be thieves or criminals in Peru. The Spanish who came here were thieves, that's what history says. From Spain came fugitives, thieves from the jails. Spain sent discoverers to kill people, to rob, nothing more. And the Incas disappeared. (Sr. Fortunato, 74 years old, lower class, retired worker)

> Yes, because Cusco is autochthonous in principle because it was the Inca capital, because it was the capital of the Inca empire. In us there still remains the *mestizaje* that we inherited from Garcilaso de la Vega. Its customs. For example, we eat the foods of the Inca region. I can enumerate: maize . . . *chuño* [freeze-dried potatoes]. These are nutritious elements that fortify the stomach, that make newborn babies healthy, or that fortify teenagers or the old folks. And we are still here, surviving in this land. (Sra. Luz Marina, 48 years old, educated, middle class, housewife)

> Of course. Since grade school, as children we've been taught, we've been inculcated with everything referring to the Incas, all of this. It's something natural, and something sentimental—but we also identify [that is, untaught, from deep down inside], certainly. (Sr. Wilbert, 44 years old, middle class, pharmacist)

> I think so. In Inca times, people were very strong, they didn't get sick. The one-hundred-percent Cusqueñas [women of Cusco] are like that. We don't go much to the doctor. We eat chuño, *kiwicha* [a native high-protein grain of the mountain zone], maize. I think that's what makes our bodies strong. That's how they ate in Inca times. In contrast, in other places it's not like that. (Srta. Francisca, 34 years old, lower middle class, handicraft shop owner)

> Because I have Inca blood in my veins. (Sr. Julio, 84 years old, lower class, retired Coca-Cola factory worker)

Of course. The first thing I say to the tourists when we are walking the Inca Road is "look at the difference in power and force and other things of our porters." (Sr. Mauro, 33 years old, lower middle class, tour guide)

Definitively yes. It makes me sad and a little angry that we've adopted the attitude of those who live in the capital [Lima], who think of themselves as very Spanish, very foreign, when in fact we're a mixture of races. Yes, I consider that I am descended from the Incas and I am very proud of this and we should emphasize this more. We don't hear a lot about our history. We don't sufficiently investigate our history. I don't know what our politicians are doing. I don't know what the INC is doing. They should much more emphatically highlight, emphasize that which there was, what the Incas used, what they did. They do some of this, but it's superfluous. They could make documentaries for television because we have five local channels. All they do is produce variety shows with games, but they don't use the space to show us "this is our history." This should be done at the national level. (Srta. Monica and Sr. Edson, 27 years old, middle-class couple, computer specialists)

Of course. We are descended from the Incas. (Srtas. Jamileth and Adelma, 18 years old, lower class, employees in a jewelry store)

Yes, it's important to me. The way the Incas worked, that's how we would like to work, but we can't. I don't know why. (Sra. Angelica, middle-aged, lower class, homemaker)

For example, as Peruvians and because we are from here, from Cusco, we feel that we are descendants of the Incas. We have Inca blood. Now we produce potatoes using fertilizers. It's all chemical. Phooey. In times past, they didn't get sick. They were stronger. But now all we do is barely survive. We don't live because, frankly, our jobs don't suffice to live as we ought to be able to, not at all. (Sra. Dolores, 50 years old, lower class, informal handicraft seller)

Yes, it's very important. I'm Cusqueño and I'm descended from the Incas. (Sr. Nelson, 24 years old, middle-class pretensions, mechanic)

Yes, it's natural. From the time you're little they tell you what your reality was. Your parents, grandparents, great-grandparents were born here. (Srtas. Marilyn and Erika, 22 years old, middle class, university students)

Truthfully, I haven't thought about being a descendant, but I know that I come from the Incas. (Sra. Giovanna, 26 years old, middle class, elementary school teacher)

Yes, I think that we have some of the Incas in us, even though in Peru there are many races and they're mixed and there are many traits, especially Spanish ones that would be the majority, but there are always Inca roots. Take me, for instance; even though I'm white, I still think, absolutely, that there are roots. The roots always remain. (Sr. Paul, 28 years old, upper class, owner of a tourist restaurant)

Whether well explained or monosyllabic, whether foregrounded or distant, the replies suggest widespread identification with the Incas in some way—cultural, racial, geographical. But this identification with the Incas is not unanimous. Señora Antonia, forty-seven years old, a lower-class housewife with strong indigenous features, said that she did not feel any tie to the Incas "because my grandparents came from another country. My grandparents aren't Peruvian." Her statement expresses the self-denial and self-protection born of five hundred years of social discrimination, economic exploitation, and political disempowerment in the Andes.

Living in a Tourist City: Perceptions of Self and Others

Whereas international organizations and heritage managers are concerned that tourists can overwhelm the local population to the point of making them feel uncomfortable in their own settings, CGPA and its professional partners do not see tourism as antithetical to the assertion of rights to space and place in the city. Rather than interpret Cusco's extraordinary architectural environment as being necessarily the cause of population displacement, they argue that "cultural patrimony is a means for obtaining quality of life" (Mesa Redonda 1998: 51), based on the recursive relationship they posit between built environment and identity.

In my study I was interested in whether Cusqueños feel excluded from the historic district, particularly the Plaza de Armas, which is Cusco's greatest public space. The answers to this question varied. Most of the young (under forty years old) Cusqueños whom I interviewed and who were able to articulate an opinion (creating, as I have indicated, a biased sample) were delighted with the presence of the tourists.

In Cusco, foreigners aren't strangers as in other cities. You are part of our social life. The Cusqueños and foreigners talk to each other. (Lic. Sonia Bárbara Escobar Loayza, early 30s, middle class, journalist)

Let more come! I like to see you. It's good for the culture of the city. (Sra. Maria, early 30s, middle class, mother of a little girl)

I'm delighted that tourists come because this is a way for us to know lots of people. When the tourist comes we should already know what he/she needs, and be able to communicate with the tourist and in what way we can help, too. (Sra. Waldina, early 40s, middle class, mother of two girls)

They don't affect us at all. To the contrary, they open the door for us to other cultures. (Sr. Hector, 21 years old, lower middle class, university student)

Economically we benefit because the tourists come. Thanks to the tourists there are hotels, restaurants, even transportation companies. (Sr. Basílides, 30 years old, lower middle class, beginning his own very small business)

However, some middle-class Cusqueños, regardless of age, recognized a negative side to the presence of the many backpackers, young tourists, and tourists overall in the city.

Sure, tourists go to the *discotecas*. I like to go too when I'm not working. Mama Afrika. Ukukus. But you know what I don't like about the tourists? Some are, well, they like to smoke a lot of marijuana. That's the problem. Especially on Procuradores [a street notorious for this problem, ascending from the Plaza de Armas]. Lots of potheads. Lots of marijuana there. It's a bit detrimental. (Sr. Julio Alberto, 23 years old, middle class, salesman)

Economically tourism benefits Cusco because it's an important resource, the most important one that Cusco has. I think it has a lot of influence in Peru. So, if we speak from this point of view, it's a necessary evil. What we've got to see is if there isn't some way to order some aspects of it. The Cusqueños have a right to be in whatever place we want, to enter wherever we want, but there's got to be some order—distinct places could be established where one could be without any kind of problem. (Sr. Wilbert, 44 years old, middle class, pharmacist)

Well, the tourists disturb me just a little because they're libertines who use Saturdays and Sundays to take drugs in the street, at least on Procuradores or in some of the discotecas, and they promote drunkenness and that contaminates the environment of the city a bit, which otherwise is still quite healthy. . . . They should show more prudence because they come from elsewhere and their behavior shocks us a bit because we're conservative. Their behavior reflects negatively on them. (Sra. Luz Marina, 48 years old, middle class, educated, housewife)

I would argue that tourist-Cusqueño interaction is predicated upon "contact zone" dynamics as described by Mary Louise Pratt (1992), with the exception of "intractable conflict." The contact zone is "the space of colonial encounters, the space in which peoples geographically and historically separated come into contact with each other and establish ongoing relations, usually involving conditions of coercion, radical inequality" (Pratt 1992: 6). Pratt goes on to assert that the "'contact' perspective emphasizes how subjects are constituted in and by their relations to each other. It treats the relations among colonizers and colonized, or travelers and 'travelees,' not in terms of separateness or apartheid, but in terms of copresence, interaction, interlocking understandings and practices, often within radically asymmetrical relations of power" (Pratt 1992: 7).

The clearest examples of the contact zone are the Plaza de Armas and the numerous discotecas that cater to Cusco's middle-class young people and the young foreign tourists (estimated ages, eighteen to thirty), who, at times, appeared to me to constitute the majority of foreign visitors to the city. The better-heeled tourists are often largely invisible in the public domain because they are shepherded around in buses on package tours and have less to time to wander.

Most Cusqueños are excluded by cost from the tourist service businesses around the Plaza de Armas and in the blocks leading away from it—especially restaurants, which could be of interest to them. And, as I indicate earlier, most of the small businesses necessary for living an ordinary life have left the historic center, especially the Plaza de Armas and the immediately surrounding area.

Even the backpackers (Figure 11.8) are perceived by Cusqueños to have disposable income, despite their grubby appearance and uncouth behavior, because they have arrived in Cusco, wear good boots or name-brand sneakers (if they're not using locally made cheap rubber-tire sandals), buy sweaters, take photographs, and so forth. Despite the vast difference in economic means, then, between tourists and locals, the articulate local population is surprisingly (in my opinion) protective of the interests of the tourists, rather than resenting them:

I always reproach my countrymen who behave badly toward tourists, who hurt them, who injure them robbing them. (Sra. Waldina, early 40s, middle class, mother of two girls)

For me, tourism is a clean industry, which we should all cultivate. But most tourists are not given proper treatment. Rather, they try to extract the last cent from the tourist, selling them food at excessively high prices. The hotels are super expensive. (Sr. Julio, 84 years old, lower class, retired Coca-Cola factory worker)

Figure 11.8. In the Plaza de Armas: *a*, "punk" tourists; *b*, back-packers (*mochileros*). They engage and/or ignore the fasci-nated young population of Cusco. Photograph by Helaine Silverman.

Cusqueños blame the difference in income not on tourists but, in a keenly perceptive argument, on the larger national and international context:

Tourism is good because it doesn't just bring economic development, it also permits us to sell or create new forms of handicrafts. But the bad thing is the economy—and this has been the case since Fujimori became president [prior to the current government of President Toledo] and spoiled everything and gave away our country at bargain prices and in shreds, selling all the state businesses and we're suffering and paying for this. I love Machu Picchu, I love Aguas Calientes, because going there is a way to absorb energy and I feel it. But I can no longer travel because it is too expensive. And who has taken the money? All of the money of the national businesses is in the hands of foreign owners. They're the owners of the train, too [the train to Machu Picchu]. They charge a ton of money, but for whom? For the Peruvian? No. We feel this deeply. My daughters are little and they can't see Machu Picchu. No. One must have a lot of money in order to travel. But I don't blame the tourist. It's the country that's the problem. And this government doesn't have an idea of what's going on. It doesn't even review its contract with Machu Picchu. It's the way tourism is managed. It's not the tourist. It's how tourism is managed. . . . The problem seems to be this globalized world. . . . At the global level we all need to share. (Sra. Waldina, early 40s, middle class, mother of two girls)

Walls versus People

Cusco is a dramatic palimpsest with three readily distinguished periods of occupation that are both vertically superimposed and horizontally spatialized: Inca, Colonial, Republican/Modern. To read the INC's declarations in Cusco's newspapers and to listen to the complaints of ordinary Cusqueños across the socioeconomic spectrum, one would think that Inca kings and Spanish viceroys were still in control, for such is the preference for their buildings over the housing needs of citizens. The INC and municipality (the exception being cases of corruption that authorize destruction or modification of the cultural patrimony in favor of the construction of new luxury hotels), as well as international heritage organizations, privilege the inanimate ancient and historical structures over those of the citizens living in these very buildings, sometimes with disastrous results. Indeed, several responses (made by individuals who requested anonymity) referred specifically to the INC in expressing dissatisfaction with current living conditions.

Some things should change. For example, if there are houses—old ones with Inca walls—that are falling down. For example, some time ago on Antonio de Lorena [a street], a wall fell down. And it killed a child. And this happened because of INC negligence because the INC refused to permit the owner to demolish in good time the wall, which was in such precarious condition. If there are houses that are falling down, what does it cost the INC to demolish the wall and build a new one with these exact same stones? (Informant who requested anonymity)

[The INC is] a very bureaucratic entity and I imagine that there is a lot of embezzlement . . . a lot of money is going into private pockets. (Second informant who requested anonymity)

Their performance is very poor. The INC is practically in the service of the capital [Lima]. From the capital the INC is told something and they do it. Instead of taking care of what's ours, they're destroying it. (Third informant who requested anonymity)

The INC is operating for the benefit of its own bureaucrats only. Nothing else. Benefit for the people—no, there's none. I think they send to Lima all the money that ingresses into the institution. . . . The money simply disappears there. (Fourth informant who requested anonymity)

The population completely rejects everything about the National Institute of Culture. (Estrada 1998: 62)

Although the argument can readily be made that without preservation of the built environment Cusco would lose its appeal for tourists and thus its economic base, the issue is far more complex. Which past and whose present will be privileged and protected in contemporary Cusco? What is authenticity (see Nara Document [ICOMOS 1994])? How are the benefits and perquisites of cultural tourism to be shared?

Framing the Gaze

The Oficina Ejecutiva del Cusco (OFEC) is the official presenter of Cusco as an open-air museum. It is the municipal office that sells the *Boleto Turístico*, the ticket providing entrance to the dozen or so attractions deemed most interesting by the municipal authorities (Figure 11.9). As I have previously argued (Silverman 2002), the *Boleto Turístico* frames the gaze of the tourist toward both Inca and Colonial monuments. But not all tourists buy the *Boleto Turístico*, since many are young backpackers who are in Cusco for the "experience" of it.

Remarkably, Cusqueños are restricted in their access to these same places that define Cusco for the international tourism industry. Again, in the sense of "museumification" that I present above, the living population of Cusco is regarded by the municipality as well as the Catholic Church as a nuisance for foreign tourists. Thus, Cusqueños have free access to pray at some of the grandest churches of the city only on a very restricted schedule, typically early morning mass. Until May 2004, Cusqueños were permitted to wander out of the central nave of the great Cathedral to see its breathtaking works of religious art of the Escuela Cusqueña only on Saturdays, Sundays, and holidays. Of course,

Figure 11.9. The *Boleto Turístico* was recently changed when several of the Catholic churches withdrew from this municipal office, and the Pachacutec Monument, Museo de Arte Popular, and Centro Qosqo de Arte Nativo were substituted. Compare the images on the three tickets and note the stamped dates of use showing rapid change in the official scripting of the municipal tourist circuit.

Cusqueños should be permitted to enter any part of any church when it is open to the public. The continuing exclusion of Cusqueños from their churches prompted a negative response from every Cusqueño I interviewed; they took umbrage for both their Catholic and civic identities.

> It's unfair. How can that be right if we're the owners of Cusco. We should be able to enter whenever we wish, to celebrate a mass, to enter. They don't let us. We should be able to enter the church as Catholics to pray, but they don't let us. Closed. Closed. The church is closed. You have to go precisely at mass time. At 10 a.m. on the dot the church is closed. (Sr. Fortunato, 74 years old, lower class, retired worker)

> It's really infuriating. We're Cusqueños and as Cusqueños we have the right to visit any place as often as we want and when we want. Sometimes we forget our DNI [identity card] and we're up at Sacsayhuaman and the guards say we can't enter because we don't have our DNI. (Srta. Monica and Sr. Edson, 27 years old, middle-class couple, computer specialists)

The Convent of Santo Domingo, which controls access to Coricancha, the Inca Temple of the Sun over which it is built, has charged its own admission fee for as long as I can remember. Here we have a fascinating issue, since the vast majority of tourists, in my experience, want to see Coricancha, not the church. For all the official discourse about Cusco as the former capital of the Inca em-

Figure 11.10. The Dominican Order contests the identification of their convent as Coricancha, the Inca Temple of the Sun. The Dominican Order has been located within Coricancha for centuries. It feels ever more empowered to reject the pagan past. In spring 2004 the Dominican priests removed the large gold letters on the front facade of the convent that had identified it as Coricancha in addition to Santo Domingo. Photograph by Helaine Silverman.

pire, and for as much as incanismo is still a strong sentiment among educated Cusqueños, Catholicism and a profound respect for the church trumps romanticism at the local level. No official entity is willing to claim Coricancha as the great archaeological site it is. And sometime between February and May 2004, when I was not in Cusco, the Dominican priests removed the gold letters on the front facade of the convent that had identified it as Coricancha in addition to Santo Domingo (Figure 11.10).

Conclusion

In this chapter, my concern has been to address the relationship between Cusco as an open-air site museum and the local and nonlocal communities that this museum serves. Cusco is perhaps the maximal expression of the many points of conflict and inconsistency that arise when an archaeological site in an inhabited area is inserted into a supralocal tourism network.

Of course, this phenomenon is not restricted to Cusco. One of the most interesting comparisons we can make is with Santa Fe, New Mexico, as analyzed by Chris Wilson (1997) in his fascinating book *The Myth of Santa Fe*. Wilson critically interrogates the museumification of the historic district of Santa Fe and the advantages and disadvantages of its recent transformation into an "exotic" international tourist destination. As summarized by Wilson, the city's "alluring image" was consciously created through a complex interaction of ethnic identity production (the commodification of Native American and Hispanic cultures), architectural/historic preservation and contrived revival, and tourist image-making. Both Santa Fe and Cusco were small, stagnating towns at the beginning of the twentieth century. Santa Fe's leaders took advantage of statehood in 1912 to consciously promote real and fake heritage so as to develop the economy around tourism. An even more dramatic event—the devastating earthquake of 1950—provided Cusco's leaders with the opportunity to modernize the city (see Silverman 2002), with tourism coming to the fore as a consequent development strategy. In both cases the deliberate creation of a marketable sense of place has involved appropriation of a mythical and historical past that is actively promoted by local people. A major point of contrast, however, is that Santa Fe's growth and insertion into the tourist circuit was largely engineered by its Anglo-American newcomers, whereas Cusco's promotion draws heavily on a century of homegrown Indigenist and Incanist ideology, embraced by the larger populace as a means of engagement with and empowerment by the central government and, ultimately, the world outside. In both cases there are resultant tensions, contradictions, paradoxes, cultural crosscurrents, and re-creations as particular details of the appropriated cultures are selected to promote tourism and a civic identity. In turn, as Wilson compellingly demonstrates, these idealized images are recursive, influencing the lived and embodied identities of residents.

This brief discussion of Santa Fe returns us to the question I pose at the beginning of this chapter: does museumification benefit the city of Cusco? In terms of the historic district, will the traditional residents be permitted and enabled to equitably co-exist with the architecture of dead Incas and dead Spanish colonial authorities? This question is ironic inasmuch as in these former times this zone was the locus of elites, be they Inca or Spanish. In its packaging for tourism and resulting social exclusion, the historic center of Cusco is reverting to its former status and original use. But one must recognize that the social and political realities and context for this reversion are far different than they were five centuries ago. Nevertheless, after recent decades of enfranchising reform in Peru (and in Cusco), one can argue that tourism—as a major phenomenon of modernization and globalization—is having some reactionary repercussions.

Therefore, in terms of the city as a whole, we need to consider this corollary problem of whether the much touted benefits of international tourism are reaching residents. I think the answer is largely negative, as evidenced by such indices as *schools* (overcrowded and poorly equipped), *health care* (primitive, even in the private clinics), *employment* (massive unemployment and underemployment), *economic diversification* (there is no other industry in Cusco to speak of, other than its small beer facility), *municipal services* (garbage pickup is irregular and insufficient, even in the historic district; electrification, sewage services, and water resources are inadequate), *environmental protection* (air pollution is rampant; the city is swallowing the agricultural land of the valley; rivers are polluted), and so on. Indeed, most residents of the larger metropolitan region appear quite cognizant of their continuing conditions of poverty and repeatedly act upon this consciousness. Thus, throughout 2003–04 (the time during which my fieldwork was conducted), there were repeated protest marches in the city by different interest groups demanding access to economic prosperity. I conclude that the global tourism industry is not creating a better life for most city residents, despite residents' largely benevolent attitudes toward tourists and despite the low-income informal sector and low-paid formal sector employment it generates.

Of related importance in this consideration of tourism's benefits is whether the patrimonial built environment can physically and aesthetically survive the industry upon which tourist interest is predicated. Here, too, Santa Fe provides a fascinating comparison. In Santa Fe, beginning around 1910, business leaders created a "City Different" proposal that specifically called for the development of a local Santa Fe style based on Spanish and Pueblo architecture and accompanied by historic preservation for the purpose of attracting tourism. In

Cusco, historic preservation is fraught with difficulties. The Inca and Colonial architecture of the historic district is what attracts tourists, yet destruction of this patrimony occurs on an almost daily basis as residents without sufficient economic resources find it more convenient to demolish old walls or let them decay into self-destruction rather than undertake INC-approvable renovations; in addition, businesses (such as hotels, restaurants, shops) wantonly open holes in Inca walls to create user-friendly entrances or window displays or enlarged spaces for commerce. Then, too, there is the problem of excessive vehicular traffic through the narrow streets of the historic district, which is both shaking the old walls to their foundations and covering them with eroding emissions. And, of course, infrastructural tourism development implicates issues of inappropriate scale (for example, hotels desperately seek to accommodate the increasing number of tourists by building up) and style (for example, maintenance of authentic architecture or re-creation of it).

For the historic center of Cusco to have a sustainable future, the global tourism industry, heritage managers, and local government are going to have to recognize the presence and rights of Cusqueños to livable space in the city, rather than offering and creating an open-air site museum as a palliative. Yes, Cusco was the glorious capital of the great Inca empire, and yes, the Spanish colonial regime constructed an extraordinarily beautiful presence in the city. But Cusco the open-air site museum is also Cusco the twenty-first-century capital city of the provincial department of Cusco in the modern nation-state of Peru. Its citizens live in the present and clamor for a decent future.

Acknowledgments

The fieldwork upon which this chapter is based was conducted in 2003–04 with an Individual Research Grant from the Wenner-Gren Foundation for Anthropological Research, whose support is gratefully acknowledged. I also thank architects Enrique Estrada Iberico, Roberto Samanez Argumedo, Ronald Peralta Tamayo, and Carlos Aguilar Castillo for the comprehensive interviews they generously gave me. The entire research project has been greatly facilitated by my outstanding field assistant and colleague, anthropologist Alex Alvarez Del Castillo, and by my fine research assistant at the University of Illinois, José Antonio Peralta.

Notes

1. The various documents of UNESCO, ICOMOS, OWHC, and so forth, are available online. The best starting point for reading these texts is the Getty Conservation Institute Web site (see bibliography).

PART 5

Museums for the Landscape/
The Landscape as Museum

12

Using the Past to Forge the Future

The Genesis of the Community Site Museum at Agua Blanca, Ecuador

COLIN MCEWAN, MARÍA-ISABEL SILVA, AND CHRIS HUDSON

Introduction

Archaeologists and anthropologists living and working in small communities inevitably find themselves sharing the intimate rhythms of day-to-day life, with all its challenges, frustrations, and occasional minor triumphs. They often perform dual roles as students and as teachers engaged in a continuous, reciprocal process of give and take. Here we describe the evolving relationship between ourselves—leading an archaeological project—and the rural *comuna* (village) of Agua Blanca, coastal Ecuador. Our contact with the community began in the late 1970s and was set against the backdrop of the newly created Parque Nacional Machalilla (Machalilla National Park). Perhaps the most visible outcome of our work together was the creation of a community site museum at Agua Blanca, which opened in 1990. This was embedded within a program of archaeological field research undertaken between 1977 and 1990 (McEwan 2003), in the course of which we developed a series of initiatives designed to address the broader needs of the community. Our efforts to pioneer an integrated approach to culture, ecology, and subsistence were motivated by the conviction that local communities have a vital role to play in meeting the combined challenge of protecting the environment and managing cultural resources wisely (for earlier reports see Hudson and McEwan 1987; McEwan, Hudson, and Silva 1994; McEwan and Silva 1993; Silva and McEwan 1989, 2000). Writing now, more than twenty-five years later, with the benefit of hindsight offers a chance to reflect on what we feel has been accomplished, what we have learned, and equally how much remains to be done. We show how the direct involvement of the community in archaeological research proved to be a catalyst for positive change, and we hope to convey a sense of what is at once a demanding and a rewarding journey shared with many friends.

Archaeological Background

Agua Blanca is located about eight kilometers inland from the Pacific coast in the Buenavista Valley, at the heart of the Parque Nacional Machalilla (Figure 12.1). In pre-Columbian times, this was an important route connecting inland settlements with those on the coast.[1] The name *Buenavista* is perhaps inspired by the fact that overland travelers making their way west toward the Pacific must traverse a rather forbidding narrow gorge before the valley rapidly broadens to afford views of an expansive floodplain. There, at the neck of the valley, lie the ruins of a very large Manteño (A.D. 800–1530) settlement that takes its modern name from the nearby community. At its apogee around five hundred years ago, the site was the nexus of a powerful alliance of coastal trading towns collectively referred to by Spanish chroniclers as the Señorio of Salangome. In fact, this site likely was Salangome itself, the *pueblo principal* (leading town) governing the señorio and a key political and religious center controlling the southern approaches to Manteño territory (Silva 1983, 1984, 1985).[2]

The stone wall foundations of several hundred structures are still visible today scattered across an area of some four square kilometers. The principal architectural complexes reveal a carefully ordered hierarchy of structures that presumably served a variety of functions, although the majority of them have not yet been excavated. They range from large public buildings up to fifty meters long and twelve meters wide, down to smaller standard domestic dwellings. The favored location for building always seems to have been the fairly limited areas of relatively level ground on the terraces and ridges adjacent to and above the active floodplain. Comuna Agua Blanca itself lies directly on top of one such *barrio* (outlying sector) of the archaeological site, and the Manteño wall foundations that underlie the village are clearly visible in places. In addition, sporadic finds of Inca ceramics at Agua Blanca are consistent with the accounts recorded by Spanish chroniclers of an imperial presence on the coastal mainland complementing the Inca burials that have been found on Isla de La Plata, twenty-five kilometers offshore (McEwan and Silva 1989, 2000).

Agua Blanca ("white water") owes its name to a nearby natural spring, which produces a continuous supply of water noted for its very high mineral content and characteristic sulfurous smell. These odorous waters and the rich black mud that accumulates in the pond created by a retaining wall are quickly gaining renown for their curative properties. In contrast, the main river channel is dry for the greater part of the year; water flows only if sufficient winter rains have fallen through January and February. The rains are eagerly anticipated toward the end of December, and in a good year these may continue for a month or two. Even when the riverbed is dry, fresh water is obtainable all year round by digging down a few meters to reach subsurface aquifers. These sources of water, together

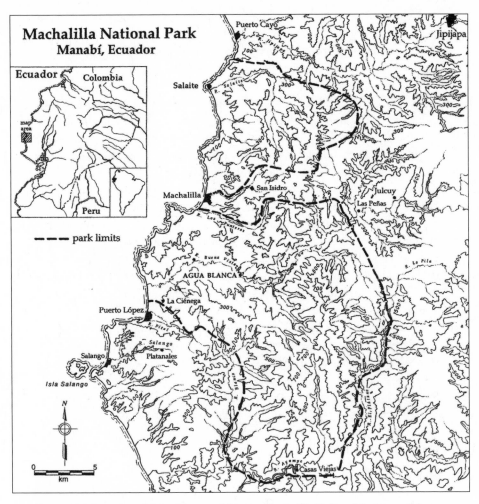

Figure 12.1. Location of Agua Blanca within the Machalilla National Park, coastal Ecuador. Map by Colin McEwan.

with a rich array of terrestrial and maritime resources, have been significant factors in attracting settlement for as long as there has been human occupation on the coast. To this day, people in the nearby fishing town of Puerto Lopez depend on their water being trucked (now piped) in from the interior valleys, and women from the neighboring port of Machalilla to the north still make the weekly journey to Agua Blanca to wash their laundry. Manteño figurines have been recovered in the course of communal *mingas* (a highland Quichua term adopted on the coast and referring to tasks undertaken collectively by the community) to clean and recondition the springs, testifying to their long use.

The arrival of the Spanish on the coast of Ecuador in 1532 brought devastating epidemics against which the indigenous population had few defenses. The ensuing demographic collapse and social disintegration resulted in the abandonment of most of the major indigenous towns. The population of the Señorio of Salangome, for example, must once have numbered many thousands, yet fifty years later, only one family was recorded as still living at Salango. Many people were most likely forcibly relocated and incorporated into the newly founded colonial provincial capital, Portoviejo, and the nearby port of Manta (formerly called Jocay), both of which soon eclipsed the principal indigenous settlements. Early maps identify a mere handful of place-names along the coast of southern Manabí, and for well over three hundred years (until the late nineteenth century), the Buenavista Valley seems to have remained rather isolated. In due course European colonists and merchants began to exploit local products such as *tagua* (ivory nut), highly valued in Europe for making coat buttons. A hacienda was established at Agua Blanca, and the clearing of natural forest to plant coffee fields was followed by the introduction of cattle. By the early 1920s, the hacienda had attracted a few migrant agricultural laborers and their families as seasonal work hands.

Some but probably not all of the *campesino* (a term referring to the rural populace) population now living at Agua Blanca may be directly descended from Manteño forebears; distinctive indigenous physical features are often evident. As is common with the great majority of the coastal mestizo populace, Spanish, rather than an indigenous language, is now widely spoken. Traces of the indigenous languages and dialects, however, are preserved in place-names and in the popular names for many plants, birds, and animals; the few remaining traditional healers (*curanderos*) still retain a deep knowledge of their habits and properties.

The Creation of the Machalilla National Park: Drought, Dire Straits, and Hard Choices

A comuna was founded at Agua Blanca in 1930, and by 1965 it had received a formal charter, thereby securing its legal status. A few years later, the hacienda went bankrupt. Its demise was a blessing in disguise, since the 1971 Agrarian Reform Law then empowered the comuna to appropriate abandoned cultivable land. By the late 1970s, however, the cumulative effects of a prolonged drought soon began to be felt. For several years in a row, the seasonal winter rains failed to materialize; unable to make ends meet, many campesinos abandoned Agua Blanca to seek a change of fortune in the sprawling shanty towns of Guayaquil, Manta, and Libertad. As with many other similarly vulnerable communities elsewhere in the rural hinterlands of Manabí, roughly one in every three families was forced to leave the village. With their crops failing, those who remained intensified their exploitation of the surrounding forest. The best lumber was hauled out by horse or donkey, destined for house and boat construction in Puerto Lopez and Machalilla.

The comuna's struggle to assert its identity and to secure rights of access to the surrounding land was sharpened by the encroachment of herds of cattle driven in from afar to forage on the moist vegetation of the upper slopes and hills. These belonged to the relatively wealthy owners of large herds, who ordered their cattle hands to burn the forest to convert it into pasture. Traditional subsistence activities, such as making charcoal for cooking fuel, yielded a meager cash income but led to continued attrition of the *algorrobo* (*Acacia* sp.) forest that carpets the valley floor. Slowly but surely the forest was being consumed. The steady degradation of the environment was becoming all too visible, especially in the immediate vicinity of the village, which was surrounded by denuded hillslopes. These had been subject to intensive foraging by goats and consisted of little more than bare bedrock bereft of vegetation—a veritable lunar landscape.

Against this backdrop, in 1979, the Parque Nacional Machalilla (henceforth referred to as the Park) was created as a 35,000-hectare reserve designed to protect and preserve the extraordinarily diverse mainland fauna and flora, as well as marine and bird life on the nearby islands of Salango and La Plata. It is the most recent such major reserve in Ecuador and harbors a range of strikingly diverse and beautiful but extremely fragile ecosystems. These include marine life and coastal fauna and flora that are akin in some respects to those found on the Galápagos Islands. On the higher slopes of the northern Colonche Hills, dry tropical forest merges into cloud forest, the delicate verdure of which is sustained by coastal fog that shrouds the ranges for much of the year.

Preparatory planning for the Park included pilot studies and surveys. Nevertheless, there was no effective consultation with the local population already living within its projected boundaries and little attempt to explain the thinking behind the creation of a natural reserve. The comuna quickly found itself at the heart of the Park and dependent for its very survival on the resources that the authorities intended to protect. Soon, attempts were being made by the Park guards to impede traditional subsistence activities that were all patently destructive of the local forest. Many members of the Park staff were drawn from other communities and towns in Manabí, and at the beginning of the enterprise, very few were local; indeed, some time elapsed before anyone from the campesino communities within the Park would be employed as a Park guard.

The advent of the Park was perceived by the comuna as a direct threat to its land and livelihood, and with good reason. The Ministry of Agriculture, which manages the Ecuadorian national park system through the Dirección Nacional Forestal (National Forestry Service), had made no provision for addressing the needs of the human population already resident within the designated protected area. It was evident that the Park was being planned primarily as a biological reserve, broadly following the North American model, and people were not factored into the equation except as an inconvenience or worse. Nothing was proffered in the way of alternative strategies for making a livelihood. In spite of good intentions, from the outset a deep mutual distrust developed between the Park officials and the campesinos, who found their misgivings confirmed by the harassment they began to suffer. From the Park's perspective, the campesinos were simply unthinking agents of the forest's destruction. To the campesinos, the very word *park* was synonymous with unsympathetic officials representing a remote government bureaucracy making decisions that would affect their lives. Worst of all, rumors were rife that the population resident within the Park boundaries was to be forcibly removed and "resettled" elsewhere, perhaps even as far away as the *oriente* (the Amazon basin) on the far side of the Andes. There was scant awareness of the duration and density of prehistoric settlement, for archaeological fieldwork in and around the Park was only just beginning around that time (McEwan 1992; Norton 1992).

Beginning the Archaeological Site Survey

We first heard mention of inland "ruins" in conversations with people in Puerto Lopez following fieldwork on Isla de La Plata—the first phase of the Sacred Isles of Ecuador Project conceived of by Presley Norton and Jorge Marcos. In 1978 Colin McEwan made a brief reconnaissance up the Buenavista Valley, where it was apparent that indiscriminate excavation was already well under way at the more visible and accessible parts of the site. Amid the larger buildings lay heaps of shattered remnants of the famed Manteño stone seats, hinting at the settlement's significance in its heyday. Parts of the site were pockmarked by recently made looters' holes. A methodical survey of the Buenavista Valley was undertaken the following year (1979), starting at the river mouth two kilometers north of Puerto Lopez and working gradually inland past Agua Blanca as far as Vuelta Larga. Members of the comuna reacted with a mixture of curiosity and wary politeness. Many also complained bitterly of sacks of charcoal being impounded and hard-earned income lost. Listening closely to local needs and aspirations made clear that everyone was apprehensive about the threat of "outside" intrusion. If the Park was to have a chance of working at all, there would need to be a decisive move beyond the traditional concepts of biological conservation to address the cultural landscape in its broadest sense and, what was more important, to involve the local populace.

Nearly everyone in Agua Blanca was keenly aware that the forest harbored archaeological remains, for the stone wall foundations of ancient buildings with associated surface scatters of ceramic and lithic material were visible amid the dense underbrush, and sometimes objects were exposed in riverbanks and gullies by winter rains. Sporadic digging by local people also yielded delicately worked figurines, impressive ceramic offering vessels, and exotic objects such as copper axes and shell ornaments, as well as the occasional item of gold jewelry. Some were kept as curiosities, but many were sold to itinerant dealers for much-needed cash, eventually finding their way into museum collections or onto the tourist and private market. Occasionally objects obtained by clandestine excavation of ridgetop sites were offered to us for sale. There was little doubt that further damage and even the eventual destruction of many sites would inevitably ensue unless more attractive alternative sources of income were found, and this fed into our developing thoughts about the research strategy discussed below. When vessels and figurines were shown, we were intrigued to see what had been discovered but made it clear that we had no interest in buying. More often than not, this provoked skeptical glances. Why else would we be wandering around in the midday heat with our gaze fixed intently on the ground? And besides, weren't we picking up bits and pieces of pottery and stone and placing them in carefully labeled bags that were then secreted away in backpacks? What possible motive could there be for this perverse behavior if it wasn't, at the end of the day, for money?

The comuna had also had firsthand experience of informal, illegal excavations by outsiders. Manteño culture is renowned for its large sculpted stone seats and stelae, most of which are known to have come from the hilltop ceremonial centers of Cerro Jaboncillo and Cerro de Hojas, some sixty kilometers to the north. The best of these have long since been removed and either were taken abroad to various museums in North America and Europe or found their way into city museums and private collections in Ecuador (see, for example, Saville 1907, 1910). The seats are an overt expression of political rank and power. Some stand up to a meter high and boast U-shaped arms surmounting either a crouched feline or a kneeling submissive male figure (illustrated in Salvat Editores Ecuadoriana 1977: 212). A splendid example occupies pride of place in the town square at Montecristi (Figure 12.2). In Agua Blanca it is said that some intact seats were still to be found as late as the 1970s. These attracted the attention of a private collector in Guayaquil who dispatched an employee to begin excavations in and around the principal structures.[3] An unknown quantity of sculpture was trucked off to Guayaquil to augment his personal collection, and

Figure 12.2. An intact Manteño stone seat is displayed in the town square at Montecristi. The seat is probably originally from the hilltop ceremonial center of Cerro Jaboncillo, some 20 kilometers to the north. Photograph by Colin McEwan.

this naturally provoked curiosity as to whether the gold that everyone knew existed might not in fact be hidden within the seats. One immediate consequence was that the remaining seats were rapidly reduced to rubble. Haphazard attempts were also made to dig intensively in certain sectors of the site, but the energy that was expended yielded little result, and enthusiasm for casual digging dwindled.

Topographical survey at Agua Blanca began in 1981, and we were soon plied with requests to explain what we were doing and why. It was clear that there was a need to respond, and we convened a meeting with the entire community, resulting in a lively encounter marked by pointed questions and energetic discussion. Proceedings came to an uproarious climax when it was discovered that the bottle of rum brought to celebrate the occasion had mysteriously disappeared, to the general consternation of all present (except presumably the authors of the crime!). And so the seeds were sown for what was eventually to grow into a fruitful collaboration between ourselves and the community. The moral of the tale is straightforward: if information is needed and questions are asked, then the willingness to offer direct, transparent answers helps to establish a genuine dialogue and to instill confidence and engender mutual respect.

Another brief visit was made in 1983 but under very different conditions, for a major El Niño event with prolonged heavy rains had occurred in the preceding nine months, and the devastation and disruption that it had caused was everywhere evident. Two years later, in mid-1985, plans were made for a longer sojourn. Opinions in the comuna were, however, sharply divided about whether outsiders should be permitted to stay. After considerable discussion, we were permitted to set up temporary living quarters in a corner of the *casa comunal* using discarded sheets of zinc and spare planks, and three *compañeros* from the comuna were hired to help clear brush and undergrowth from the ruins. The casa comunal provided space where we could assemble and sort the finds coming in from surface collections. Since this material was accessible for all to see, questions could be freely asked and readily answered, and so relations with the comuna developed gradually over the next five years.

Whose Seat?

Early in 1986 a chance discovery was to prove to be a pivotal moment in galvanizing the comuna's attitude toward archaeological finds (the following discussion of the event may be compared with the one recounted by Ann Cyphers concerning her discovery of a colossal head at San Lorenzo; see chapter 3, this volume). In the course of a minga to dig trenches through Agua Blanca for the introduction of a potable water system, a *comunero* hit upon an intact stone seat. Because this was the first such find in many years, news of the discovery spread rapidly. Within days the seat had been spirited away from the comuna and sold to a local businessman in Machalilla, who proudly put it on public display on the front patio of his shop on the main street. Machalilla is best known in archaeological circles for the eponymous type site of the Early Formative Machalilla Culture and also gives its name to the national park. Ironically, in the vicinity of Machalilla today, little is visible in the way of cultural remains—no obvious tangible cultural site or objects in which to invest local pride. The advent of the Manteño seat from Agua Blanca provided an attractive, if temporary, substitute.

The obvious course of action might have been for us to take a direct hand in negotiating the return of the seat from Machalilla. The Park director urged us to get the police involved on the grounds of "illegal removal and trafficking of antiquities." It is possible that the conspicuous intervention of the Park and police authorities on behalf of Agua Blanca might have safeguarded the seat and earned some much-needed respect. Nevertheless, we decided against this approach, for recourse to legal action probably would have led to lasting resentment and loss of trust in terms of the kin bonds and ties between Machalilla and Agua Blanca. It also ran the risk of subverting the possibility of future open engagement and consultation in such cases and the likelihood that future discoveries would be kept secret. Moreover, although a nominal sum had originally been paid for the object, we strongly felt that further monetary transactions would have the unfortunate effect of equating cultural objects with the prospect of immediate and expedient financial gain. A different kind of value had to enter into the equation: not only a sense of place and where the object had come from but also who would identify with it and who would ultimately benefit. The answers began to emerge from Agua Blanca itself, where a palpable feeling was growing that something properly belonging to the community had been unfairly appropriated. We emphasized that the primary responsibility for recovering the seat lay with the comuna and said that if everyone was willing to take the first steps toward assuming that responsibility, then we, in turn, would be prepared to look at how we might find a suitable way of putting it on permanent display.

When we approached Olaf Holm (an expatriate Dane and for many years director of the Anthropological Museum of the Banco Central), he offered to buy the seat at the going market rate for the museum's collections—which would, of course, have entailed ownership passing outside the comuna. It seemed imperative to seize the opportunity to try to reverse this pattern, and we persuaded him instead to let us use the money to house the seat on-site at Agua Blanca. Chris Hudson was working at that time on the site museum at Salango and offered to design and oversee the construction of a small archaeological exhibit. After due discussion at comuna meetings, everyone agreed that the best place for the exhibit would be in the casa comunal, a cement structure located at the center of the village that had been built some years previously by the comuna with assistance from a German volunteer organization.

The money provided by the bank helped to purchase materials such as glass and paint needed for the display, and the comuna contributed the labor. Knowing that almost all households in the comuna held archaeological objects that had turned up over the years, we invited everyone to donate these to the exhibit, which consisted of two glass display cases to hold objects, a scale model of the site, and an open plinth to support the larger sculptures. All the donor families were listed in the credits on an introductory panel, thereby helping to reinforce a sense of collective identity and pride and to demonstrate the comuna's willingness to assume responsibility for caretaking objects originating from the site.

On one occasion Olaf Holm, accompanied by Presley Norton (then director of the neighboring Banco Central Archaeological Project at Salango), paid a weekend visit to check on progress. Upon seeing the level of involvement, they supposed that the enthusiasm was attributable to the fact that most people were being paid. Upon being reassured that young and old alike were volunteering their time, they departed slightly incredulous.

As the inauguration day approached and the exhibit neared completion, a special place had been reserved for the seat to form the focus of the display. The shop owner in Machalilla was asked to return it, but he held out right up until the day before, no doubt hoping not only to get his money back, but also perhaps to profit from the exchange. The comuna representatives made it clear that the seat's disappearance amounted to unauthorized removal. People felt that the seat should be returned to its rightful home and, what is more, returned voluntarily without any compensating payment. On the day of the inauguration, the seat appeared and was duly installed in pride of place. This magnanimous gesture left a good feeling all around, and from that point on, the display formed the backdrop for all the activities taking place in the field laboratory, such as washing, labeling, and classifying of excavation finds (Figure 12.3; see Hudson and McEwan 1987).

Figure 12.3. Alciviades Martínez and Charo Merchan processing excavated finds in the *casa comunal*. The first archaeological display that opened in 1986 is in the background and features the intact seat found at Agua Blanca. Photograph by Colin McEwan.

Figure 12.4. The sign above the door claims Agua Blanca's archaeological patrimony as cultural heritage. It reads, "This culture is ours: together we'll protect the archaeological site." Note the iconic use of the stone seat in this assertion of identity. Photograph by Colin McEwan.

News of the impending inauguration spread rapidly by word of mouth. On that day, family and friends materialized from neighboring hamlets and villages, schoolteachers made the journey from Puerto Lopez and Machalilla, and museum colleagues came from Manta and Guayaquil. The exhibit established a visible expression of the community's involvement with the ongoing process of investigation, recovery, and protection. As they guided visitors through the site and site museum, the comuna archaeological team explained in their own words their experiences of discovering the past. The Manteño seat was an overt and readily recognizable expression of autochthonous pre-Columbian social organization and cultural achievement (Figure 12.4). The seat symbol soon became synonymous with Agua Blanca and began to feature as a logo on T-shirts and pennants declaring the comuna's commitment to protecting its archaeological heritage, as well as on signs to that effect (Figure 12.4). It quickly came to embody both a potent link with the past and a sense of community solidarity. Placing archaeology literally and symbolically at the heart of the community and its day-to-day activities was a defining step forward in an incremental process.

Encouraged by the success of this initial endeavor, we worked closely with the comuna to organize an *encuentro cultural* (cultural festival) each year in which villagers share and celebrate their experience with community leaders, artists, and musicians from all over Ecuador. The key feature of these *encuentros* is that they take place at (and indeed on) the archaeological site, and visitors are adopted by host families who provided accommodation and meals. We trained the members of the archaeological team to build on what they learned on-site to present their perceptions of the Park ecology as well as the archaeological discoveries in their own words. They gradually became equipped to give well-informed guided tours to the increasing flux of national tourists visiting from towns and cities, especially during the holiday season. Learning about an archaeological site through local eyes was a novel experience for many Ecuadorian and international visitors and had a palpable effect on their response and the kinds of questions they asked. This was a marked contrast to traditional ways of viewing objects in city museums far removed from their sites of origin and their adjacent communities.[4] The evident pride that members of the archaeological team take in explaining their role in the investigations along with other aspects of daily life opened up entirely new insights for many visitors.

A Research Strategy Based on Community Involvement

Early on in the project, we made a conscious decision about what we felt would be a responsible research strategy to pursue. Excavations would be bound to turn up interesting and quite possibly spectacular finds, a likely consequence of which would be to trigger a renewed wave of indiscriminate and destructive digging. The central question then was how to break that cycle to avert further degradation and destruction of the site. We elected to avoid deep excavation of trenches, cemeteries, and tombs and instead to prioritize the mapping and drawing of the many hundreds of visible wall foundations and structures. In addition, we focused on piece-plotting the surface distributions of artifacts in selected structures, combined with limited excavation of visible surface features such as pits and postholes. This offered a chance to orient and train the team in routine procedures that could be readily learned and gave compañeros a better firsthand understanding of what archaeologists are interested in and why (Figure 12.5).

In 1986 support from the Anthropological Museum of the Central Bank of Ecuador enabled the scope of the project to grow. We gradually incorporated members of the comuna into the mapping and excavation teams according to their ability and potential. Instructed by topographers Aurelio Iturralde and Franklin Ordonez, the mapping team cut sight lines and mastered the intricacies of plumb bob, tape measure, and stadia rod to lay out site grids. The practiced eyes of the compañeros in the excavation team were adept at detecting subtle differences of soil color and texture during the excavation, which would have eluded others unfamiliar with the local terrain. At each midday recess, we chose a different find for discussion, and animated debates developed. Where

Figure 12.5. Members of the archaeological team engaged in the excavation and plotting of artifacts on-site. Photograph by Colin McEwan.

was the material for a certain stone tool found? Why was lime encrusted on the inside of a vessel? How had the Manteños smelted the copper used to fashion a delicately spiraled earring? Why were the dead buried in funerary urns? Did the Manteños suffer droughts too? It soon became apparent that we were interested in all the varied debris of prehistoric occupation that people were accustomed to seeing in and around the ruins: dense scatters of broken pottery, fragments of stone tools, bone, and marine shells. We held impromptu classes in the gullies in and around the comuna. This served as an introduction to archaeological stratigraphy, for beneath the discarded tins, plastic, broken bottles, and other "archaeological" debitage of modern activities, we could discern successive flood deposits. These alternated with cultural levels comprising clay floors and hearths with ash, pottery, and bones, all visible in profile. Many meters beneath the present ground surface, a deeply buried soil horizon with associated cultural material indicated an Early Formative occupation in the valley. There was abundant evidence in and around Agua Blanca to suggest that human intervention had been a destabilizing factor in the past. The deep profiles exposed in gullies revealed up to eight meters or more of alluvial sediments, and the rates of erosion appeared to have been greatly accelerated in the past, probably as a result of deforestation. Another soil horizon visible slightly more than a meter below the present ground surface suggested that the natural cover probably recovered notably after the population collapse and effective abandonment of the area brought about by the Spanish conquest. Clearly, for better or for worse, human agency has been a significant factor in the environmental history of this part of the coast during the Late Quaternary.

We trained new team members in the various tasks of drawing and excavating on-site (Figure 12.5) and encouraged those with the most aptitude and motivation to learn how to reconstruct excavated finds such as large ollas (vessels used for preparing food and storing water) in the field laboratory (Figure 12.6). Careful measurements were taken to confirm the alignment of the largest Manteño structures on the sun's rising and setting points on the horizon around the solstices. We coordinated the preparation of reference collections of shells gathered during expeditions to local beaches. Using a published guide to Pacific seashells, one member of the team memorized all the Latin names for the genus and species of each. When a visiting botanist (Fernando Ortiz Crespo) put him to the test with a comprehensive quiz, he passed with flying colors.

Extending Horizons, Forging Friendships

In tandem with the fieldwork, we arranged meetings with universities, government ministries, and nongovernmental organizations (NGOs) in Quito. At one

Figure 12.6. Restoration of a Manteño funerary urn in the field laboratory by members of the archaeological team, Hugo Ventura and Enrique Ventura. Photograph by Colin McEwan.

meeting with the National Forestry Service, it was clear that their plans envisaged locating the future park infrastructure well away from the comuna. Facilities such as reception offices and gatehouses were to consist of cement structures with tin roofs. Forestry Service representatives explicitly stated that their highest priority was to keep contact between visiting tourists and campesinos to an absolute minimum, claiming that tourists would not want to see an "untidy" campesino village. The prospects for the employment of local campesinos as guards, guides, and interpreters in the park seemed to be far down the list of priorities. When we suggested that campesinos ought to play a central role in environmental conservation and responsible management of the archaeological site, the proposal was something entirely new for the park planners and managers (Paucar et al. 1987).

It seemed to us that any attempt to keep the site and community separate would only serve to exacerbate divisions and mistrust and ultimately be self-defeating. Such an attempt also was at odds with our demonstrable progress at involving the comuna in taking positive steps toward the protection of both natural and cultural resources. We realized that we would have to take the initiative in finding independent sources of support to develop some of the on-site infrastructure and hope that the park authorities would sooner or later catch up. Slowly, we secured backing for the task of building up the site infrastructure. The British Council responded to a request for funds to install two rest shelters and scale relief models to better accommodate and inform visitors. Finally, realizing that the archaeological site was fast becoming a major attraction for tourists, the park director secured funds from the National Forestry Service to build a boundary fence around the site, construct stairways, and consolidate footpaths that we had laid out. As the excavation progressed, the casa comunal became the venue for evening classes by candlelight with the archaeological team. Together we addressed different aspects of Manteño culture, using the available didactic pamphlets in Spanish to study such things as the representation of native birds and animals in Manteño iconography (see, for example, Holm 1982). Further, mingas enabled us to build a small storeroom and guest room adjoining the casa comunal.

As part of a conscious strategy of extending horizons, we took members of the archaeological team all over the country to visit national museums as well as other archaeological projects and sites. The sites included those that are protected and equipped to receive visitors, as well as other sites that have suffered severe depredation and damage. The visit to La Tolita in Esmeraldas Province made a lasting impression, since this site has been very heavily looted and panning for gold artifacts was still going on. One or two sites had modest museums, and where these had fallen into disrepair and closed—such as at Valdivia on the Santa Elena Peninsula—the consequences of neglect and disinterest were all too apparent. These visits exposed the team to the scope and variety of archaeological investigation and enabled them to see how other sites were being managed, mismanaged, or even neglected altogether. It was an opportunity to learn first-hand about what local sites and museums can mean in a larger cultural and political context.

At the same time, we encouraged Ecuadorian colleagues to visit the project and to share their knowledge and expertise. Specialists such as geologists Ramón Vera and Marcela Mosquera undertook fieldwork on the fluvial geomorphology of the valley and led field excursions and contributed lectures to explain their research (Mosquera 1989). We organized a three-day visit to Agua Blanca by archaeologists working on other Banco Central projects so that they could get to know the comuna and share their experiences of "archaeology in action" in different settings. This recognition and active interest and involvement by supportive colleagues helped validate and reinforce the unfolding initiatives in the comuna. We began to take selected members of the archaeological group to attend conferences, creating a chance to see how archaeological research is presented and shared and also encouraging firsthand experience of this aspect of professional activity. Key members of the team could appreciate that the participatory approach to archaeology that we were pioneering together at Agua Blanca was something new, and they could come to understand the responsibilities that this entailed.

Ecology and Community: The Need to Subsist

During the long process of building a consensus in favor of protecting the archaeological site, we were always keenly aware of the harsh realities of day-to-day subsistence. The temporary employment generated by the archaeological project brought an immediate and welcome cash income for many families, and this was spread across the comuna as fairly as possible. The core archaeological team consisted of about twelve compañeros, added to which there were up to eight more working in the topographic teams and four or five at any given time in the field laboratory. Up to twenty-five compañeros were thus employed at the peak of the project, out of a total population of around two hundred at that time living in and around the comuna. Even so, many families still derived all or part of their income from direct exploitation of the forest. Since no archaeological project goes on forever, clearly the successful long-term protection of the site would be as much about creating viable subsistence and income alternatives as anything else. Here we listened carefully to the comuna's own perceptions and aspirations. These were voiced at meetings presided over by the *cabildo,* which consists of representatives (namely, the comuna president, vice president, treasurer, and *sindico*) who are elected anew each year. This is the comuna's mechanism for self-governance and is the main forum for dialogue, exchange of views, and long discussions. A typical meeting might begin on Saturday afternoon and go on until well after midnight.

One example of a good idea being translated into practical action was an irrigation system set up in 1981 by the *club femenino* (women's group) with support from rural development funds. This enterprising initiative began on a modest scale using durable plastic drainage tubes to pipe the sulfurous water issuing from the spring across the riverbed to an irrigable area of floodplain on the other side. There was a unanimous feeling that expansion of this system would bring benefits to nearly everyone, with potentially far-reaching positive outcomes. We approached the British Embassy with a request for assistance, and embassy officials helped channel Overseas Development Association support for this project. When the extension was implemented in 1987, it resulted in a wider range of fruits and vegetables being grown and also generated a surplus that could be sold. This brought direct improvements in the range and quality of the diet and a small but important source of independent income for some women.

We then contacted Fundación Natura (Nature Foundation), an Ecuadorian NGO, to seek alternative ways of generating employment and income for people in the comuna who, for one reason or another, were not directly involved in the archaeological project. The foundation facilitated a comprehensive evaluation of the comuna's resources and prospects, and in collaboration with the national rural development organization, Comunidades y Desarrollo en el Ecuador (Communities and Development in Ecuador or COMUNIDEC), we secured financial support from the Inter-American Foundation for a pig project. Training in project management and accounting was given. Unfortunately, not only did obtaining the right kind of high-quality feed prove difficult and costly, but also swine fever struck unexpectedly and undermined the viability of this project, which eventually failed. Something similar had also happened to the *vivero forestal* (a plant nursery), which was set up to encourage the cultivation of seedlings of native species for sale but did not prosper. In yet another initiative, a practical course was organized in organic agriculture that included composting, mulching, and crop rotation designed to maintain productivity and avoid exhausting the soil. Likewise, instruction was given in the use of natural sprays and other techniques to avoid applying highly toxic chemical insecticides for dealing with destructive and persistent pests. This, however, was not effectively followed through.

The contrasting fortunes of these projects reveal the kinds of challenges and difficulties that must be faced in pursuit of sustainable subsistence alternatives. Whether through poor judgment, irresponsibility, or sheer bad luck, even apparently promising initiatives can easily founder. It was not for nothing that the park director once exclaimed with an exasperated sigh, "Con los campesinos no se puede" (with peasants you can't do anything). However, when projects do work, they represent an affirming step toward achieving an integrated approach to environmental and cultural resource management. The support given by the archaeological project to these kinds of ancillary initiatives has aided in the community's struggle to achieve a viable livelihood in the face of the vagaries of climate and the park's policy of environmental protection. A bottomless reservoir of patience, perseverance, and endurance is required. Working shoulder-to-shoulder digging ditches, clearing wells, and collecting trash on community mingas also contributes visibly to communal projects and helps advance the collective interests of the entire community.

A Decisive Year

By late 1988 Olaf Holm realized that the initiatives we had taken had grown much bigger in scope and intent than the original archaeological project funded by the Banco Central. This was a period when the Banco Central's major archaeological projects on the coast were nearly all directed by foreign archaeologists overseen by Holm. In the case of Agua Blanca, the radical departure from the more traditional way of running a project was not to his liking, and he made his displeasure increasingly evident, stating adamantly that things "had gone too far." Meanwhile, the momentum we had generated was beginning to produce tangible results. As we will describe in the next section, we were also in the midst of securing support for the site museum and were convinced that in the longer term much would hang on the outcome of these efforts. Regrettably, in 1989 Holm withheld all support for the project. We resolved to stay the course, and with Ecuador's National Archaeological Congress due to take place in Cuenca later that year, we set our sights on sharing our experiences of this kind of participatory approach with its potential benefits. The majority of the archaeological team committed to make the journey to Cuenca, and each contributed a share of the costs. This was the first time that a team of campesinos working on a project had attended a professional meeting; we presented the results of the archaeological work to date, underlining the success of the participatory approach in action and prompting a generous acknowledgment of the team from Agua Blanca by all who were present at the conference. This overwhelmingly positive and heartening response was a powerful and decisive moment. With the evidence before his eyes, Holm offered warm congratulations to everyone for all that had been accomplished.

Conscious of the Past, Building for the Future: The Creation of a Community Site Museum

One idea that arose from discussions with the cabildo was to create a permanent cultural center and site museum in the heart of the comuna. We were excited by the idea of a purpose-built building that would serve to display finds from the excavation and extend the facilities available to both the archaeological project and visitors. While this building is often referred to here as a site museum, we rarely used that term literally but always described it as the *casa cultural* (cultural center). We felt that it should be built using local materials and traditional construction techniques to create a structure that would fit into the village and landscape. By employing labor from the comuna, we felt strongly that it could serve to help validate building skills and techniques that were on the verge of being lost because of the trend toward building brick houses with zinc roofing. Not least, it would be more economical to build and offered a better chance of ensuring regular maintenance and refurbishment when necessary. We hoped, too, that by participating in its construction, the community would identify closely with the new building.

In 1988, cognizant of incipient plans for a pipeline to be built through the park by the Ecuadorian Oil Corporation (CEPE), we approached the company's Community Relations Department. After lengthy consultations, we submitted a detailed proposal and were granted funding. The British Council agreed to offer a travel grant to enable Chris Hudson to return to the village to supervise construction. Labor for the project was entirely drawn from the village; in addition, three mingas were organized to marshal collective involvement and support. At the suggestion of the village president, one of these was made up of schoolchildren, who enthusiastically collected river cobbles for the foundations. Nearly all the foundation holes yielded evidence of the Manteño occupation, including hearths, potsherds, and animal bones. In two places, Manteño stone wall foundations were uncovered. These were excavated, mapped, and photographed by the archaeological team and then roped off to become an in situ exhibit right at the entrance to the museum. A balsa-wood scale model was made of the structure, and this proved to be an invaluable tool for discussing and refining the design with the carpenters (Figure 12.7). The building is composed of materials that were all obtained locally: timber, split bamboo, palm thatch, and *quincha* (a render made of manure, earth, straw, and water). So far as we know, the casa cultural is the largest structure to be built for many decades in southern Manabí using traditional techniques (Figure 12.8). A balcony on the main level affords a magnificent panorama of the valley, while upstairs are an office, storeroom, and living accommodations for members of the archaeological project. The entrance porch provides welcome shade in which to sit and rest, and on the wall above, the painted logo of a Manteño seat affirms the comuna's affinity with this symbol of cultural prowess and achievement.

The opening of the casa cultural (Figure 12.9) repeated the success of the smaller archaeological exhibit in the casa comunal several years before, and attention was focused on the new structure in the heart of the comuna—the outcome of a process that had been over a decade in the making. The inaugural celebrations were infused with the spirit of the encuentros that had taken place in the intervening years. Among the many ethnic groups represented were Salasaca musicians (Figure 12.10), whose presence embodied the links that were

Figure 12.7. Designer Chris Hudson with the *comuna* team using a balsa-wood model to discuss the construction of the *casa cultural*. Photograph by Colin McEwan.

Figure 12.8. Colin McEwan and members of the archaeological team in front of the newly completed *casa cultural*. Photograph by María-Isabel Silva.

Figure 12.9. Inauguration of the site museum in the heart of Comuna Agua Blanca in 1990. Photograph by Colin McEwan.

Figure 12.10. A visiting troupe of Salasaca musicians celebrates the opening of the site museum. Photograph by Colin McEwan.

Figure 12.11. A view of the archaeological display and graphics inside the museum, with photos of *comuna* members on the back wall serving as a backdrop for archaeological figurines of Manteños. Photograph by Colin McEwan.

being established between highlands and coast. The display inside the museum (Figure 12.11) is designed to orient visitors to the extent and significance of the archaeological site before they tour it on foot. Simple glass modules on plywood bases protect the exhibits, and larger objects, such as stone seats and burial urns, are on open display; there is also a "please touch" table. Information is provided by text, photos, maps, and a simple time-chart incorporating real potsherds.

This and many subsequent gatherings have become a practical means of sharing knowledge about this past and fostering interactions between visiting community representatives, as well as provoking discussion and debates about indigenous identity and interethnic relations (Figure 12.12). These experiences play a vital role in reaffirming the links between past and present and in cultivating identification with and pride in past cultural achievements. They also provide powerful motivation for envisioning how to bring about change.

Looking Ahead

After more than a decade of sustained involvement with Agua Blanca, the time came to create space for the comuna to assume full responsibility for running the site museum, providing guided tours, and maintaining the site. We felt that it was imperative to guard against fostering a dependency on ourselves as the principal means of obtaining support for community initiatives.

Figure 12.12. A member of the archaeological team from Agua Blanca shows a visitor from a highland community around the museum. Photograph by Colin McEwan.

One of the principal challenges over the longer term has been how to ensure that sufficient income is generated within the comuna so as to guarantee the regular upkeep and maintenance of the site and site museum. We emphasize above that the National Park Service had never really had to address the challenge of managing cultural resources within a designated natural reserve anywhere in Ecuador. A vexing problem has always been the relationship between Agua Blanca and the park authorities, who levy an admission charge on all visitors entering the reserve. Tourists who arrive at the comuna have already paid an entry fee and therefore expect to find the appropriate infrastructure, guiding services, and interpretive signage relating to the site. While the inauguration of the site museum offered a significant step in the right direction, it is, of course, managed and maintained internally by the comuna and therefore provides a valuable attraction at little or no cost to the park. By 1990 Olaf Holm had come to recognize the need for a modest budget to assure year-round maintenance of the site. This amounted to the equivalent of three monthly salaries, whereas the core archaeological team of comuneros numbered around a dozen. The team devised a regular weekly rotation to staff both the site museum and the control point at the entrance to the valley and also take care of clearing vegetation and maintaining paths and drainage channels on-site. The bank support, however, lasted little more than three years, as Ecuador plunged into political and financial crisis in the early 1990s. As this support dried up, the archaeological team maintained the rotation but relied on tips and donations from visitors as a source of income. This continues to be a sore point and a source of friction and resentment, although more formal arrangements for payment by large visiting groups are now in place.

At the time of writing, some thirty families (out of some fifty in the comuna) derive all or most of their income from activities related to tourists (national and international) drawn to the archaeological site and site museum. There has been a marked reduction in the impact of subsistence activities; this is most evident in the regeneration of the forest, especially in the immediate environs of the comuna. The site is being successfully maintained and managed, and no looting or sale of objects has occurred in the intervening years. The advent of the site museum has stimulated a mini-renaissance of other smaller structures, such as cabins for visitors, which are being built using local materials and traditional techniques, by conscious choice.

However, there is a pressing need for a long-overdue refurbishment of the site museum. The second-generation archaeological team is anxious to receive proper training and orientation, and at the time of writing, we are about to re-engage in this process. In parallel with this effort, it will be vital to develop didactic materials for use in the school curriculum so that the new possibilities in the cultural life of the community can prove to be a tool for education in the broadest sense.

Archaeology and Community: Reflections on the Bigger Picture

Public perception of Ecuador's indigenous past has been constrained in large measure by the relatively few sites that have gained wide public recognition and are accessible to visitors. This situation contrasts with that of Mexico and Peru, both of which boast abundant and impressive monumental evidence of past cultural accomplishments. There, pyramids and temples stand as powerful, visible expressions of this past and have been woven into the construction of an evolving national ethos and identity. Renowned sites such as Teotihuacan in Mexico and Machu Picchu in Peru have been adopted as potent symbols of the indigenous contribution to nationhood and have won international recognition. By comparison, Ecuador suffers from a relative paucity of archaeological sites with distinctive architectural remains. Those that come to mind are nearly all to be found in the highlands, and most of them are, in fact, the product of Inca imperial expansion. Only rarely is there direct visible evidence of monumental construction by autochthonous cultures—such as at Cochasqui, where large ramped *tolas* date to approximately A.D. 900–1200. Elsewhere, a strong identification with and connection between local indigenous populations and nearby archaeological sites is not often readily apparent.[5] This is even more apparent on the coast, where archaeological sites with any kind of conspicuous architecture are equally scarce. Sites such as Real Alto on the Santa Elena Peninsula and Salango in southern Manabí encompass deep histories but possess little in the way of pyramids and walls that is intelligible to the untutored eye. What we tend to see instead is the appropriation of key objects, which are held to embody a powerful historical legitimization of indigenous identity, and their incorporation into new urban settings. A case in point is the forcible removal of the celebrated Huancavilca sculpture known as San Biritute from its original site to a museum in Guayaquil. This impressive 2.5-meter-tall monolith with an erect phallus once stood in the small village of Sacachun, having served as a focus for indigenous belief for many centuries. It has been the subject of heated polemic between the community exhorting its return and the political authorities in Guayaquil, who have appropriated and subsumed the object into their own cultural agenda (Benavides 2004).

For all its relative isolation on the southern Manabí coast, Agua Blanca has come to represent something of a turning point in Ecuador in terms of stemming the movement of objects from their sites of origin into museums in towns and cities. In this chapter we have tried to show in practice how efforts to research, preserve, and protect archaeological sites and objects must be incorporated into the social, political, and economic fabric of local communities (see Benavides 2001; Lumbreras 1974). We have described how the location of Agua Blanca within a national park presented a special set of circumstances and opportunities. In common with many rural communities throughout Latin America, the comuna faces the overwhelming reality of inherent limitations imposed by scarce material and financial resources. In such situations, the deleterious impact of certain daily subsistence activities upon the natural environment is increasingly widely recognized. Where there are vulnerable archaeological sites in close proximity, economic need and sometimes outright greed can easily fuel a rapidly accelerating and usually irreversible process of *huaquerismo* (uncontrolled excavation) and destruction.

The advent of the archaeological project at Agua Blanca introduced a valuable new dynamic into the equation. Not only has the archaeological research offered insights into the relationship between earlier human communities and the environment over many millennia, but with the patient nurturing of a participatory approach, archaeology has also acted as a catalyst for positive change. A respect for (and willingness to work with) the comuna has gone hand in hand with a recognition of the pressing economic realities of a community whose surrounding environment was in jeopardy. Everything we have attempted together has been based on careful deliberation and discussion. We have invested time and energy in a continuous process of consultation and discussion with the comuna to identify priorities and to determine what was feasible and what the likely outcomes and benefits might be. Of vital importance has been recognizing that the community's strength lies in its capacity for governing and shaping its own ambitions and through delegating responsibility by collective decision making on important issues. This community-based approach provides a viable alternative to "top-down" development strategies, which risk excluding or deliberately overriding the creative contribution that a local population can make toward solving problems of environmental and cultural resource management. While we take justifiable pride in what has been accomplished, in common with other site museums in rural settings, Agua Blanca does not represent a tale of unqualified success. It was conceived and delivered under difficult and often discouraging circumstances. The process has met with many obstacles—some stemming from ignorance, some from indifference, and some from outright hostility toward new ways of working. Nevertheless, we made a conscious attempt to involve a wide range of institutions and individuals and enjoyed support and encouragement from unexpected sources. After over a decade of preparatory work, the creation of the site museum was perhaps the most visible expression of what was a larger ongoing process underpinned by many less visible interrelated activities. We believe that this case study shows how local communities can be instrumental in protecting and managing both biological and cultural heritage in an integrated way and thus become key agents in promoting sustainable approaches to development. We have learned and continue to learn from each other's experiences—not only the things that have worked, but also (and of equal importance) the things that have not. There is no prescriptive formula to ensure success; nevertheless, we hope that the experiences described here can be usefully compared with similar kinds of initiatives elsewhere (see, for example, Moser et al. 2003 in Peers and Brown 2003).

Acknowledgments

We are part of a larger network of friends and family whose involvement in ways large and small has often been critically important at different stages in the project. We especially wish to acknowledge the many colleagues who have worked alongside us in different capacities and whose personal commitment has often far exceeded the normal demands of fieldwork. The work described here was made possible by the skills and dedication of the original members of the archaeological team: Isidro Ventura, Hugo Ventura, Carlos Maldonado, Jorge Alban, Pedro Ventura, Enrique Ventura, Nilo Soledispa, Alciviades Martínez, Charo Merchan, Marco Asunción, Raúl Ventura, Leoncio Soledispa, Jairo

Ventura, Camilo Martínez, Alejo Ventura, Galo Ventura, and Augustín Ventura. We also wish to acknowledge the current members of the team—many of whom are the sons of the compañeros listed above—who "carry the torch": Paul Martínez, Gonzalo Asunción, Alejo Avila, Carlos Ventura, Arturo Maldonado, Leopoldo Ventura, Plinio Merchan, Stalin Maldonado, Pablo Tomala, Jaime Martínez, Alfredo Ventura, Favian Avila, and Milton Ventura. In addition we want to record our special thanks to Samuel and Mariana Martínez and to Zoila Ventura. We also acknowledge Yolanda Kakabadse (Fundación Natura), Carlos Zambrano (Parque Nacional Machalilla), Gonzalo Rivas, Catalina Pazmiño, Aurelio Iturralde, Adela Silva, and Franklin Ordoñez. Among Ecuadorian and other professional colleagues, particularly noteworthy are Ramón Vera, Marcela Mosquera, Alfredo Carrasco, Diego Quiroga, Alfredo Moreira, Maritza Freire, Francisco Valdez, Ernesto Salazar, Jorge Marcos, Fabian Penaherra, José Chancay, Tamara Bray, Richard Lunniss, Karen Stothert, and Dorothy Hosler. Modest but vital funding from the following institutions supported the earlier stages of the archaeological research at Agua Blanca: the Gordon Childe Bequest Fund (Institute of Archaeology, London), the Tinker Foundation, the British Museum (Elizabeth Carmichael), and the Graduate College of the University of Illinois. Initial logistical assistance provided by Presley Norton together with the generous support of the Anthropological Museum of the Central Bank in Guayaquil (and facilitated by Olaf Holm) enabled the project to develop continuously over a period of several years. The 1989 field season was supported by a bequest left by Peter McEwan.

Notes

1. This route once connected the inland town of Jipijapa (originally, Xipijapa) via Joa, Julcuy, and the Buenavista Valley to the coast and is still used on occasion to bring in contraband and avoid the checkpoints on the main highways. It goes without saying that in the course of traversing the hill trails, the local inhabitants acquire a detailed knowledge of both the natural and the cultural landscape. Many paths have evidently been in use since Manteño times (and probably very much longer), because they link the main site of Agua Blanca with a number of outlying settlements.

2. María-Isabel Silva analyzes the indigenous toponyms within the context of precontact social organization and economic and political relationships.

3. A private businessman, Ing. Luis Piana, employed an assistant, Hans Morotzke, to begin "exploration" of the site. This was, perhaps, well intentioned, since notes, diagrams, and photos record some of this work and a typescript draft report was prepared. However, the excavations were in due course abandoned, having been left open.

4. During the oral presentation of this paper in Montreal, Colin McEwan noted that the SAA meeting was taking place far removed from the site settings that all the partici-

pants were describing. He commented on the fact that the SAA annual meeting rarely travels outside the continental United States. The International Congress of Americanists (ICA), by contrast, alternates between Europe, North America, and Latin America. He suggested that the ICA could be one means of arranging visits to and support for local site museum initiatives. These and other conferences can be used much more actively and imaginatively to help overcome the sense of isolation and lack of resources that can beset promising projects. The unstinting support and visible presence of the professional community is essential if these kinds of projects are to flourish.

5. The cultural politics shaping Ecuadorian archaeology in recent decades have been addressed by Benavides (2004) and Andrade (2004) and merit further critical reflection. This is the subject of a separate paper presently in preparation.

13

The Sicán Museum

Guardian, Promoter, and Investigator of the Sicán Culture and the Muchik Identity

CARLOS G. ELERA AND IZUMI SHIMADA

General Considerations

Archaeologists need to play a more active, if not proactive, role in guiding public conception, use, protection, and understanding of the past and its remains (for example, Pyburn and Wilk 1995; Sabloff 1998). Fieldwork must be viewed as an interactive process built on reciprocal relationships with local communities. The social reality of the fieldwork setting must be well understood to develop congenial and productive forms of interaction and information dispersal. Possession of a permit from some distant, governmental, supervisory institution does not preclude the need to inform and coordinate with the local population in various ways and at different levels.

In Peru, national and foreign archaeologists often do not adequately inform the public of the objectives and results of their investigations. Foreign projects tend to publish their research results first in their own countries and only some time later in Peru, if at all (Shimada 1995: vii). It would behoove us all to promptly inform the Peruvian public and professionals alike of advances in our investigations through conferences, exhibits, publications, and/or mass media at local and national levels (Shimada 1995: vii). Archaeological investigations concerning past human relationships should seek to encompass contemporary human relationships, particularly between archaeology and the public.

Some notable discoveries and interpretations reach the public through exhibits, news, and other media along with the occasional research summaries of archaeological fieldwork conducted in Peru. However, the latter are, by and large, ephemeral, sporadic, and/or oriented toward professional archaeologists. No formal organizations or regulations exist in Peru to ensure regular, broad, public dissemination of archaeological research results. The National Institute of Culture (Instituto Nacional de Cultura, or INC), which supervises all archaeological fieldwork in Peru, has detailed regulations governing the content of reports to be submitted by all archaeologists to whom they grant permits. Yet it has no requirements or recommendations regarding presentation of research results (including the display of significant artifact finds) to the public. Similarly, proper storage and conservation of recovered materials are largely left to each archaeologist to decide.

Furthermore, existing regulations and concerns with archaeology and the Peruvian cultural heritage are overly weighted toward the fieldwork/recovery phase and the benefit to be derived by the capital city of Lima. Local (provincial) populations and postfieldwork phases of archaeology receive little attention. But these deserve much more emphasis from both the INC and the archaeologist. We argue that museums—both small and large—need to assume a more active role as a key nexus between the archaeological community and the public, and they should receive greater support from the government.

Peruvian museums have the additional important task of facilitating better understanding of the contemporary Peruvian reality with its deep, kaleidoscopic, multicultural roots. Few countries in the world have as rich and diverse a cultural legacy as Peru, which, ironically, is a fact not well understood by the majority of Peruvians. Moreover, many Peruvians have a widespread prejudice against and indifference to aboriginal Andean cultural values. The formation of a Peruvian identity has been a slow and at times antagonistic process. Peruvians must understand that the cornerstone for a mature and unbiased cultural identity should be the appreciation of the richness and diversity of their cultural and ethnic heritage. A broad-based, patient, long-term educational effort is necessary to build solid bridges among the different segments of Peruvian society. Public museums have the potential to be a major player in this process.

Provincial museums in Peru are, however, handicapped in achieving their primary missions by their relatively low status within the highly centralized, Lima-centered national museum system. They habitually face financial, logistical, and staff shortages, as well as the long-term challenge of securing the public interest and support that are crucial to long-term viability.

With the foregoing remarks as background, in this chapter we discuss the factors that led to the establishment of the Sicán National Museum (SNM) (Figure 13.1); its scientific, educational, and social aims; and some of strategies and steps we have devised to implement them. We archaeologically and socially situate the SNM in regional context.

The Establishment, Agendas, and Characteristics of the Sicán National Museum

The SNM is situated on the northern edge of the small city of Ferreñafe (approximately eight hundred kilometers north of Lima) in the province of Fer-

Figure 13.1. Frontal view of the Sicán National Museum in the small city of Ferreñafe. Photograph by Yutaka Yoshii.

reñafe, department of Lambayeque, on the north coast of Peru (Figure 13.2). It was opened to the public in November 2002. Carlos G. Elera is the museum director; Izumi Shimada serves as its scientific adviser. The SNM is responsible for the protection and preservation of archaeological sites within the province of Ferreñafe, particularly the more than thirty sites in the approximately sixty square kilometers of dense, semitropical thorny forest of the Poma National Historical Sanctuary in the mid–La Leche Valley to the northwest. The site of Sicán is the inferred capital of the Sicán culture and is the largest and best-known site in the sanctuary (Figure 13.3).

The SNM is an outgrowth of the Sicán Archaeological Project (SAP), which Shimada directed from 1978 to 2002. Both the SAP and SNM strive to be archaeologically and socially embedded in regional context and holistic in coverage. As a student, Elera was a member of this project and later served as its Peruvian codirector. The project was a long-term, international, interdisciplinary, regional study aimed at a holistic understanding of the Sicán (also known as Lambayeque) culture that was centered in the Lambayeque region on the north coast of Peru circa AD 750–1375. Excavations of regional sites of different period, character, size, and location were augmented by a variety of approaches, including archaeometry, experimental archaeology, and ethnoarchaeology. Since its inception, the SAP has integrated Peruvian students and professionals through a number of long-term scientific collaborative agreements with various

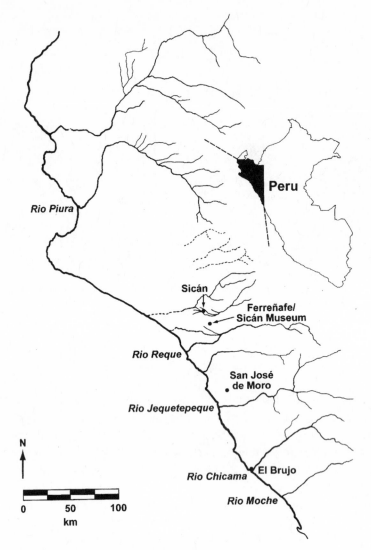

Figure 13.2. Locations of the site of Sicán and the small city of Ferreñafe (where the National Sicán Museum is situated). Map by Steve Mueller.

institutions (for example, the Museo de la Nación and the Archaeology Program of the Pontificia Universidad Católica del Perú). Project headquarters and living quarters were located in the midst of local communities and maintained an open-door policy. In addition to actively publishing in Spanish and English with Peruvian participants, we regularly provided news releases regarding our research to local and national television and newspapers. Public talks were given regularly at local schools and community centers to introduce project members;

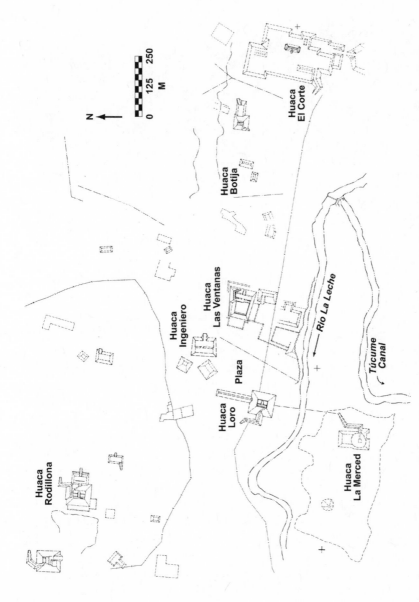

Figure 13.3. Architectural map of the site of Sicán in the Poma National Historical Sanctuary in the mid–La Leche Valley. Map by Izumi Shimada.

Figure 13.4. One of the workshops that comprise the Aldea Artesanal within the Sicán National Museum compound. Photograph by Victor Curay.

explain the background, aims, field activities, and results of the project; and request assistance in successful implementation of our fieldwork and combating looting of archaeological sites. We also invited local schoolteachers to come see our excavations and laboratory for firsthand understanding of our archaeological investigation. They, in turn, were asked to pass on to their students what they learned. We then paid for gasoline for school buses to bring hundreds of local students to our excavations. As a result, tests in Peruvian history classes in local schools now regularly include questions about the Sicán culture as well as the difference between illicit grave looting and archaeological research. Our goal was to socially integrate ourselves in local communities and play an active role in educating local populations about archaeology and their cultural heritage.

Most of the local residents find it difficult to relate to abstract discussions regarding the importance and protection of their cultural heritage. We are often asked what will become of the excavated remains—whether they will be taken to Lima or outside of Peru, and, if not, where and when the local people can see them. When we planned for the excavation of a thousand-year-old Middle Sicán elite shaft tomb at the major temple mound of Huaca Loro in the site of Sicán, these questions were very much in our minds. Accordingly, when we excavated the tomb in 1991–92, we invited local people and the Peruvian mass media to visit our excavation, and we also sought and obtained funds for two years of intensive conservation work by American, British, and Peruvian specialists. These efforts were replicated when we excavated another major Middle Sicán elite shaft tomb at Huaca Loro in 1995–96.

Given that our 1991–92 work at Huaca Loro represented the first scientific excavation of a Sicán elite tomb and an impressive quantity of gold and other precious metal objects were recovered, we considered prompt publication of the excavation results and public exhibition of the excavated grave goods to be of the utmost importance (see Shimada 1995; Shimada and Montenegro 1993). For decades, until the mid-1970s, similar tombs had been systematically ransacked by looters for gold objects, which were either melted down or sold to private collectors throughout the world (Carcedo and Shimada 1985; Pedersen 1976; Shimada 1981a, 1981b; Tello 1937a, 1937b, 1937c; Valcárcel 1937). The first public exhibit of a small selection of our excavated gold objects took place in the nearby Brüning Regional Archaeological Museum in 1992. Subsequently, a major exhibit was held at the Museo de La Nación in Lima (1992–93). Only then were exhibits held outside of Peru, first in eight cities in Japan (1994–96) and later in Zürich (1996–97).

Following the exhibit in Japan, Alberto Fujimori (then president of Peru) proposed a plan to construct a new museum based on the accumulated results of the Sicán Archaeological Project, including the grave goods from the two shaft tombs at Huaca Loro. The Japanese government agreed to fund the construction, and Shimada was given the task of coming up with the basic conceptual plans for the museum building, mission, organization, exhibits, equipment, and personnel.

President Fujimori provided an opportunity to forge a unique synergy between a Peruvian public institution and a long-term archaeological research project; in other words, we saw that these two entities together could more effectively accomplish the primary missions of the SNM. The aims of the SNM are to promote and advance Sicán archaeology, disseminate the resultant knowledge and understanding, and identify and conserve the material and immaterial remains of the Sicán cultural tradition.

The SNM has a number of additional distinctive features reflecting the basic philosophy, aims, and approaches of the SAP and the belief that successful communication requires a clear understanding of the message to be conveyed and its audience. The SNM is dedicated to scientific research of a single culture—Sicán—and dissemination of its results, as well as protection of its legacies. In addition, the SNM is intended to serve as the primary research center of the Sicán culture, and it stores all artifacts recovered during the eighteen seasons of fieldwork conducted by the SAP.

The SNM also emphasizes a holistic vision of the Sicán culture—from its chronology and environment to the daily life of commoners and craft production. In contrast, displays in traditional museums in Peru are dominated by looted funerary pottery, thereby sending a misleading message regarding the aims of archaeology and giving the Peruvian public little basis upon which to relate to their cultural heritage.

Our museum exhibits focus on the presentation of meaningful contexts and the entirety of productive processes rather than isolated objects selected on the basis of their rarity and fine technical and/or artistic qualities alone. The clear majority of exhibit space is used to present life-size or scale reconstructions of tombs and workshops. The latter are based on information gained from our excavations of ancient smelting, smithing, and pottery-making workshops as well as replicative field experiments and ethnoarchaeological research (for example, Shimada and Merkel 1991; Shimada and Wagner 2001). Videos, CD-ROMs, and other graphic media are used to illustrate archaeological fieldwork, laboratory analysis, and the resultant reconstructions.

Our "hands-on" exhibits include adobe bricks and full-scale replica artifacts and tools. As with the "open-air" or "living" museums popular in Europe (for example, Stone and Molynaux 1994; Stone and Planel 1999), reconstruction is perceived to facilitate experimental learning, including concepts of process and context. Visitors are encouraged to be active participants in learning about the Sicán culture.

Lastly, all displayed artifacts are derived from either scientific fieldwork or careful replication using what we have documented of pertinent ancient technologies. Not a single looted object is exhibited, reinforcing our message against looting.

Along with the above features and aims, the SNM strives to build bridges among different segments of Peruvian society for better appreciation of the region's multicultural roots. The north coast of Peru, in spite of its impressive pre-Hispanic cultural achievements and the political and economic importance it has held since Colonial days, suffers from the ambiguous cultural identity to which we allude earlier in this chapter. The province of Ferreñafe, where the SNM is located, subsumes mestizos in the lower elevations who trace their ethnic origins to Hispanic and aboriginal Muchik (Mochica) populations, as well as Quechua peoples in the mountainous region farther inland (east).

On the basis of historically documented distribution of Muchik/Mochica speakers and toponyms and lexical and other linguistic analyses, Torero (1986, 2002) sees Muchik/Mochica as a stable and persistent language that existed in the Lambayeque valley complex at least for the past fifteen hundred years (also see Schaedel 1987, 1989). Ethnic identity and interethnic relations remain an important structuring principle and transformational force in many complex societies, and archaeological exploration of ethnic issues can "assist in providing identities for local groups and in the process politically empower them" (Emberling 1997: 296; see also Shennan 1989a). At the same time, we are cognizant of the risk of political misuses and abuses of ethnic information, and we thus remain vigilant to this danger. In contextualizing the SNM and its activities, the task of identification and preservation of the Muchik/Mochica ethnicity serves as an effective bridge connecting us to the local population of the province of Ferreñafe.

As detailed below, the SNM has worked hard to establish strong ties with local communities and governments. While the archaeological tasks of the SNM might be achieved with infusions of funds, such achievements would be of little social consequence without the comprehension and support of local and regional populations and institutions. This understanding and support, however, must be sought proactively through various avenues to displace the widespread indifference toward museums, which are too often perceived as static collections of artifacts pertaining to prehistoric peoples with whom they do not identify. In this regard, we conceive of our museum not only as a scientific and educational institution, but equally as an agency for educating and empowering the predominantly mestizo and disadvantaged population of the area for better adaptation in modern Peru.

Scientific and Educational Agendas and Their Realization

To advance knowledge and understanding of the Sicán culture, the SNM actively supports new analysis of our artifact collection; provides laboratory space and equipment to those who are conducting archaeological investigations in the province of Ferreñafe and/or into aspects of the Sicán culture; and carries out new fieldwork of its own.

In regard to the last point, in September 2001, in collaboration with Hirokatsu Watanabe, a leading Japanese expert of ground-penetrating radar (GPR), Elera, Victor Curay (staff archaeologist of the SNM), and their crew conducted a GPR survey and accompanying test excavations around the base of the Middle Sicán monumental mound of Huaca Rodillona in the Poma Sanctuary. The work documented the presence of buried auxiliary constructions and inferred the existence of deep shaft tombs much like those found at the contemporaneous Huaca Loro mound, located less than a kilometer to the southeast (see, for example, Shimada et al. 2004). During the summer of 2003, Elera and his museum team conducted an excavation of what proved to be an elaborate but largely looted tomb at the site of Huaca Sontillo (approximately 1.5 kilometers to the north of Huaca Rodillona) in the Poma Sanctuary. Results of these activities are displayed in the SNM hall reserved for temporary exhibits, establishing the critical linkage between research and public interest. In both cases, fieldwork was supported by small research grants garnered by the nonprofit Asociación

Amigos del Museo Sicán (Association of the Friends of the Sicán Museum) from the Tokyo Broadcasting System in exchange for the latter's filming rights to the fieldwork. Filming further ensured public dissemination of our fieldwork results.

Our efforts to establish the SNM as an active center of Sicán research have been greatly facilitated by fully equipped guest quarters on the museum grounds earmarked for visiting investigators. Visiting scholars are asked to submit a brief research proposal, pay a small house maintenance fee, and give an informal talk about their research results to museum personnel. The SNM is also gathering reprints and books on the Sicán culture as well as broader Lambayeque archaeology, history, and ethnography to serve as a regional archival center.

Conservation and analysis of the existing artifact collection go hand in hand with dissemination of archaeological information through museum exhibits. With this in mind, during the summer of 2003, Elera and Curay participated in a program organized by the U.S. Embassy in Lima, Peru, aimed at improving exhibits and artifact conservation in Peruvian museums. They also took advantage of a series of preceding artifact conservation workshops sponsored by the U.S. Embassy as well. During the same summer, Kimberly Machovec-Smith, a student in the M.A. degree program in conservation at Buffalo State University (in consultation with her professor, Dr. Aniko Bezúr, and Dr. Ruth Norton, head conservator at the Field Museum of Natural History), worked with the museum staff on much-needed conservation of various major metal objects and their subsequent display. In coordination with Dr. Bezúr, the SNM is establishing a long-term collaborative program in conservation, which will provide valuable firsthand experience for conservation students and much-needed artifact analysis and conservation for the museum.

To implement our goal of not just disseminating archaeological information but making it socially relevant, we are working together with local and regional educational institutions. As part of this ongoing effort, the SNM recently signed an agreement with the Province of Ferreñafe Educational System to train primary and secondary teachers on the subject of regional cultural identity in the hope that it will eventually be part of the school curriculum. Instruction on relevant archaeological and historical data and issues ran from March through November 2004, taking place at the SNM, with visits to regional archaeological and historic sites. This is the first time that formal training focused on the issue of cultural identity has been offered to schoolteachers by an archaeological museum in the Lambayeque region of Peru. Most recently, the SNM helped the Municipality of Ferreñafe draft a broadly conceived ordinance (see appendix) to collaborate in strengthening local cultural identity.

Social Agendas and Their Realization

A major social agenda of the SNM is to protect and sustain the cultural and natural heritage that is the Poma Historical Sanctuary. The long-term protection and maintenance of the sanctuary cannot be achieved without addressing the challenges posed by impoverished farming communities that surround much of the sanctuary. Traditionally, these communities have gathered firewood and pastured their animals in what is now a protected sanctuary. They have also, at times, attempted illegal occupation, often accompanied by grave looting and the felling of trees for charcoal making.

One measure that the SNM is taking to alleviate the economic and social problems of the above farmers is to revive the traditional technologies and crafts of their pre-Hispanic cultural heritage. In support of this plan, the government of the province of Ferreñafe and the central government of Peru recently approved a plan that Elera presented to construct the Aldea Artesanal Sicán (craft village) within the SNM grounds (Figure 13.4). This construction project has been accepted as a part of the national developmental program known as "A Trabajar Urbano" ("Let's Put People to Work in the City"). Funds for training of artisans—to be recruited from the aforementioned farmers—and necessary materials and equipment are being provided by the International Cooperation Agency of Spain (Agencia Española de Cooperación Internacional) and the Ministry of Trade and Tourism of Peru.

The village will be built following Sicán architectural canons, style, and materials. It will house a series of craft workshops, a native food restaurant, and a shamanism study-demonstration center. The crafts targeted—such as replica blackware pottery, sheet metalwork, native cotton weaving (including painted cloth), and pyro-engraving of gourds—are distinctively Sicán and have been archaeologically documented. Concurrently, Sicán-inspired original works designed and made by modern artisans will also be promoted. No less important in this endeavor will be the documentation and preservation of traditional Muchik ethnic food and beverages and shamanistic and folk-curing practices.

The village as a whole is envisioned as becoming a self-sufficient enterprise that will serve and promote local artisans and boost tourism. In the process, we hope to help preserve the Sicán cultural heritage and strengthen the artisans' sense of identity and self-confidence with a better appreciation of their cultural and historical roots. The SNM will help with implementation of the above plans for the village and auxiliary centers and with their operation by providing relevant archaeological and ethnohistorical information to artisans and acting as liaison with local, national, and international tourism and development agencies. We aim at successful integration into the emerging north coast–northern highland tourist circuits.

Through more than two decades of sustained, interdisciplinary research, the SAP has achieved a comprehensive understanding of the pertinent raw materials, operational sequences, and technologies of the targeted crafts, particularly ceramics and metallurgy (for example, Merkel et al. 1994; Shimada and Merkel 1991; Shimada and Wagner 2001; Shimada et al. 2003). We expect that the early stage of the village's operation will be much like conducting ethnoarchaeology and replicative experiments, in that we will be able to not only test and refine our models, but also gain a new understanding of associated behavior, skills, beliefs, and social relations of production. Overall, the village will allow productive feedback between and fulfillment of both scientific and social agendas of the SNM.

In relation to the above initiative, the SNM has designed a project that was recently approved by the Innovative Technological Center (Centro de Inovación Tecnológica) of Peru's Ministry of Trade and Tourism to conduct a census of local native colored cotton (*Gossypium barbadense*), its production, and weavers, as well as to organize workshops to ensure survival of its weaving. Native cotton and its weaving have been deeply intertwined with Muchik ethnic and cultural values (for example, Shimada 1994: 206–10; Vreeland 1978, 1982, 1986). This project differs from earlier attempts to revive and commercialize native cotton production and weaving in that management and training will be community based rather than in the hands of external individuals or institutions.

As a part of the original conception of our museum, within its walled compound we already have an "ethnobotanical garden" with a wide range of local native cultigens (for example, gourd, cotton, squash, maize) of economic, medicinal, and/or handicraft use. Many of these cultigens are quickly disappearing from the local landscape, as farmers increasingly favor cash crops. We are interested not only in having museum visitors become familiar with these native cultigens and their traditional values, but also in preserving their Muchik names and genes and explaining and promoting organic or traditional cultivation of these cultigens to local farmers.

The recent establishment of La Asociación Rural Muchik "Naymlap" del Eco-Caserio de Poma III by 60 farmers and their families—representing some 350 individuals in the area that borders the northwestern sector of the Poma Sanctuary—is an important development in respect to the task of protecting the Poma Historical Sanctuary. This nonprofit organization is dedicated to the development of sustainable eco-tourism and protection of the Poma Sanctuary in close coordination with the SNM and the National Institute of Natural Resources (Instituto Nacional de Recursos Naturales, or INRENA) of the Ministry of Agriculture of Peru.

The Asociación represents an important grassroots effort by the residents to improve their quality of life by recognizing the long-term potential in nondestructive, sustainable use of the archaeological and ecological resources of the Poma Sanctuary. For example, Asociación members have expressed enthusiasm to learn more about their ethnic heritage and hope to familiarize themselves with the archaeology of Poma so as to serve as tourist guides. Their knowledge of the impressive variety of birds and other ecological features will also be brought to bear. Museum staff will assist them in this learning process and also in the establishment of an archive of relevant information sources that will be managed by Asociación members.

Conclusion

The conception of our museum as more anthropological and holistic than archaeological is an extension of our belief that provincial museums such as ours should be archaeologically and socially embedded in regional context and be active learning or cultural centers. Accordingly, the museum has scientific, educational, and social agendas and roles to play. These diverse agendas complement each other. The various strategies and steps described here are admittedly quite ambitious. Should the eco-tourism project in Poma prove viable, we hope it will serve as a model for achieving a long-term solution for other communities that border the sanctuary. Several years must pass, however, before success can be properly assessed. Museum involvement in education is an extension of our strong belief in and commitment to making this institution socially relevant and empowering the local mestizo population. Clearly, for any small museum with limited personnel and funds to be successful, long-term planning, close coordination, and symbiotic relationships with local, regional, national, and even international institutions are critical.

Acknowledgments

We express our sincere appreciation to numerous members of the Sicán Archaeological Project and the Sicán National Museum Museography Project for their tireless efforts that resulted in the opening of the museum. We are also grateful to the Tokyo Broadcasting System, particularly Tetsuji Nishino and Yutaka Yoshii, the Asociación Amigos del Museo Nacional Sicán, and the Municipality of Ferreñafe and its mayor, Juan J. Salazar, for their continuing interest and support of the Sicán National Museum.

Appendix: Ordenanza Municipal No. 015-2004-CMPF

Ferreñafe, 30 de Abril del 2004

El Señor Alcalde de la Municipalidad Provincial de Ferreñafe

POR CUANTO: El Concejo Municipal Provincial de Ferreñafe, en Sesión Ordinaria de fecha 30 de Abril del 2004

CONSIDERANDO:

Que, de acuerdo con el Art. 191° de la Constitución Política del Estado, las Municipalidades tienen autonomía, económica, administrativa y política, atributo que reconoce la potestad legislativa de los gobiernos locales.

Que en concordancia con la autonomía política de la que gozan las Municipalidades, el artículo constitucional citado en el párrafo anterior ha otorgado expresamente al Concejo Municipal, órgano conformante de la estructura orgánica de cada gobierno local, la función normativa respecto de aquellos asuntos que son de su competencia.

Que el Concejo Municipal cumple su función normativa, entre otros mecanismos, fundamentalmente a través de las Ordenanzas Municipales, las cuales de conformidad con lo previsto por el Art. 200°, Inc. 4) de la Constitución Política en concordancia con el Art. 194° arriba glosado, ostentan rango normativo de Ley, en su calidad de normas de carácter general de mayor jerarquía dentro de la estructura normativa Municipal, calidad reconocida por el Art. 40° de la Ley No. 27972, Ley Orgánica de Municipalidades vigente a la fecha.

Que el Art. 82° de la acotada Ley de Municipalidades promulgada en Lima el 27 de Mayo del 2003, en materia de Educación, Cultura, Deportes y Recreación, tiene como competencias y funciones específicas compartidas con el Gobierno Nacional y el Regional entre otras las siguientes funciones signadas con los números 19 y 20 que dicen "Promover actividades culturales diversas" y "Promover la consolidación de una cultura de ciudadanía democrática y fortalecer la identidad cultural de la población campesina, nativa y afroperuana" respectivamente.

Que, la presente Ordenanza establece el marco general que ha de promover la puesta en marcha de la consolidación de la identidad cultural en los seis (06) distritos de la pluricultural provincia de Ferreñafe la misma que será coordinada y alentada por el Concejo Provincial de Ferreñafe y el Museo Nacional de Sicán, en una perspectiva orientada al fortalecimiento de la identidad cultural ferreñafana encaminada hacia el desarrollo sostenible, sustentada en la practica de la concertación y la participación ciudadana y democrática dirigidas a garantizar la coordinación y articulación de las políticas culturales de los diversos organismos del Estado vinculados a la gestión municipal.

Que, en la provincia de Ferreñafe existe una falta crónica de identidad cultural la misma que se refleja en una falta de conocimiento del rico legado histórico-cultural local así como una rica biodiversidad que tiene la provincia; falta de auto confianza, orgullo y autoestima de poblaciones mestizas algunas de ellas de predominante ancestro nativo así como desdén y burla de los valores culturales Muchik y Quechua frente a los valores culturales de origen europeo y de otras latitudes.

Que diversos estudios realizados por organismos públicos y privados han evidenciado una rica producción intelectual nacional e internacional sobre el patrimonio cultural con énfasis al ámbito rural costeño de la provincia de Ferreñafe siendo por el momento a menor escala en los distritos alto andinos de la misma que debidamente dosificado por una alianza estratégica entre el sector educación de la provincia y el Museo Nacional Sicán bajo un lenguaje sencillo lleguen a todos los sectores de la población ferreñafana.

Que han habido experiencias significativas de investigación arqueológica que dan cuenta bajo un enfoque multidisciplinario modelo sobre la importancia de Ferreñafe como centro político, religioso y económico de la Cultura Sicán o Lambayeque la misma que servirá como parte del afianzamiento de la matriz étnica y cultural Muchik o Mochica que es predominante en la realidad rural mestiza costeña de los distritos de Ferreñafe, Pueblo Nuevo, Mesones Muro y Pitipo así como el entendimiento, revaloración y promoción de la rica realidad cultural y lingüística Quechua de los distritos alto andinos da Inkahuasi y Kañaris de la provincia de Ferreñafe.

Que, el centro del poder de la cultura Sicán o Lambayeque en el santuario Histórico Bosque de Pomac, en Ferreñafe encierra complejos culturales pre-Sicán de producción semi-industrial de cerámica, constituyéndose en las áreas de producción alfarera más antigua de América (Cultura Cholope: 600–400 B.C.) así como la producción sin parangón de objetos de bronce arsenical, oro y plata, considerándose que el 85% de objetos de oro del antiguo Perú que se encuentran en colecciones estatales y privadas en el Perú y en el extranjero provienen de las tumbas de elite Sicán del Santuario Histórico Bosque de Pomac el mismo que hay que conservar como patrimonio cultural y natural de todos los peruanos.

Que, hay ricas manifestaciones artísticas y folklóricas en Ferreñafe alrededor de la plástica, poesía, tradición oral, cumananas, pregones, pasacalles, tonderos, marineras, vals criollo, triste y huaynos que hay que conservar, valorar y promover, incentivando, apoyando y dando los homenajes en vida correspondientes a los actores de tan rica producción literaria, plástica y musical cuyo prestigio rebasan las fronteras de la provincia de Ferreñafe y tiene alcance nacional e internacional.

Que en el territorio de la provincia de Ferreñafe existe una riqueza extraordinaria de monumentos arqueológicos que junto con el patrimonio colonial y republicano en conjunción con la naturaleza circundante constituyen para el ferreñafano de hoy y mañana fuentes de conocimiento, orgullo e inspiración del legado de sus mayores.

Que, los caballos peruanos de paso, perros peruanos sin pelo, peleas de gallo, juegos de tejos, arcos con frutas, yunsas, procesiones de cruces de algarrobo y otras manifestaciones de religiosidad popular deben de conservarse, promocionarse y difundirse.

Que, el acervo gastronómico y de bebida tradicional que son parte indisoluble de la identidad de un pueblo es uno de los más ricos del Perú y se hace necesario documentar, destacar y promocionar permanentemente.

Que, hay que realizar y conservar la vestimenta tradicional típica del ámbito rural costeño y serrano de Ferreñafe usándolo con orgullo como símbolo de pertenencia a esta tierra.

Que, uno de los aportes tecnológicos artesanales mas representativos de la etnicidad Muchik gira alrededor de la textileria del algodón nativo de colores naturales la cual hay que revalorar, potenciar y difundir.

Que, hay que instaurar símbolos de la provincia de Ferreñafe inspirados en su rica tradición cultural, los mismos que servirán para hacer reconocimientos públicos a personalidades cuyos aportes intelectuales, científicos y artísticos son de gran trascendencia para la ferreñafeneidad.

Que, la presente Ordenanza es resultado del festival cultural anual "Ferreñafe Canta y Baila para el Perú" llevado a cabo en el Museo Nacional Sicán y que se ha considerado como parte gravitante del fortalecimiento de la identidad cultural ferreñafana. Por lo expuesto, y en uso de las atribuciones que confiere la Ley Orgánica de Municipalidades No. 27972, Artículos 9°, numeral 8), 39° y 40°, por Unanimidad y con dispensa del Trámite de Lectura y Aprobación del Acta, se aprobó la siguiente.

ORDENANZA:
SEMANA DE LA IDENTIDAD CULTURAL DE LA PROVINCIA DE FERREÑAFE

Artículo Primero.—Declárese de interés provincial la instauración de la Semana de la Identidad Cultural de la Provincia de Ferreñafe en la cual se promoverá el encuentro con las raíces pre- y post-hispánicas que dan sentido a la idiosincrasia del pueblo ferreñafano costeño y serrano. Exposiciones, mesas redondas, publicaciones, desfiles y festivales serán el eje de la semana de la identidad. La Semana de la Identidad Cultural de la Provincia de Ferreñafe se llevará a cabo la última semana del mes de Abril de cada año considerándose el día central el último domingo de dicha semana bajo la denominación del festival cultural "Ferreñafe Canta y Baila para el Perú" teniendo como sede el Museo Nacional Sicán.

Artículo Segundo.—El patronato del Museo Nacional Sicán junto al Concejo Provincial de Ferreñafe coordinará acciones en conjunto para lograr que los objetivos de la Semana de la Identidad Cultural de la Provincia de Ferreñafe se cumplan a plenitud.

Artículo Tercero.—Durante la Semana de la Identidad Cultural de la Provincia de Ferreñafe se incentivará en oficinas públicas y privadas como público en general el uso de trajes típicos del ámbito rural ferreñafano a fin de afirmar la identidad de la provincia.

Artículo Cuarto.—Como símbolo de agradecimiento el Concejo Provincial de Ferreñafe empleará una medalla de oro inspirada con el icono del Dios Sicán en un contexto marino el mismo que será sujetado por una cinta tejida en algodón nativo de colores naturales.

Artículo Quinto.—Se gravará con un 10% al área de transportes a fin de contar con un fondo base para la ejecución anual de la Semana de la Identidad Cultural de la Provincia de Ferreñafe.

POR TANTO:

Regístrese, Comuníquese, Publíquese y Cúmplase

14

Landscape Site Museums and Adventurers in Peru's Cotahuasi Valley

JUSTIN JENNINGS

Introduction

A travel advertisement in *Condor Journeys and Adventures* reads, "While hiking or rafting through the [Cotahuasi] canyon, we marvel at the geography and the beauty of the Andes. We stop to explore numerous unknown sites, discover gravesites with pottery, cloth from the mummies, water channels, Andean terraces, and more human remains than you thought possible from the Huari and Inca cultures. This all adds up to one of the best journeys in the world." Similar advertisements hawk thundering whitewater, star-lit nights, rugged topography, intact mummy bundles, and unexplored ruins to those willing to pay almost three thousand dollars for what one of my rafting guidebooks called the "ultimate river trip"—a rafting expedition down the middle reaches of southern Peru's Cotahuasi River (Figures 14.1, 14.2).

The twenty to thirty clients who raft down the Cotahuasi River each year are one example of a rising tide of trekkers, spelunkers, climbers, and other adventure travelers who are seeking out extraordinary activities in the farthest reaches of the globe. During their travels these tourists are now visiting archaeological sites that have long been insulated against destruction by their isolation (Figure 14.3). The long-term management of these remote sites, especially in the developing world, presents enormous challenges that remain unaddressed.

In this chapter I consider the impact of adventure tourism on one particular ensemble of archaeological sites that together I define as a "landscape site museum." My argument draws on ideas taken from the cultural heritage literature and my interactions with rafters and rafting guides over the last seven years that I have conducted archaeological fieldwork in the Cotahuasi Valley, especially during a ten-day rafting trip that I took down the river in 2003 (Jennings 2003). That trip was part of an ongoing collaborative project to manage archaeological sites along an archaeological tourism "river corridor" that I am trying to develop with the participation of several fine rafting guides (Marc Goddard, Gian Marco Velluntino, José Francisco Giraldo, Santiago Ibáñez Corpancho),

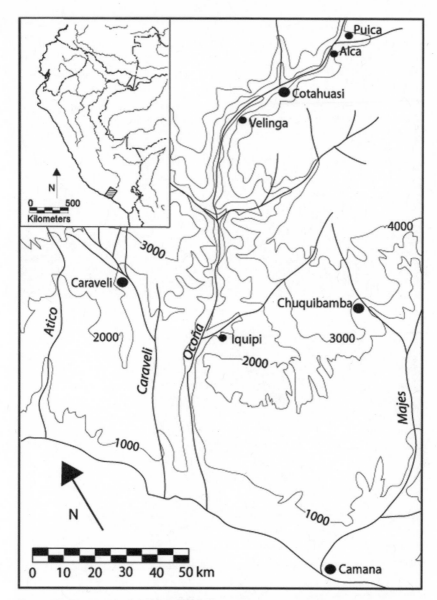

Figure 14.1. Location of the Cotahuasi-Ocoña river drainage, with the hatched area on the inset map of Peru indicating the location of the drainage. The remote area where the author advocates the "open museums" approach is located between Velinga and Iquipi. Map by Justin Jennings.

Figure 14.2. View of the Cotahuasi Valley. Photograph by Justin Jennings.

Figure 14.3. Adventure travelers exploring a looted tomb at the site of Toccec, Cotahuasi Valley. Photograph by Justin Jennings.

local Cotahuasi authorities (Genaro Cacilino Mejía Espinal, Efrain Guillermo Sánchez Medina, Gregorio Elfer Ale Cruz), and a cultural anthropologist–rafting guide (Dr. Robert Fletcher) (see Goddard and Jennings 2003).

This chapter presents a first attempt to address some of the important issues of effectively managing marginal archaeological sites that are impacted by adventure tourism. More fieldwork will test the tentative ideas that I present and, I hope, will turn the landscape site museum concept into a reality.

Ethical and Practical Challenges for Archaeologists

The most fundamental ethical responsibility of archaeologists is to serve as stewards of the past (Lynott 1997; Wylie 2003). We are bound to "work for the long-term conservation and protection of the archaeological record" (Lynott 1997: 592) and urged to "reach out to and participate in cooperative efforts with others interested in the archaeological record with the aim of improving the preservation, protection and interpretation of the record" (Lynott 1997: 593). While some archaeologists continue to ignore their responsibilities for conservation and education (Palumbo 2002), many more now embrace these duties (for example, Erickson 2003; Lerner and Hoffman 2000; McManamon 2000a).

As the chapters in this volume demonstrate, site museums in many cases can admirably fulfill our ethical duties to inform the public and preserve the past (see, especially, the explicit discussion of the SAA's ethical principles in Silverman's introduction). While differing in detail on how these duties should be carried out (see, for example, Sivan 1997), all of this volume's authors rightly advocate the construction of site museums and the exercise of some degree of scholarly control over the information presented at these museums (Manzanilla's chapter is the most insistent in this regard) and throughout the site. These management schemes are most feasible at sites that enjoy a mixture of marketability, accessibility, and monumentality sufficient to attract tourists and outside funding. Most "ruins," however, are not as "lucky," because they are too poorly preserved, too far away from comfortable population centers (see, for instance, the case of Kuntur Wasi described by Onuki in this volume), and/or too "insignificant" to be of interest to the tourist. Nonetheless, archaeologists have an ethical responsibility to protect these more marginal sites and educate the few tourists who visit them.

I propose that the most effective means of managing many of the world's most remote and difficult-to-reach sites is to turn them into landscape site museums managed by adventure guides who are trained by archaeologists and who would be overseen by local political authorities, ideally in cooperation and consultation with archaeologists from the nearest governmental office (in Peru this would be the Instituto Nacional de Cultura [INC], or National Institute of Culture).

Managing Marginal Sites

In Peru all archaeological sites and the objects found within them are owned by the state. The state has delegated control over these sites to the INC. The INC has aggressively asserted its control over Peru's greatest archaeological sites, such as Machu Picchu, Sipán, Pachacamac, and Chavín de Huántar (Alva 2001; Bonavia 1986). The INC's budget, however, is quite limited. In 2004, the INC received only 22 million nuevo soles (6.75 million dollars), or 0.084 percent of the total state budget (INC 2004). Since the INC's budget does not give it the financial and infrastructural capacity to effectively manage all sites, it entrusts de facto management of lesser archaeological sites in remote areas to local government officials.

Such remote areas in developing countries such as Peru are often quite poor. Faced with poverty, local authorities and nongovernmental organization (NGO) workers have sometimes sought to improve local conditions by attracting tourist dollars on the basis of a region's cultural resources. In Cotahuasi, for example, a development plan for the valley seeks to leverage the archaeological sites to attract "natural-adventure tourism of international quality" (AEDES 1998: 71). Since the INC is generally unable to provide aid to manage sites in Cotahuasi and other poor regions, the preservation and promotion of cultural heritage falls to local authorities. Although these local authorities may be sympathetic to site preservation, they lack sufficient resources for effective involvement. Even without such resources, some local authorities have made unsanctioned, occasionally disastrous, attempts to make the sites in their region more tourist-friendly in the hope of attracting visits (Jennings 2002). As archaeologists, it is our ethical responsibility to conserve sites and educate the public (Lynott 1997; Wylie 2003). The challenge is to find a way to work with local people, the INC, and other stakeholders in these particular contexts where state involvement in culture heritage is occasional or lacking.

I argue that effective management and education programs for archaeological sites in places like Cotahuasi can only be achieved by tailoring our strategies to the kinds of tourists who will visit these sites (Demas 1997; Gale and Jacobs 1986). In remote areas of the world, such as the middle Cotahuasi, site visitors are adventure travelers. Site museums, as traditionally conceived, are infeasible in these locations. Construction and maintenance, for instance, would be logistically difficult and expensive. Moreover, an isolated site museum at a less than spectacular or not highly significant site could not be maintained through admission fees, since large numbers of tourists would not visit them.

A more feasible means to productively manage many of the world's remote archaeological sites is to turn them into landscape site museums managed by trained adventure guides who are overseen by local political authorities. Landscape site museums could be effective in these regions because they would meet the best interests of different stakeholders in the region by allowing guides and locals to profit from the cultural patrimony, while preserving the sites over the long term. At the same time, landscape site museums require very little investment of capital and make few demands on an overtaxed state government.

Adventure Travel and the Authentic in the Cotahuasi Valley

Adventure travel, encompassing such diverse activities as rock climbing, whitewater rafting, trekking, heli-skiing, dog sledding, and storm chasing, are physically (and, some would say, spiritually) challenging leisure activities that take place in locations that are seen by the participant as unusual, exotic, and/or remote (Beedie 2003: 208–10; Vester 1987: 237–38). Creating adventures is big business. Adventure travel accounted for $245 billion in products bought and trips booked in 2000 (the last year from which statistics were available to me) and is one of the fastest growing segments of the tourism industry (Neirotti 2003: 14; USA Weekend 2003: 6). Adventure experiences are made special not only by the activities done during the trip, but also by the location where the trip occurs. With the industry seeking to expand into places that can provide the authentic experience their clients crave, adventure tourism presents enormous economic opportunities for places that can be marketed as "adventuresome" (Beedie and Hudson 2003).

Fleeing the "septic, air-conditioned bubble of the luxury bus" (Van der Berghe 1994: 8), adventure travelers hope to find themselves by challenging their bodies and souls through actions undertaken among "untouched" natives and "unspoiled" environments. Adventure is not adventure unless you can step off increasingly crowded tourist circuits (Tourtellot 2000; Yamashida 2003). The sustainability of adventure tourism is therefore linked to the perceived integrity and authenticity of the place, qualities that are judged in large part by how far removed the location seems from the tourist's way of life. With more tourists, and more tourist infrastructure, a location becomes less desirable. The most adventuresome locations are therefore often found in the poorest and most remote parts of the developing world. One of these locations is the Cotahuasi Valley.

The Cotahuasi Valley (Figures 14.1, 14.2) is located at the terminus of an unpaved road that winds up, down, and through the Andean Cordillera beyond the city of Arequipa. Although the valley is occasionally mentioned on the English- and Spanish-language advertising placards that are sprinkled around Arequipa's central plaza, most tourists balk at the bumpy twelve-hour (or more, depending on road conditions) ride to Cotahuasi. Cotahuasi's local government keeps no official figures for tourism, but the numbers are unlikely to reach into the thousands. Of these visitors, almost all are Peruvian, and many come during the valley's tourism festival in late May. I estimate that fewer than two hundred foreign tourists visit the valley each year. For the most part, visitors come to the valley to wander through the towns, hike in the countryside, soak in the hot springs, and visit a handful of the more accessible archaeological sites, such as the Inca administrative center of Maulkallacta and the Wari-influenced center of Collota.

Many of the visitors who come to Cotahuasi can be classified as adventure tourists. The most extreme adventurers in this group might be the approximately forty people each year who venture deep into the canyon on multiday rafting trips. In the summer of 2003, I joined a group of twenty clients and guides on a six-day white-water plunge down the Cotahuasi River (Jennings 2003). During that trip, we visited three extremely isolated archaeological sites (Figure 14.3). An understanding of how my companions experienced these ruins provides insights on how archaeologists and their collaborators might be able to best manage marginal sites in this and in other parts of the world.

The adventurers who went on my trip did not come on the expedition to learn about Peru's people and past. They came to go down the river. Every person on this trip stated to me that his or her primary motivation in undertaking the expedition was to challenge himself or herself against the river's Class IV and V rapids. Advertisements for our expedition promised the trip of a lifetime, and the trip delivered on that promise. Clients described their experience in gushing terms such as "transformative," "otherworldly," "mystical," and "life changing." Eric Arnould and Linda Price (1993) have heard words like these many times during their studies of Colorado River rafters and suggest that rafter responses are the result of what they call "river magic," a concept coined to describe the cultural script that transforms these trips into rites of intensification, in which initiates are separated from their everyday environments, and integration (Hollyfield 1999). It is not just the river, however, that makes these trips magical. A trip's appeal is also clearly intertwined with a sense that a river valley is untouched, unexplored, and unspoiled (Patterson et al. 1998). For my companions in Cotahuasi, the valley's extreme remoteness was a key selling point for the trip.

While the valley's archaeological sites were not a particularly important draw for most clients before our trip, they became increasingly more important as our trip continued. I recognize that curiosity about the valley's past was piqued by my presence (I told everyone I was an archaeologist). As the expedition proceeded, the rafters on my trip often talked about the excitement of "discovering" and "exploring" Cotahuasi's ruins, with one of the men comparing himself to Indiana Jones and a second man being left "awe-inspired" by his "small part in history" as one of the first Westerners to see these places. I suggest that clients saw the valley's well-preserved and unreconstructed ruins as signs of the valley's remoteness and unspoiled character—authenticating Cotahuasi as a place where one could experience a true adventure. Had these sites been scripted by boundary walls, roped-off paths, guards, and traditional site museums, these adventure tourists would likely have complained, since their newly discovered goal during the expedition was to see "real ruins" in their "natural" state of decay.

Cotahuasi's archaeological sites and artifacts were also interesting to my fellow adventurers because they were markers of the valley's "timelessness." I talked to members of our group over the course of our trip about Peruvian prehistory. Most of the questions posed to me were about the Incas, and most of the rafters were either incredulous or dismayed when I told them that the Inca empire had lasted for less than one hundred years. Their new knowledge of the Incas' brief reign, however, did not stop the word *Inca* from quickly becoming a pseudonym for anything that looked old. All agricultural terraces were Inca, all trails were Inca, and all structures were Inca. The local people whom we met were *not* Inca, but, in the words of one woman, "they live today in the same way that the Incas had." For some of the members of our party, the juxtaposition of deserted sites and inhabited villages suggested a landscape that was both ancient and timeless. A valley trapped in its past is inherently untouched by westernization and globalization and therefore provides an ideal location for the adventurer to "get away from it all."

The rafters on my trip suggested that museums and managed sites were fine while they were on the tourist circuit, but all but one of them did not want to see these same things when they ventured off the circuit. Cotahuasi is quintessentially off that circuit. As I indicate above, the people who come to Cotahuasi think of themselves as adventurers: they are searching for the "authentic" Peru, and the real Peru is a Peru in its "natural" state with its "ruins" in their "natural" state of decay. For my rafting companions, "untouched ruins" served as a sign of the region's authenticity as an adventure destination. Site museums, by their very creation, suggest that there is a pre-existing tourist market in the region. A site that looks managed suggests that true adventure lies elsewhere.

Why Landscape Site Museums?

Museums are traditionally buildings in which objects of historical, scientific, artistic, or cultural interest are preserved and exhibited (see discussion in Silverman's introduction to this volume). The two primary functions of museums are to conserve objects and to educate the public. Site museums fulfill these functions by exhibiting artifacts found at the site (or occasionally elsewhere) and by providing interpretative displays that educate visitors who pass through the museum. Site museums, and other traditional management schemes, are effective and proven techniques to conserve sites and educate the public (Matero et al. 1998). These schemes, however, run counter to the expectations and desires of the adventure tourists who visit the most remote sites. The cost of building and maintaining boundary walls, displays, and other features would be a heavy burden for the local government, and the result of this investment might drive tourists away instead of attracting them. While scholars can rightfully condemn the expectations of adventurers to find an untouched and timeless Peru as a corrosive search for the non-Western "other" (Said 1979), I argue that archaeologists and other heritage professionals have a moral responsibility not to deny potential tourist revenues to the people who live in poor, remote regions. If site museums in remote areas are likely to drive away tourists and their dollars, then we should not advocate such museums in the middle Cotahuasi. We should instead work in partnership with local groups to find other ways that they can profit from their cultural patrimony.

While building museums is infeasible, leaving these sites completely unmanaged is equally unsatisfactory. It may come as no surprise that adventurers who compare themselves to Indiana Jones can cause significant damage to sites (the Inca Trail syndrome). On past trips down the Cotahuasi, travelers have returned home with textiles, ceramic sherds, and other ancient souvenirs, not to mention the physical damage they cause to sites during their visits, whether by casual surface collection and subsurface probing or by careless wandering that inadvertently topples precarious walls. Despite my best efforts, the expeditioners on my rafting trip caused noticeable damage during our descent down the river. At each site, people eagerly and quickly dispersed to "explore" sites individually. The mad scramble of feet up the steep slopes of the sites often sent down a cascade of dirt, lithics, and ceramics. One man destroyed a terrace wall when he flung himself over it, and the various digestive difficulties endured by members of our group occasionally created "toilet paper gardens" on or adjacent to sites.

The solution to site destruction does not lie in denying or lambasting the power of the adventure search for the "other" (contra Schmidt 1999). Instead, I argue that we need to subtly turn the "unexplored ruins" that tourists seek into landscape site museums.

Guides, Local Authorities, and Landscape Site Museums in Cotahuasi

The critical agent in the landscape site museums concept cannot be the INC, archaeologists, or even local authorities. In remote regions like the middle Cotahuasi, the ruins are too isolated to be effectively overseen during the few visits made each year to the sites. Adventure guides, in contrast, are well positioned to be "archaeological messengers" (McManamon 2000b: 5) who can educate tourists and protect the sites on the trips that the guides run. While relationships between guides and archaeologists can be acrimonious, I have found that most guides with whom I have talked are genuinely interested in the past. On my trip down the river, I had many long conversations with guides on a wide range of topics, such as how ancient Andean terracing worked and marriage patterns among the Inca nobility. I gave several of them some of my publications, and Marc Goddard, the leader of the expedition that I was on, even voluntarily slogged through portions of my dissertation.

If adventure guides can be convinced to serve as archaeological stewards, then it is likely that they will be able to lead by example, since adventure guides tend to have much more authority than regular tour guides. Just as "river magic" deepens the experience of rafting, the authority of the guides is deepened because they are seen as the providers of this "river magic" (Arnould and Price 1993; Arnould et al. 1999). This elevated position allows adventure guides a greater degree of control over their clients, as well as a greater ability to influence clients' behavior by their own (Jonas 1999). During my trip down the river, I convinced the guides to enact a "take nothing but pictures, leave nothing but footprints" policy for all sites in the Cotahuasi Valley after I had stressed the archaeological importance of leaving all artifacts in situ. We agreed that groups should not build fires on terraces or hang heavy equipment on terrace or structure walls. We also decided to choose specific areas for camping and cooking and to keep these areas the same for future visits. Finally, we agreed on the importance of developing a set path within all ruins to mitigate the damage done by individual exploration. The guides immediately and happily adopted all of these procedures during my trip down the river. These actions by the guides impressed upon the clients the importance of protecting the sites that we visited. Marc and his colleagues are now even considering more costly mitigation measures, such as carrying out all of the human waste generated on each trip.

The ability of guides to act as archaeological stewards would be further enhanced if they can convincingly discuss the prehistory of the region and justify the heritage management schemes that they ask their clients and colleagues to follow. In Cotahuasi, I am now working with Marc to develop a short, easy-to-read, archaeological primer in Spanish and English for each of his clients and guides. The primer will include a brief history of the Central Andes with emphasis on the Cotahuasi Valley, short descriptions of the archaeological sites found in the middle reaches of the valley, and guidelines for visiting the sites. In addition, the primer will provide the link to my fieldwork project Web page, which contains much more information. For future expeditions, I am also working with Marc and other guides to incorporate visits to the more accessible sites in the valley.

A landscape site museum program is feasible because it plays to the long-term best interest of adventure guides. Since clients on these trips are interested in the places that they will see, knowledgeable guides are a critical selling point in the highly competitive tourism industry. Guides have an incentive to work with archaeologists and local authorities because we can endorse their training and give their knowledge legitimacy. Simple conservation measures at sites, such as those the guides and I agreed upon during my trip, require little to no money to implement and will help to keep the sites "unspoiled" for clients who expect pristine ruins as part of their experience. Furthermore, guides who implement mitigation plans can market themselves as eco-friendly—another major draw in the market.

Although adventure guides would be the major agents in maintaining the landscape site museums, local authorities also need to be deeply involved in managing the sites in the more remote regions of the valley. The Peruvian government recognizes the importance of local involvement to sustainable tourism (PromPerú 2001), but there is currently no local oversight of rafters in Cotahuasi. Rafters do not need the permission of local authorities to go down the river; nor do local representatives oversee rafters. This lack of oversight has occasionally been a source of frustration for local leaders.

In the United States, rafting guides must generally obtain permits for trips from park authorities. Activities in and around sites are restricted, and companies that fail to follow conservation policies are denied permits for subsequent trips (National Park Service 1989; United States Code 2003). Such a system is currently untenable on the national level in Peru because of logistical and financial constraints, but perhaps a similar system could be put into place informally in the valley. As guides, local authorities, and other interested parties begin to work more closely together, I hope that we can agree upon a level of local oversight. While Cotahuasinos would benefit by having a greater control over their cultural patrimony, guides would benefit by having a bar set for proper conduct at the sites. Just as in the United States, companies failing to follow conservation policies would be denied permits for subsequent trips. Without such restrictions, I fear the rafting corridor will soon become a "tragedy of the commons," where commonly held resources are destroyed by personal interests (Hardin 1968).

Conclusion

As adventure tourism continues to expand, travelers are visiting more and more remote sites. To protect them, a heritage program for remote sites must walk a fine line between guaranteeing the economic interests of adventure guides and local populations and fulfilling the ethical responsibilities of heritage professionals and state governments (for example, Thorsby 1997). Landscape site museums are my attempt to walk this line.

Over the next few years, I will continue working with adventure guides, local authorities, state officials, and NGOs to formalize plans for the protection of archaeological resources in the Cotahuasi Valley. I advocate a landscape site museum approach for remote sites in the valley. Other sites are more easily accessible, and we are formulating a plan that will call for other kinds of management strategies at them; for instance, at some of the most accessible and impressive sites, state-supported site museums are an option. And where there are nearby communities, sites could be managed by trained local guide/stewards with simple museographical displays mounted in village houses (for example, Zilhào 1998; see Castillo and Holmquist's discussion of San José de Moro in this volume).

The growth of tourism is fundamental to the livelihood of the Cotahuasi Valley. I believe that archaeologists have an ethical responsibility to foster this growth if at all possible. The valley's sites are a potentially important tourist draw. There are, of course, multiple stakeholders in Cotahuasi's sites, and an effective plan will be successful only if it addresses the interests of all parties. Guides, local people, and the state need to ensure that the cultural patrimony can be enjoyed for generations to come. By working together with these parties, archaeologists can implement a conservation/education plan that adapts to the different circumstances of each location. With more fieldwork and greater collaboration, we can evaluate the landscape site museum concept and other ideas to create a sustainable heritage program in the Cotahuasi Valley.

PART 6

Comments

15

The Museums' Object(ive)s

LAWRENCE S. COBEN

The authors in this volume have addressed an unusually stimulating and thought-provoking set of issues. Many should be praised for their efforts and courage in trying to establish, develop, sustain, modify, and maintain a museum. These are truly noteworthy, since practical site museum studies are not part of any archaeological curriculum with which I am familiar. Congratulations are due for the successes achieved to date as well as for those that the future will bring. In my comments I elucidate and expand upon some of the themes running through these chapters, and I consider some of the key issues they present.

The first question might be what is a museum, in both a physical and a non-material sense. Only Silverman (Chapter 11) actually offers a definition while most, to paraphrase Justice Potter Stewart (in *Jacobellis v. Ohio*, 378 U.S. 184 [1964]), "know one when they see one." Museums in this volume range from a single-room hut to an archaeological site to a city to an entire river valley. Moreover, these museums possess a variety of not necessarily internally consistent goals: the safe storage of artifacts; site preservation; the claiming and expression of identity, primarily local; education (again, mostly local); and economic development through tourism or crafts development, to name a few.

As archaeologists studying museums, we might be expected to examine these physical structures as we would any building—that is, what the layout, location, size, and type of rooms and access tell us about what is transpiring therein and what are the most important activities of the structure or area. Such an examination of the museums discussed in this volume would, to varying degrees, suggest that most space is given over to conservation and protection, whether of artifacts in a structure, museumification of a city, or preservation and indeed reconstruction of an archaeological site. Indeed, I suspect that anyone excavating many of these site museums in the future might conclude that we had found a storeroom and not a museum. We might then move on to the second-largest area, the lab, describing it as some kind of work space, then a small living area, and then a small room with single entrance, that is, the guard booth.

It is, of course, not surprising that archaeologists would want to support the construction of buildings dedicated to material preservation. But if instead the goal is tourism, economic development, or local empowerment, would we necessarily design and build the same structures, not to mention museums themselves, and adopt the other social policies regarding the objects therein? I suggest that the answer might be no, and that the light of reflexivity, which has swept through anthropology in recent decades, should be shone upon this privileging of object conservation in museum development. In making this and indeed some of the other observations that follow, I am, of course, not unmindful that archaeologists are not the sole arbiters of what type of building is built and that museums are the product of negotiation, contestation, and social context. Nonetheless, I query whether the archaeologist's role in that process is always that of protector of material culture.

Second, who is visiting the museum, whom do we want to attract to the museum (a different question closely tied thereto), and what message do we desire to impart to them? Local groups, to the extent that one can define local in a meaningful way? People from the region? Domestic or foreign tourists? Scholars? Not all authors discuss these questions, no doubt in part because the requisite statistical data have not been kept or are otherwise unavailable. Nonetheless, it is obvious that the type of museum one creates and constructs is closely tied to these questions, as Castillo and Holmquist's (Chapter 10) modular human-scale museum makes quite clear. If one desires to attract tourists from the United States, English-language placards are a must. If one is seeking scholars, reasonably priced accommodations and an excellent library might be helpful, while for conservators a lab might be the most important feature (see Elera and Shimada, Chapter 13). Manzanilla's (Chapter 2) wonderful proposed redesign of the Teotihuacan museums brings this issue home starkly. I have little doubt that archaeologists would enjoy spending time in her revised museums far more than the present ones at the site, but would this be true for other groups? We all have seen busloads of tourists racing through large museums on the one-hour tour that encompasses a museum's ten most famous objects. Would these groups have the added time to grasp the more complex anthropological tale proposed by Manzanilla? Could that tale be told in the same hour, and would the tourists want to hear it? Should we care about them and the effect on museum revenues if they no longer come? Is this building designed well for this purpose, or are modifications necessary? And why are we privileging anthropology in the first place, other than self-empowerment? While I have used the Teotihuacan example here—and do not mean to detract from Manzanilla's thoughtful proposal—I think all of these questions could be asked equally of Jennings's (Chapter 14) river rafters, Mortensen's (Chapter 4) stones, Castillo and Holmquist's (Chapter 10) tourist circuit, and those visitors traveling to Cyphers's (Chapter 3) more out-of-the-way museum.

A third issue that appears in most of these chapters is identity and local empowerment. While I recognize that these are not identical, they are certainly closely related. The scale of such identity and empowerment varies, as discussed chapter by chapter—and, of course, most museums have identities that nest in multiple and sometimes crosscutting scales. The majority of the chapters, however, focus on the communities in which the museums are located and the scholar is working (though some have a more regional or even national focus). Interestingly, the relationship between the predominant scale of empowerment only sometimes is tied by authors to the scale of the underlying culture studied. Identity and empowerment seem to take a few varying forms: local control of objects as opposed to their shipment to regional or national museums, education of local people, pride in and preservation of sites and artifacts, and economic benefits, primarily by either craft production or tourism. Hastorf (Chapter 7) neatly summarizes the people of Chiripa as "marking their place within the rich historical heritage" of the region. Various of the chapter authors note extensive education programs (see, especially, Weinstein in Chapter 9) and, among others, Elera and Shimada (Chapter 13) and Paredes, Fattorini, and Klarich (Chapter 6) describe pottery production programs.

All authors recognize the need to place this identity and empowerment question into a broader political, social, or economic context. Nonetheless, I believe that deeper consideration of the relationship between identity/empowerment on the one hand and sustainable economic betterment on the other would be beneficial. Elera and Shimada (Chapter 13), Cyphers and Morales-Cano (Chapter 3), McEwan, Silva, and Hudson (Chapter 12), and Weinstein (Chapter 9), among others, address this question to varying degrees, arguing that successful museums are predicated upon what McEwan calls the creation of viable economic alternatives. I believe that few people will maintain and preserve their museums without an inherent belief that it is in their economic best interest to do so; indeed, I think all parties involved in this issue would agree that identity and its politics are closely tied to a desire to obtain some material or power-related goal, though I suspect we might dispute the degree of correlation.

There are, of course, resources and jobs associated with museum construction. Onuki (Chapter 5) describes the devoted support that the Kuntur Wasi Museum receives from the local community and the *comuneros'* belief that numerous beneficial public works have come to the region as a result of that support. The jobs for Weinstein's (Chapter 9) guides may also provide a similar basis for support and preservation, while Stothert (Chapter 8) demonstrates the relationship between the absence of resources and community fragmentation and the correspondent threat to the museum's future. Interestingly, there is little if any discussion by authors in this volume of what I think could be a primary basis of sustainability: admission fees. In my own work at Inkallacta in Bolivia, the placement of a gate and charging of a fee to enter the site has led not only to revenue generation, but also to the salutary prohibition of grazing and soccer games in the *kallanka* (an enormous single-room, multidoored structure) and monumental center of the site. I suggest that when measurable economic value is placed on protection, rather than the sale of objects, the historic value is more likely to be recognized.

In other efforts related to sustainability, I find Elera and Shimada's (Chapter 13) attempt to reintroduce traditional ceramic technologies as a job creation device to be fascinating, and I look forward to hearing more data regarding this project as a potential continuable, sustainable economic rationale for site and artifact protection that might survive the presence of these archaeologists in the region. Indeed, something that strikes me about many of the chapters, particularly those with a local focus, is the importance of the continued presence of the archaeologist and his/her education skills, fortitude, charisma, contacts, and funding. Weinstein (Chapter 9) recognizes a decline in Agua Blanca now that Colin McEwan is no longer working there (and see McEwan and coauthors' discussion in Chapter 12), and I have to wonder how many of these museums will survive and prosper when the archaeologist is no longer present. Even the most cursory review of the chapters in this volume suggests that those museums with outside sources of money are more sustainable, have broader programs, better preserve their artifacts, and are visited by more tourists than those with no funding, and much of the funding is obtained through the efforts and sales talent of the archaeologist.

If we are creating a museum that will not endure much beyond the length of our projects, are we creating a community benefit or merely a temporary institution to assist in our own research? Shouldn't our goal be to create an economically self-sufficient and sustainable museum, and what skills must we have (see discussion by Castillo and Holmquist in Chapter 10) and what actions must we take to do so? Stothert (Chapter 8) frames this issue most starkly, as her museum's management and planning structure endanger its future, and another museum was formed with similar lack of forethought. This is an issue to which I have given much thought (see below), but let it suffice now to say that many nongovernmental organizations and other hyperacademic models designed by so-called specialists that do not recognize the primacy of food, shelter, clothing, and other economic considerations are generally destined for failure and are a primary cause of the many untended, empty, and abandoned site museums that dot the region today. What aspects should we be focused on sustaining: education, tourism, preservation?

Local identity and empowerment also run particularly crosswise to another stated goal: tourism. Archaeological tourism is, for the most part, a regional or national phenomenon. Tourists are far more likely to travel on circuits with multiple attractions, such as that which has grown up in northern Peru as shown by Castillo and Holmquist (Chapter 10), than to remote single sites, unless they are particularly grandiose or famous. If one could visit only one Mochica site, there would be far fewer tourists visiting San José de Moro than might eventually be the case with the development of a "Ruta Moche" along the north coast. This fact necessitates regional cooperation in infrastructure and planning that frequently runs contrary to local identity politics, as Paredes and coauthors (Chapter 6) have discovered.

I now turn to what Silverman (Chapter 11) describes as "social justice" and what others call economic development or betterment, a theme underlying every chapter in this volume. Every presenter believes that through the development of a local site museum, he or she is improving the lives of the residents in the community, many of whom suffer from abject poverty and its unwelcome consequences. I think by any reasonable measures, most of the authors have succeeded in making positive contributions in their communities. But I think we must look self-critically at what we mean by such justice and betterment and at the costs inherent therein.

Most of the chapters in this volume and the Society for American Archaeology's Code of Ethics coincide in associating good social policy with conservation and preservation; tourism without cultural, ecological, or archaeological damage; local empowerment and control; minimal disruption of and maintenance of traditional cultures ("cultural continuity," but Silverman worries about "museumification"); and a corresponding distrust of larger and more regional, national, and global institutions. Every proposed notion of social justice and economic betterment incorporates all or most of these principles as a given upon which programs and development are predicated. I would suggest that rather than take these principles as a given, we must examine and justify anthropologically, socially, and economically the costs and tradeoffs associated with this ideology of preservation as we would any other ideology. This is not, I should note, unique to poorer regions of the world such as Latin America: less than thirty years ago, the U.S. Supreme Court faced a similar question regarding the landmarking of twentieth-century buildings in New York City, ruling six to three that New York City could landmark Grand Central Station and prevent the cantilevering of a skyscraper over it even when such construction would avoid a catastrophic bankruptcy (*Penn Central Transportation Co. v. City of New York,* 438 U.S. 104 [1978]). Silverman's (Chapter 11) chapter regarding the museumification of Cusco deals with such social costs, though I suggest that the inhibition of continued touristic development might result in more sewage, less tourist infrastructure, and thus fewer jobs and more poverty. Keeping archaeological sites in their pristine states and conserving and preserving every artifact in secure storage bins are every bit as much economic, political, and social choices as are building power plants or mining in the middle of an archaeological site. Might not the plant provide more jobs, housing, and economic betterment than a small site museum? I am not here arguing one way or the other, but rather pointing out the lack of reflexivity in failing to consider that which we privilege.

Let me draw particular attention to the privileging of objects through their preservation in museum vaults. Here I play devil's advocate. Might we not better the lives of local people by enabling them to legally sell some small portion of these infrequently displayed and studied artifacts, which might have the added benefit of hurting the looting market by increasing supply and driving down prices? Might not local potters sell more of their own pots if they could include an authentic sherd for comparison? How do we justify the expense and social cost of building museums or preserving every artifact? And why not use some of these sale proceeds to achieve desired ends: archaeological research and conservation, local education, and so forth. My proposal will horrify many archaeologists, particularly those of Latin American countries whose beautiful looted pottery brings exorbitant sale prices at Sotheby's and who are rightly concerned about the loss of opportunity to study deaccessioned pieces. But if such sales could feed, better the lives of, and empower local people and even help to preserve artifacts, doesn't our concept of social justice require at the very least its consideration? Are neoliberal market solutions and economic development so inherently evil that they can never be part of the solution? Must the solution always be archaeo- and eco-tourism, which is, of course, every bit as market based? Silverman and I would argue that this kind of tourism is as problematic as any other industry, though for different reasons. And, coincidentally, if adopted at every site where proposed, such tourism would be economically impossible to sustain, since there are not sufficient tourists or dollars. Do we not have an obligation to present alternatives that do not privilege our principles, so that decision makers (whether they be local, regional, or national) can make a truly informed decision? And can we engage in discourse with other interests until we recognize our biases and privileged concepts?

The chapters in this volume are so thought-provoking that I have ranged far in my comments on them. I have only scratched the surface of the many issues raised by these fine authors. I have not even considered notions of authenticity and replicas. I recognize the extraordinary efforts made by each of the authors in the creation and development or study of their respective museums, and

I realize that I have exercised a discussant's privilege in making suggestions without expressing consideration of many of the difficulties of implementation. I would welcome such discussion as a further topic for consideration at a later date. I thank all authors for a most stimulating volume of extraordinarily high standard.

16

Exhibiting Archaeology

Site Museums and Cultural Resource Management in Latin America

K. ANNE PYBURN

It has been a great pleasure to review the excellent work described in this volume that is now under way to integrate archaeological research into the living world in a politically and socially conscious way. All these contributions are being made by people with a stake in the archaeological record and a high profile in the academy, who have begun to take the need for community involvement and educational outreach seriously. Our need for data on what archaeologists are doing to situate research in its contemporary context and work with varied communities of stakeholders is reaching crisis proportions. We still are dealing only with anecdotes and chance bits of information about what works and what has caused disasters for people and cultural resources. Site museums are obviously key to sustainable conservation strategies in many parts of the world; they are often requested by local communities and increasingly aided and abetted by archaeologists.

In fact, for most archaeologists, public outreach and community engagement have become part of our professional responsibility and an important consideration in the design of our scientific research. Just a decade ago, sensitivity to local needs and values was hardly on any archaeologist's radar (Trigger 1984). Archaeologists who considered public opinion did not regard it as directly related to their investigations, except that the digging supplied the pots for the museum cases. So the blossoming of this topic is one of the many results of the revolution in archaeology that has taken hold of the majority of practitioners only in the past ten years. Stewardship, education, stakeholders—indeed all of the Society for American Archaeology's principles of archaeological ethics (Lynott and Wylie 1995; Zimmerman et al. 2003b) are integral to the programs described in these chapters. Archaeology has turned a corner, and standard professional practice has come to involve treating the archaeological record as a global resource (Barkan and Bush 2002; Bernbeck and Pollock 1996; Derry and Malloy 2003; Folorunso 2000; Medina 2000; Nicholas and Andrews 1997) rather than the preserve of a narrowly defined science.

The chapters in this volume offer a wealth of ideas and experience for working with local people to develop community museums in Latin America. Recently I proposed a set of guidelines for archaeologists working to support the economies and develop the archaeological resources of local communities, based on my work in Belize; that all the programs outlined in this book are grappling with the issues I enumerated is probably not a coincidence. We live in a globalized present where factors generated by the world system repeat themselves over and over at the local level.

The communities discussed in this volume have important similarities: all are economically disadvantaged, and all are near if not literally on top of spectacular ancient monuments (of one sort or another); all stand to benefit significantly from forging links to the past. All the contexts discussed have a legacy of European domination, especially Spanish colonialism, and were the loci of ancient urban cultures. These commonalities offer comparative data with generalizable implications for what the archaeologist should expect when designing a museum program.

But New World cultures did not all experience European invasion in the same way; some suffered less, some had been colonized for generations already. Disease hit some groups harder than others. Not all Europeans saw with the same eyes, and not all had the same impact. Some sites are still in urban contexts; others have become rural over the centuries since the Spanish conquest. Consequently, the groups considered in this book have varied relationships to their pasts. In some cases, memory seems almost continuous into deep prehistory, and children grow up with cultural identity that is unselfconsciously rooted in heritage. In other cases, the people living in the research areas are learning their connection to the past for the first time, and children are learning to turn reconstructions of the past into memory.

For these reasons the paramount requirement for development of a successful site museum is a secure ethnographic foundation to facilitate collaboration. Local communities usually have had a great deal of experience with visitors and even with archaeologists (see Chapter 4, this volume; Castañeda 1996; Hollowell 2004), but most of us would not like to be held responsible for the behavior of our predecessors. The only way to accomplish our goals as educators, advocates, and preservationists and to keep our research options open is to know whom we are teaching and what we are advocating and what we are preserving and reconstructing in terms that translate (Bender and Smith 2000).

In effect, all these projects are doing applied anthropology (Pyburn and Wilk 1995; Shackel and Chambers 2004), which is development work in less-developed nations. After all, the point of community museums is not abstract. Knowledge for its own sake and aesthetic entertainment are not the immediate goals—rather, economic improvement through tourism and the establishment of positive and dynamic identities in the modern world are the focus of all these efforts, along with preservation of the resources that are fundamental to both scientific knowledge and cultural well-being.

Not that the road is an easy one. Cyphers (Chapter 3) gives us the lowdown on competing interests that drag archaeological data into a tug-of-war with results that may be less than positive, despite good intentions and careful consideration. Jennings (Chapter 14) reminds us that unregulated use of global resources can destroy them. Manzanilla (Chapter 2) worries about the inadequacy of the information given to visitors. Hastorf (Chapter 7) wonders why people are eager to commodify their heritage. McEwan, Silva, and Hudson (Chapter 12), Elera and Shimada (Chapter 13), and Paredes, Fattorini, and Klarich (Chapter 6) provide positive scenarios in which local communities are empowered and enriched by their museums and able to incorporate ideas about stewardship, education, and archaeological heritage into their value system and economic needs (see also Chapter 5, this volume; Rockwell 2002). All this information about strategies and experience, both the negative and the positive, is invaluable to the rest of us for the way ahead. Every community is different, every museum is special—but as social scientists, we all believe that accumulated data and expertise will improve our ability to help and protect.

As Cyphers (Chapter 3) points out, without a background in museums or sustainable development, these are necessarily "seat of the pants" efforts. The authors are intelligent, educated people from developed nations making heroic efforts to do right and to do well by the people who suffer from economic disadvantages and political stresses of various kinds and who live where the archaeologists work. There is no one else to do the work that must be done, and archaeologists are stepping into the breach. Most archaeologists are understandably not familiar with the resources available to guide good intentions and address local needs that manifest themselves in a cry for site museums. Few archaeologists have the resources and time to research economic development, museum function, and public education. There are numerous scholarly and practical works on applied anthropology that can help us (see, for example, Bentley 1992, 1999; Cernea 1995; Chapin and Threlkeld 2001; Harrison 2001; LeCompte et al. 2001) and a huge database on outreach to less-developed countries (see, for example, Appleton 1983; Aronowitz and Giroux 1991; Arratia 1997; Hornberger 2000; Schensul and Schensul 1992; Sillitoe 1998). Work on museums has recently burgeoned as anthropologists have become more interested in issues of representation (for example, Anderson 2004; Carbonell 2003; Hall 2001; Handler 1989; Karp and Lavine 1991; Karp et al. 1992).

So while all these programs across Latin America work toward something good for local people and the public, most do not problematize the decisions about what that good might be so that the next generation of researchers and advocates can easily stand on their shoulders (Gathercole and Lowenthal 1990). Some site museums presented here are working well, while others have fared more poorly. By situating these experiences in the wider scholarship on outreach and aid to less-developed countries, archaeologists may be able to develop some proactive strategies for new contexts where site museums seem appropriate. Clearly, the most successful projects have been able to invest enormous amounts of money—providing information, resources, and technology to local communities but also putting a great deal of time, energy, and specialist knowledge into creating the infrastructure within the community where archaeologists work that must underwrite a successful venture. Problematizing issues of representation and identity (Layton 1989a, 1989b) immediately foregrounds local issues (Archibald 1999; Mbunwe-Samba 2001; Muringaniza 2002) and may save valuable time by shortening some of the time required to mount a collaboration. And familiarity with the results of collaborative programs within applied anthropology programs may also make it possible to save time, and therefore money.

By problematizing the issues, I mean asking at the outset of the project, "What should the museum teach?" Manzanilla (Chapter 2) is clearly concerned about this issue, but general improvements that are up-to-date and more comprehensive may not satisfy the stakeholders in the site museum of Teotihuacan. Certainly the beautiful suite of information she proposes would be a dramatic improvement and pleasing to many visitors, but how was this list of things to include developed? There are always other things that might need to go on someone else's "complete" list. Museologists have argued that the way to make sure your list is complete is to decide at the beginning what you want the museum exhibit to do (Hall 2001; Karp et al. 1992). As Manzanilla (Chapter 2) points out, the first glimpse of material culture should be carefully planned. But what exactly should visitors be taught? Perhaps the answer to this question is the key to understanding why an art historical approach is more often government supported. Display of a world-class artistic heritage may have more political legs than does evidence of a thriving ancient city (see Silverman 2005b). I would argue that the problem of the art historical approach is not exactly that it is incomplete, although of course it is, but that it sends two messages that bear consideration. One is that the focus of archaeology is objects instead of knowledge (an issue that Manzanilla is concerned about, too), which places emphasis on the values that drive looting (Pyburn 2003b). Another is that a focus on elite culture suggests that all significant cultural achievement lies with the rich and powerful, naturalizing class boundaries. So the question for any museum exhibit is, "What does it teach about human beings, about culture, about the past?"

Literature on education and tourist development (for example, Shaffer 2001) might prompt us to ask, "Is the customer always right?" Jennings (Chapter 14) describes the situation in which adventure travelers are likely to be displeased by what they see as spoiled or inauthentic local culture and landscape. But why should we worry about protecting the ignorance of tourists, especially ones like the rafters, who leave little or no money behind in the authentic villages they pass through? Rather than protecting the fantasy land that they expect, the function of a museum—even an outdoor museum—is to educate. Accepting an attitude that has unpleasant roots and undesirable consequences is probably not a good idea, and the museum experience needs to be shaped to bring visitors out of their fantasies and into the real world that is interesting and beautiful and relevant to living people. Allowing this situation to continue will soon have worse results than toilet paper gardens, since ignorant tourists added onto local need in the absence of heritage awareness will soon result in serious looting.

Jennings' (Chapter 14) point that haranguing visitors about their essentialist attitudes and the colonialist origins of their ideas about the past is worse than useless is extremely well taken. The reality of the situation he describes is that no protection of archaeological resources is going to come soon enough for the Cotahuasi Valley to maintain its archaeological record intact, and adventure tourism is not only *not* going to cease but is also providing the only possible support for preservation and development. His solution of working with guides to create a tour experience that not only thrills but educates is an excellent one. In my experience, if the information is presented in an engaging way, people easily see through essentialist rhetoric and eagerly take up the genuine plight of living people over their fantasy about living in the past. It is not only archaeologists who care about needy communities and deteriorating monuments.

Most of these programs promote identity formation and pride in cultural heritage; both are obviously important supports for preservation and are possibly beneficial political tools. But there is a vague line between an essentialism that elevates and an essentialism that destroys, and these are issues that many anthropologists understand (Cleere 2000; Meskell 1998; Olson 2001). Unconsidered promotion of cultural revivalism is not always a good idea, and the possible consequences need to be carefully considered—by the people involved.

This issue is of concern to Elera and Shimada (Chapter 13) and is particularly vexing to archaeologists since no rule applies to all stakeholders or even to all factions within a group of stakeholders. Here is where long-term commitment and personal relationships with stakeholders become essential. Essentialism is both necessary and dangerous to subaltern groups, and the anthropologist's role can only be that of educator and advisor. It is our job not to make decisions about representation that most deeply affect local communities but to educate these stakeholders about the potential consequences of their choices. Elera and Shimada's (Chapter 13) concern to be "ever vigilant" is laudable, but someday the archaeologists will have to depart; the vigilance must be homegrown.

Archaeologists readily fall in with the idea that we know what local people need from us and what will solve the problems we see. But development specialists call this sort of assistance "top down," and they know well that programs imposed from above last for only as long as the money lasts and as long as the "helpers" hang around and continue to help. We are going to have to release some of our authority and listen to what people really want if the programs we support are going to have a sustainable effect. The question "How can I help stakeholders to do what I think they should with their material heritage?" must become "How can I explain the potential value of this cultural resource so that stakeholders can make informed decisions about representation, development, and preservation?" (Layton et al. 2001)

One particularly apt example comes from Bentley (1992, 1997, 1999), whose style of collaboration deserves emulation. Bentley worked with a group of subsistence farmers in Honduras on crop pests. He gathered interested participants at the Zamarano extension college for long enough to explain scientific information about the life cycles of the insects that were affecting yield. A year later, the farmers returned to Zamarano and taught Bentley how they had used their new information to reduce predation on their food supply. The object of archaeology-based community development projects should be to similarly provide empirical information on strategies and consequences of museum development and other types of cultural resource management (CRM) that can be used by stakeholders to solve their own problems in sustainable ways. Castillo and Holmquist's (Chapter 10) modular museum provides an excellent example of how collaborative innovation can create viable solutions that are less costly but still engage multiple groups of stakeholders in an educational development project.

Talking openly about possible development strategies or museum plans or local exhibits or scholarly research designs and then listening carefully and openly to objections and suggestions—as the teams of Stothert (Chapter 8), Weinstein (Chapter 9), McEwan and colleagues (Chapter 12), and Elera and Shimada (Chapter 13) have done—will stretch our communication skills, but anthropologists are supposed to be able to accomplish cross-cultural understanding.

Stothert (Chapter 8), in particular, has shown that we need to move away from the dichotomy between *their* heritage and *our* research design. We need to pay careful attention to local culture, and we have to create situations in which we can both teach and learn about community needs. From these communities, archaeologists can learn history and myths and benefit from the observations of people with an indigenous sense of place. But we must also learn what people think about their needs and learn how to make the material past relevant to them so that it is worth preserving in their terms. Once we share enough information about the archaeological record and what it has to offer, community members can often help us figure things out—villagers talking about villagers, farmers talking about agriculture, isolated people talking about communication and trade, poor people talking about need. And they can teach us humility: if we explain our work so that people really understand, then we have to be willing to reconsider its value. The long-term partnership described by McEwan, Silva, and Hudson (Chapter 12) offers a stellar example of this sort of democratic approach that I believe holds the greatest hope for community enrichment through engagement with cultural resources.

Hastorf (Chapter 7) asks why site museums are popular these days. A similar idea preoccupies Mortensen (Chapter 4): Why is authenticity the focus of considerable interest and conversation about the past? The literature on globalization suggests that the possession of a museum is a ticket to inclusion in an important social group (Appadurai 2000; Wilk 2000). Governments need museums full of art to enter the global beauty pageant of high culture (Wilk 2000); communities need museums to join the group of tourist-worthy destinations and also to reify the glorious past that demonstrates that the present strained circumstances are not of their making, are not deserved. Museums are a kind of cultural solid that makes heritage into an artifact, a pageant entrant, a commodity. Importantly, in these cultural competitions, local variation has been delineated by global vocabulary; whatever heritage has been in the past, today it is defined to the world by its presentation in a museum. We must realize that the beauty of the art or the authenticity of the heritage or the completeness of the record of the past is not what has power. The winner of the beauty pageant may gain authority, but the power resides with the judges, with those who have the power to identify authenticity, evaluate art, and measure completeness (Wilk 2000). Once upon a time these decisions were the prerogative of archaeologists, the source of our power to control the material past. But if we really want to protect the past, if we want the material record to outlast our good intentions and our good works, it is time to let that go.

Each of these chapters is grappling with what I have called "the rules of engagement" (Pyburn 2003a). Though not exactly rules, these talking points are a way to organize important considerations that underlie all successful development work:

1. Relinquish interpretive control responsibly; do not try to restore "the" past

We cannot "give people back their history." As Eric Wolf (1982) beautifully revealed, all peoples have history. The choices to be made about authenticity and connection to the past, whether through oral histories or through archaeological reconstruction, are crucially related to the self-determination that defines human rights and opportunity in the modern world.

This is what all the outcry regarding cannibalism is really about (Askenasy 1994; Billman et al. 2000; Goldman 1999; Gonzales and Rodriguez 2000; Turner and Turner 1999; White 1992). When we recount the menu of the Donner Party or describe the human sashimi used to sustain plane-crash victims, we do not thereby identify cannibalism with the pioneers of the American West or use the plane-crash data to elaborate a model of the protein needs of a winning soccer team. These incidents become part of our understanding of human beings in extremis, providing lessons for "all humans," not another example of an exotic "them."

So the important thing about history is that it exists in the present (Collingwood 1939) and that there are many facts in history from which to select a pattern. Not all constructions of the past are equally good or equally factual or equally politically motivated or socially blind. However, there has been a pattern to archaeologists' claims about ancient people that cannot be explained merely by appealing to "the facts." Looking more carefully at how we approach our data to see what factors are influencing our interpretations can only make it better science.

Choosing one hypothesis over another, one data set over another, one methodology or research design over another is never the result of completely objective reasoning. No one could argue convincingly that within a cultural context of media hype, politically motivated funding agencies, and a public fascination with violence, archaeologists' research designs just happen by coincidence to focus on warfare, human sacrifice, cannibalism, and sex. Other connections are less obvious and may well be benign, but we cannot know this without examination. For example, the fact that a male-dominated discipline (Zeder 1997) reconstructs a male-dominated past (S. Nelson 1997) may not be without undesirable consequences (Pyburn 2004).

This is possibly the trickiest part of site museums: we have to provide the information that we currently have to help disadvantaged groups make their own choices about how their cultural and ethnic identity will be presented to their peers, their government, their guests, and the world. And we have to do this well enough to be comfortable with (or at least able to tolerate and work with) the decisions that communities make.

2. Do not try to be "nice": real help takes time

It is nice to bring wages into a poor village. It may not be nice to undermine the local political order by paying wages and giving power to village factions who oppose the local majority. It is nice to be in good standing with the national governments; it is not so nice when the local authorities use the project vehicle to transport political prisoners. It is also not really nice to tell local people who have been in mortal conflict with their government for generations over their land rights that you have come to take away the ancient altar their ancestors put on the land, so that the government can protect it for them.

For an anthropologist, doing the right thing must be based on a careful analysis of what will be the repercussions of the action. Just how nice are the results of this going to be, and for whom? This is what all the furor about Napoleon Chagnon (1997; see Tierney 2000) comes down to: not whether he did excellent science, but whether the science was good enough to justify certain costs and who had the right to evaluate the costs. The result was a backlash that imagined evil intent and undermined the scientific and humanistic value of what Chagnon accomplished. Every step in a research program involves choices; heritage can affect people's life chances in the modern world, and consequently archaeologists cannot be the only arbiters of the past that we hope to reclaim.

3. Do not confuse poverty with tradition or tradition with material culture

Archaeologists are accustomed to one-way interactions with another culture; after all, the dead do not answer back. Many of us have sophisticated models designed to compensate for this, to make the other side of the conversation more lively. But we tend toward visions of culture as a sealed package, since no amount of sensitivity or empirical accuracy is going to make it possible to change what happened to Pompeii when Vesuvius erupted or to the cultures of the New World after Columbus landed.

I think this immersion in the past has affected how we think about living people. We take the gap between vernacular perceptions of the world and ours, between local people's life chances and ours, between informal education and ours to be unbridgeable cultural gaps. "They don't know what tuberculosis is, so how can they decide whether I should be allowed to dig up these bones showing the progression of disease?" Or similarly, "These people are not interested in what I am doing; it makes no sense to them; so I can't explain my project." This is really an antiempirical form of cultural relativism. Proponents of such arguments implicitly treat other cultures as unchanging wholes that are broached at the risk of introducing damaging new knowledge. This attitude dooms many groups of stakeholders to ignorance of what archaeologists do, because of the archaeologist's belief in an incommensurability of perspectives. But if incommensurability really made cultures opaque to each other, there would be no point in any anthropology—least of all archaeology, so none of us really believes this. Translating one culture into another to create understanding is our job.

I have proposed elsewhere that the difference between archaeologists and living people is more economic than cultural (Pyburn 1998). People mostly use outmoded tools and practice non-Western medicine not from choice, but from necessity. A lack of technological, economic, and sociopolitical change is not characteristic of any wealthy culture, past or present. To say that local people do not have the information that they need to make decisions about the disposal of their cultural patrimony need not be disrespectful if we are willing to provide the information in usable form and also if we are willing to get out of the way when the decision is made. Archaeologists have to relinquish the idea that if everyone understood the practice and the value of science and archaeological research, then everyone would agree that it was a good thing. Science cannot stand apart from the culture of its origin or the political context of its expression. This is an empirical fact of great historical significance that behooves the genuine engagement of any responsible social scientist.

4. Do not encourage fundamentalism; local knowledge is not scholarship, and religion is neither the equivalent nor the obverse of science

The political ramifications of essentialism are what showed anthropologists the error of such reasoning. While it seems fair to encourage oppressed peoples to fight their oppression using the culture concept that has been used to marginalize them, social scientists know well what the consequences can be, no matter how well-meaning; for us to tell only a part of what we know is irresponsible.

To disregard the distance between the past and the present is unscholarly. Current practices may relate to the past, and living people may make uncritical connections; archaeologists, however, as students of social process who understand the complexities of social change, must regard such similarities as a source of hypotheses. Rather than undermining cultural integrity in the present day, current anthropological knowledge argues that flexibility and change are more reliably attendant on cultural survival than are rigidity and stagnation. What this means is that descendant communities and other stakeholders cannot do archaeology without training and education any more than archaeologists can. To pretend otherwise is disingenuous and patronizing. There are non-empirical strategies for interpreting archaeological patterns (for example, goddess worship, dowsing, oral history, mythology) that may provide the basis for testable hypotheses, but on their own they are not archaeology. True collaboration requires not only that we listen carefully to what stakeholders tell us but also that we teach what we know about the methods of science and the limitations of social science. We do no one any favors if we demote religion to a limited version of science or pretend that the scientific goal of disproof is just another religion. Science is not a system of belief, it is a system of disbelief; rather than a way of knowing, it is the perpetual emphasis on what we do not know. Equating science with religion not only misunderstands both, it also denies members of descendant groups and stakeholders from many religious traditions the opportunity to make use of the scientific method or to themselves become scientists (Pyburn 1999).

5. Do no harm; be modest (dress, behavior, and claims about the past)

Archaeologists have become quite sensitive to their impact on the people with whom they work. Respect is clearly a two-way proposition, and the first step toward genuine understanding is adherence to the values people express in the modesty of their dress and social behaviors (Watkins et al. 2000). But archaeologists should also be modest in their claims about the past. If evidence appears to support migration into the area within the past hundred years, are research conclusions really strong enough to support the disenfranchisement of residents of the local community from their land (Wilk 1999)? Even if this is not an issue today, might it become an issue tomorrow? I am not suggesting that we curb intellectual freedom but advocating that we be honest about the reliability of our evidence and its applicability to the present. No archaeologist I know would intentionally violate human rights; it is up to us to make clear how far our interpretations can be taken, and why. If the only possible use (or even the most likely use) of the data we are generating is negative, perhaps it is time to examine what responsibilities are entailed by the privilege of intellectual freedom (Pyburn 1999; Watkins 2000).

So the next step for archaeologists, after we have worked more deeply into the scholarly literature on development and more carefully into the issues of presentation entailed in the concept of a museum, and after we have acquired sufficient ethnographic knowledge to teach and also to learn from the stakeholders we target, is the development of collaboration on our scholarly research designs. It is not only in the public setting of a museum that we will need to begin to make our work palatable and interesting, it is in the kernel of the intellectual endeavor itself. I believe that with honesty and effort, and a measure of creativity, we will be able to employ our skills in support of research designs that have been truly collaboratively conceived with stakeholders from outside the academy. This is not a small charge, since I do not propose that we give up scholarly integrity or scientific reasoning or pander to political context to achieve it. Nevertheless, I believe that the future of our discipline hangs on our ability to take this step, and the chapters in this volume give me great confidence that we can rise to the challenge.

Bibliography

Addyman, Peter V. "Reconstruction as Interpretation: The Example of the Yorvik Viking Centre, York." In *The Politics of the Past,* edited by Peter Gathercole and David Lowenthal, 257–64. London: Routledge, 1990.

Advantage Mexico. Teotihuacan museums. http://www.advantagemexico.com/mexico_city/teotihuacan.html (accessed 2005).

AEDES (Asociación Especializada para el Desarrollo). *Agenda Local 21: La Unión—Arequipa. Plan de Desarrollo Estratégico Provincial.* Arequipa, Peru: Tipografía "El Alva," 1998.

Agurcia Fasquelle, Ricardo. "La Depredación del Patrimonio Cultural en Honduras: El Caso de la Arqueología." *Yaxkín* 7, no. 2 (1984): 83–96.

Alva, Walter. "Discovering the New World's Richest Unlooted Tomb." *National Geographic* 174, no. 4 (1988): 510–48.

———. "The Destruction, Looting, and Traffic of the Archaeological Heritage of Peru." In *Trade in Illicit Antiquities: The Destruction of the World's Archaeological Heritage,* edited by Neil Brodie, Jennifer Doole, and Colin Renfrew, 89–96. Cambridge, England: McDonald Institute of Archaeology, 2001.

Alva, Walter, and Christopher B. Donnan. *Royal Tombs of Sipán.* Los Angeles: Fowler Museum of Cultural History, University of California, 1993.

Ames, Michael M. *Cannibal Tours and Glass Boxes: The Anthropology of Museums.* Vancouver: University of British Columbia Press, 1992.

Anderson, Gail. *Reinventing the Museum: Historical and Contemporary Perspectives on the Paradigm Shift.* Lanham, Md.: Rowman and Littlefield, 2004.

Andrade, Xavier. *Burocracia: Museos, Politicas Culturales y la Flexibilización de la Fuerza de Trabajo en el Contexto Guayaquileno.* Quito, Ecuador: Revista ICONOS, 2004.

Appadurai, Arjun. "The Production of Locality." In *Modernity at Large,* by Arjun Appadurai, 178–99. Minneapolis: University of Minnesota Press, 1996.

———. "Grassroots Globalization and the Research Imagination." *Public Culture* 12, no. 1 (2000): 1–19.

Appadurai, Arjun, and Carol A. Breckenridge. "Museums Are Good to Think: Heritage on View in India." In *Museums and Communities,* edited by Ivan Karp, Christine Mullen Kreamer, and Steven D. Lavine, 34–55. Washington, D.C.: Smithsonian Institution Press, 1992.

Appenzeller, Tim, Daniel Clery, and Elizabeth Culotta. "Archaeology: Transitions in Prehistory." *Science* 282 (1998): 1441–58.

Appleton, Nicholas. *Cultural Pluralism in Education: Theoretical Foundations.* New York: Longman, 1983.

Archibald, Richard. *A Place to Remember: Using History to Build Community.* Walnut Creek, Calif.: AltaMira Press, 1999.

Arnold, Bettina. "Germany's Nazi Past: How Hitler's Archaeologists Distorted European Prehistory to Justify Racist and Territorial Goals." *Archaeology* (July/August 1992): 30–37.

Arnould, Eric J., and Linda L. Price. "River Magic: Extraordinary Experience and the Extended Service Encounter." *Journal of Consumer Research* 20 (1993): 24–45.

Arnould, Eric J., Linda L. Price, and Cele Otnes. "Making Magic from Consumption: A Study of White-Water River Rafting." *Journal of Contemporary Ethnography* 28, no. 1 (1999): 33–68.

Aronowitz, Stanley, and Henry Giroux. *Postmodern Education: Politics, Culture, and Social Criticism.* Minneapolis: University of Minnesota Press, 1991.

Arratia, Maria-Inés. "Daring to Change: The Potential of Intercultural Education in Aymara Communities in Chile." *Anthropology and Education Quarterly* 28, no. 2 (1997): 229–50.

Askenasy, Hans. *Cannibalism: From Sacrifice to Survival.* Amherst, N.Y.: Prometheus Books, 1994.

Ball, Joseph W. *Cahal Pech, the Ancient Maya, and Modern Belize: The Story of an Archaeological Park.* San Diego: San Diego State University Press, 1993.

Barkan, Elazar, and Ronald Bush, eds. *Claiming the Stones, Naming the Bones: Cultural Property and the Negotiation of National and Ethnic Identity.* Los Angeles: Getty Research Institution, 2002.

Bawden, Garth. "Galindo and the Nature of the Middle Horizon on the North Coast of Peru." Ph.D. diss., Department of Anthropology, Harvard University, 1977.

———. *The Moche.* Malden, Mass.: Blackwell Press, 1996.

Beedie, Paul. "Adventure Tourism." In *Sport and Adventure Tourism,* edited by Simon Hudson, 203–39. New York: Haworth Hospitality, 2003.

Beedie, Paul, and Simon Hudson. "Emergence of Mountain-Based Adventure Tourism." *Annals of Tourism Research* 30, no. 3 (2003): 625–43.

Benavides, O. Hugo. "Returning to the Source: Social Archaeology as Latin American Philosophy." *Latin American Antiquity* 12, no. 4 (2001): 355–70.

———. *Making Ecuadorian Histories: Four Centuries of Defining Power.* Austin: University of Texas Press, 2004.

Bender, Barbara. *Stonehenge: Making Space.* Oxford, England: Berg, 1998.

Bender, Susan, and George Smith, eds. *Teaching Archaeology in the Twenty-First Century.* Washington, D.C.: Society for American Archaeology, 2000.

Bennett, Tony. *The Birth of the Museum.* London: Routledge, 1995.

Bennett, Wendell C. "Excavation in Bolivia." *Anthropological Papers of the American Museum of Natural History* 35, no. 4 (1936): 331–505.

Bentley, Jeffrey W. "Alternatives to Pesticides in Central America: Applied Studies of Local Knowledge." *Culture and Agriculture* 44 (1992): 10–13.

———. "On the Ethics of Biological Control of Insect Pests." *Agriculture and Human Values* 14, no. 3 (1997): 283–87.

———. "Farmer Knowledge and Management of Crop Disease." *Agriculture and Human Values* 16, no. 1 (1999): 75–81.

Benzoni, Girolamo. *La Historia del Mondo Nuovo (Relatos de Su Viaje por el Ecuador, 1547–1550): Traducida por Primera Vez en Lengua Castellana por Carlos Radicati de Primeglio.* Guayaquil: Museo Antropológico y Pinacoteca del Banco Central del Ecuador, 1985.

Bernbeck, Reinhard, and Susan Pollock. "Ayodhya, Archaeology, and Identity." *Current Anthropology* 37, no. 1 (1996): 138–42.

Beverido Pereau, Francisco. "San Lorenzo Tenochtitlán y la Civilización Olmeca." M.A. thesis, Facultad de Antropología, Universidad Veracruzana, Xalapa, Mexico, 1970.

Billman, Brian R., Patricia M. Lambert, and Banks L. Leonard. "Cannibalism, Warfare, and Drought in the Mesa Verde Region during the Twelfth Century A.D." *American Antiquity* 65, no. 1 (2000): 1–34.

Bonavia, Duccio. "Peru." In *Approaches to the Archaeological Heritage: A Comparative Study of World Cultural Resources Management Systems,* edited by Henry Cleere, 109–15. Cambridge, England: Cambridge University Press, 1986.

Bond, George Clement, and Angela Gilliam, eds. *Social Construction of the Past.* London: Routledge, 1994.

Boylan, Patrick. "Museums and Cultural Identity." *Museums Journal* 90, no. 10 (1990): 29–34.

Browman, David L. "The Temple of Chiripa (Lake Titicaca, Bolivia)." In *El Hombre y la Cultura Andina,* edited by Ramiro Matos M., vol. 2, 807–13. III Congreso Peruano: El Hombre y La Cultura Andina. Lima: Editores Lasontay, 1978.

Brüggeman, Jürgen, and Marie Areti-Hers. "Exploraciones Arqueológicas en San Lorenzo Tenochtitlán." *Boletín del INAH* 39 (1970): 18–23.

Bruner, Edward. "Abraham Lincoln as Authentic Reproduction: A Critique of Postmodernism." *American Anthropologist* 96 (1994): 397–415.

Carabias, J., Enrique Provencio, and Carlos Toledo. *Manejo de los Recursos Naturales y Pobreza Rural.* Mexico City: Universidad Nacional Autónoma de México y Fondo de Cultura Económica, 1994.

Carbonell, Bettina Messias, ed. *Museum Studies: An Anthology of Contexts.* London: Blackwell, 2003.

Carcedo, Paloma, and Izumi Shimada. "Behind the Golden Mask: Sicán Gold Artifacts from Batán Grande, Peru." In *Art of Pre-Columbian Gold: Jan Mitchell Collection,* edited by Julie Jones, 60–75. London: Weidenfeld and Nicolson, 1985.

Carlevato, Denise. "Late Ceramics from Pucara, Peru: An Indicator of Changing Site Function." *Expedition* 30, no. 3 (1988): 39–45.

Castañeda, Quetzil. *In the Museum of Maya Culture: Touring Chichen Itza.* Minneapolis: University of Minnesota Press, 1996.

Castillo, Luis Jaime. "The Last of the Mochicas: A View from the Jequetepeque Valley." In *Moche Art and Archaeology in Ancient Peru,* edited by Joanne Pillsbury, 306–32. Studies in the History of Art 63. Center for the Advanced Study of the Visual Arts. Washington, D.C.: National Gallery of Art, and New Haven: Yale University Press, 2001.

———. "Los Ultimos Mochicas en Jequetepeque." In *Moche: Hacia el Final del Milenio,* edited by Santiago Uceda and Elías Mujica, vol. 2, 65–123. Actas del Segundo Coloquio sobre la Cultura Moche, Trujillo, 1 al 7 de Agosto de 1999. Lima: Universidad Nacional de Trujillo and Pontificia Universidad Católica del Perú, 2003.

Castillo, Luis Jaime, and Christopher B. Donnan. "Los Mochicas del Norte y los Mochicas del Sur: Una Perspectiva desde el Valle del Jequetepeque." In *Vicús,* edited by Krzysztof Makowski et al., 142–81. Lima: Colección Arte y Tesoros del Perú, Banco de Crédito del Perú, 1994a.

———. "La Ocupación Moche de San José de Moro, Jequetepeque." In *Moche: Propuestas y Perspectivas,* edited by Santiago Uceda and Elias Mujica, 93–146. Trujillo: Universidad Nacional de La Libertad; Lima: Instituto Francés de Estudios Andinos, 1994b.

Cernea, Michael M. *Putting People First: Sociological Variables in Rural Development.* Washington, D.C.: World Bank, 1995.

Chagnon, Napoleon A. *Yanomamö.* Fort Worth, Tex.: Harcourt Brace College Publishers, 1997.

Challenger, Anthony. *Utilización y Conservación de los Ecosistemas Terrestres en México: Pasado, Presente y Futuro.* Mexico City: Comisión Nacional para el Conocimiento y Uso de la Biodiversidad (CONABIO)/Instituto de Biología–UNAM/Agrupación Sierra Madre, 1998.

Chapin, M., and B. Threlkeld. *Indigenous Landscapes: A Study in Ethnocartography.* Arlington, Va.: Center for the Support of Native Lands, 2001.

Chávez, Karen L. Mohr. "The Organization of Production and Distribution of Traditional Pottery in South Highland Peru." In *Ceramic Production and Distribution*, edited by George J. Bey III and Christopher A. Pool, 49–97. Boulder, Colo.: Westview Press, 1992.

Chávez, Sergio J. "The Conventionalized Rules in Pucara Pottery Technology and Iconography: Implications of Socio-Political Development in the Northern Titicaca Basin." Ph.D. diss., Department of Anthropology, Michigan State University, 1992.

Childs, S. Terry. "The Curation Crisis." *Federal Archaeology* 7, no. 4 (1995): 11–15.

Cleere, Henry F. "Introduction: The Rationale of Archaeological Heritage Management." In *Archaeological Heritage Management in the Modern World,* edited by H. F. Cleere, 1–19. London: Unwin Hyman, 1989.

———. "The World Heritage Convention in the Third World." In *Cultural Resource Management in Contemporary Society: Perspectives on Managing and Presenting the Past,* edited by Francis P. McManamon and Alf Hatton, 99–106. One World Archaeology 41. London: Routledge, 2000.

———. "The Uneasy Bedfellows: Universality and Cultural Heritage." In *Destruction and Conservation of Cultural Property,* edited by Robert Layton, Peter G. Stone, and Julian Thomas, 22–29. London: Routledge, 2001.

Clifford, James. *Routes: Travel and Translation in the Late Twentieth Century.* Cambridge, Mass.: Harvard University Press, 1997.

Coe, Michael D., and Richard A. Diehl. *In the Land of the Olmec,* 2 vols. Austin: University of Texas Press, 1980.

Collingwood, R. G. *An Autobiography.* Oxford, England: Oxford University Press, 1939.

Comisión Nacional para el Conocimiento y Uso de la Biodiversidad (CONABIO). Prioritized terrestrial regions. http://www.conabio.gob.mx/conocimiento/regionalización/doctos/terrestres.html (accessed spring 2004).

Cordero Miranda, Gregorio. "Las Ruinas de Chiripa." Unpublished manuscript, dated 1978. On file. Directorate of Archaeology, La Paz, Bolivia.

Cyphers, Ann. *Informe del Proyecto Arqueológico San Lorenzo Tenochtitlán: Temporada 1992.* Report to the Consejo de Arqueología, Instituto Nacional de Antropología e Historia, Mexico City, 1992.

———. "Olmec Sculpture." *National Geographic Research and Exploration* 10, no. 3 (1994): 294–305.

———. *Escultura Olmeca de San Lorenzo Tenochtitlán.* Mexico City: Instituto de Investigaciones Antropológicas y Coordinación de Humanidades de la Universidad Nacional Autónoma de México, 2004.

Daltabuit, M., H. Cisneros, L. M. Vázquez, and E. Santillán. *Ecoturismo y Desarrollo Sustentable: Impacto en Comunidades Rurales de la Selva Maya.* Mexico City: Centro Regional de Investigaciones Multidisciplinarias de la Universidad Nacional Autónoma de México, 2000.

Davis, Hester. "From the Ethics Committee: What If . . . ?" *SAA Bulletin* 16, no. 4 (1998): 14–15.

del Río Alvarez, María de la Soledad. Teotihuacan museum images. http://www.inaoep.mx/~sole/turismo/Edo_Mexico/Teotihuacan/Museo.html (accessed 2005).

Demas, Matha. "Ephesus." In *The Conservation of Archaeological Sites in the Mediterranean Region,* edited by Marta de la Torre, 127–49. Los Angeles: Getty Conservation Institute, 1997.

Derry, Linda, and Maureen Malloy, eds. *Archaeologists and Local Communities: Partners in Exploring the Past.* Washington, D.C.: Society for American Archaeology, 2003.

Docter, Catherine. "Notes from Copán." In *Copán Maya Foundation: Inauguration Article.* http://www.Copánmayafoundation.org/inauguration.htm (accessed 2002).

Dongoske, Kurt E., Mark Aldenderfer, and Karen Doehner. *Working Together: Native Americans and Archaeologists.* Washington, D.C.: Society for American Archaeology, 2000.

Donnan, Christopher B., and Luis Jaime Castillo. "Finding the Tomb of a Moche Priestess." *Archaeology* 45, no. 6 (1992): 38–42.

Downum, Christian E., and Laurie J. Price. "Applied Archaeology." *Human Organization* 58, no. 3 (1999): 226–39.

Doyle, Mary. "The Ancestor Cult and Burial Ritual in Seventeenth and Eighteenth Century Central Peru." Ph.D. diss., Department of History, University of California at Los Angeles; Ann Arbor: University Microfilms International, 1988.

Duitz, Mindy. "The Soul of a Museum: Commitment to Community at the Brooklyn Children's Museum." In *Museums and Communities: The Politics of Public Culture,* edited by Ivan Karp, Christine Mullen Kreamer, and Steven D. Lavine, 242–61. Washington, D.C.: Smithsonian Institution Press, 1992.

Duncan, Carol. *Civilizing Rituals: Inside Public Art Museums.* London: Routledge, 1995.

Emberling, Geoff. "Ethnicity in Complex Societies: Archaeological Perspectives." *Journal of Archaeological Research* 5 (1997): 295–344.

Erickson, Clark. "Agricultural Landscapes as World Heritage: Raised Field Agriculture in Bolivia and Peru." In *Managing Change: Sustainable Approaches to the Built Environment,* edited by Jeanne Marie Teutonico and Frank Matero, 181–204. Los Angeles: Getty Conservation Institute, 2003.

Errington, Shelly. "Progressivist Stories and the Pre-Columbian Past: Notes on Mexico and the United States." In *Collecting the Pre-Columbian Past,* edited by Elizabeth Hill Boone, 209–49. Washington, D.C.: Dumbarton Oaks Research Library and Collection, 1993.

———. "Nationalizing the Pre-Columbian Past in Mexico and the United States." In *The Death of Authentic Primitive Art and Other Tales of Progress,* by Shelly Errington, 161–87. Berkeley: University of California Press, 1998.

Esteban, Fabio. "Central American Site Managers Meet in Copán, Honduras." *World Heritage Newsletter* 14 (1997). http://whc.unesco.org/news/14newsen.htm#story3.

Estrada Iberico, Enrique. "Comments" cited in "Visión del Centro Histórico del Cusco." *Crónicas Urbanas* (Cusco) 6–7 (1998): 60–62.

Estrada Iberico, Enrique, and Luis Nieto Degregori. "Cuzco en la Encrucijada. Análisis del Registro Catastral del Centro Histórico." *Crónicas Urbanas* (Cusco) 6–7 (1998): 3–38.

Fajardo, Carmen Julia. "Archaeological Investigation and Conservation in Honduras." *SAA Bulletin* 15, no. 1 (1997): 22–23.

Fash, Barbara, and William L. Fash. "Maya Resurrection." *Natural History* (April 1996): 24–29. [1996a]

———. "Saving the Maya Past for the Maya Future." http://www.peabody.harvard.edu/profiles/fash.html (accessed 1996). [1996b]

Fash, William, and Barbara Fash. "Investing in the Past to Build a Better Future: The Copán Sculpture Museum in Honduras, Central America." *Cultural Survival Quarterly* (Spring 1997): 46–51.

Fash, William, and Ricardo Agurcia Fasquelle. *History Carved in Stone: A Guide to the Archaeological Park of the Ruins of Copán.* Copán Ruinas: Asociación Copán, Instituto Hondureño de Antropología e Historia, 1998.

Findlen, Paula. *Possessing Nature: Museums, Collecting, and Scientific Culture in Early Modern Italy.* Berkeley: University of California Press, 1994.

Florescano, Enrique. "The Creation of the Museo Nacional de Antropología of Mexico and Its Scientific, Educational, and Political Purposes." In *Collecting the Pre-Columbian Past,* edited by Elizabeth Hill Boone, 81–103. Washington, D.C.: Dumbarton Oaks Research Library and Collection, 1993.

Flores Ochoa, Jorge. *El Cuzco: Resistencia y Continuidad.* Cusco: Centro de Estudios Andinos, 1990.

Folorunso, C. A. "Third World Development and the Threat to Resource Conservation: The Case of Africa." In *Cultural Resource Management in Contemporary Society: Per-*

spectives on Managing and Presenting the Past, edited by Francis P. McManamon and Alf Hatton, 30–39. One World Archaeology 41. London: Routledge, 2000.

Franquemont, Edward. "The Ancient Pottery from Pucara, Peru." *Ñawpa Pacha* 24 (1986): 1–30.

Gale, Fay, and Jane Jacobs. "Identifying High-Risk Visitors at Aboriginal Art Sites in Australia." *Rock Art Research* 3, no. 1 (1986): 3–19.

Gathercole, Peter, and David Lowenthal, eds. *The Politics of the Past.* London: Unwin Hyman, 1990.

Getty Conservation Institute. UNESCO, ICOMOS, OWHC documents. http://www.getty.edu/conservation/research_resources/charters.html.

Goddard, Marc, and Justin Jennings. "Rafts and Ruins: Cooperative Efforts to Save the Archaeological Heritage of the Cotahuasi Valley." *SAA Archaeological Record* 3, no. 3 (2003): 30–32.

Goldman, Laurence R. *The Anthropology of Cannibalism.* New York: Bergin and Garvey, 1999.

Gonzales, Patrisia, and Roberto Rodriguez. "Cannibalism and the End of Archaeology." http://content.uclick.com/content/cm.html (accessed 2000).

González, Alicia M., and Edith A. Tonelli. "Compañeros and Partners: The CARA Project." In *Museums and Communities: The Politics of Public Culture,* edited by Ivan Karp, Christine Mullen Kreamer, and Steven D. Lavine, 262–84. Washington, D.C.: Smithsonian Institution Press, 1992.

Greenwood, Davydd J. "Culture by the Pound: An Anthropological Perspective on Tourism as Cultural Commoditization." In *Host and Guest: The Anthropology of Tourism,* edited by V. L. Smith, 171–85. 2nd ed. Philadelphia: University of Pennsylvania Press, 1989.

Grinder, Alison L., and E. Sue McCoy. *The Good Guide: A Sourcebook for Interpreters, Docents, and Tour Guides.* Scottsdale, Ariz.: Ironwood Publishing, 1985.

Hall, Martin. "Cape Town's District Six and the Archaeology of Memory." In *Destruction and Conservation of Cultural Property,* edited by Robert L. Layton, Peter G. Stone, and Julian Thomas, 298–311. One World Archaeology 41. London: Routledge, 2001.

Ham, Sam H. *Interpretación Ambiental: Una Guía Práctica para Gente con Grandes Ideas y Presupuestos Pequeños.* Golden, Colo.: North American Press/Editor Fulcrum, 1992.

Handler, Richard. "Ethnicity in the Museum." In *Negotiating Ethnicity: The Impact of Anthropological Theory and Practice,* edited by Susan Emley Keefe, 19–26. NAPA Bulletin 8. Fairfax, Va.: American Anthropological Association, 1989.

Handler, Richard, and Eric Gable. *The New History in an Old Museum: Creating the Past at Colonial Williamsburg.* Durham, N.C.: Duke University Press, 1997.

Hardin, Garrett. "The Tragedy of the Commons." *Science* 162, no. 3859 (1968): 1243–48.

Harrison, Barbara. *Collaborative Programs in Indigenous Communities: From Fieldwork to Practice.* Walnut Creek, Calif.: AltaMira Press, 2001.

Hastorf, Christine A., ed. *Early Settlement in Chiripa, Bolivia: Research of the Taraco Archaeological Project.* Contributions, Archaeological Research Facility Monograph Publications 57. Berkeley: University of California, 1999.

———. "Community with the Ancestors: Ceremonies and Social Memory in the Middle Formative at Chiripa, Bolivia." *Journal of Anthropological Archaeology* 22 (2003): 305–32.

Hayden, Dolores. *The Power of Place: Urban Landscapes as Public History.* Cambridge, Mass.: MIT Press, 1999.

Henderson, Justin. *Museum Architecture.* Gloucester, Mass.: Rockport Publishers, 2001.

Hewison, Robert. *The Heritage Industry: Britain in a Climate of Decline.* London: Methuen, 1987.

Hobsbawm, Eric. "Introduction: Inventing Tradition." In *The Invention of Tradition,* edited by Eric Hobsbawm and Terrence Ranger, 1–14. Cambridge, England: Cambridge University Press, 1983.

Hollowell, Julie J. "'Old Things' on the Loose: The Legal Market for Archaeological Materials from Alaska's Bering Strait." Ph.D. diss., Department of Anthropology, Indiana University, 2004.

Hollyfield, Lori. "Manufacturing Adventure: The Buying and Selling of Emotions." *Journal of Contemporary Ethnography* 28, no. 1 (1999): 3–32.

Holm, Olaf. *Cultura Manteña-Huancavilca.* Guayaquil: Museo del Banco Central, 1982.

Holmquist, Ulla. "Mita, Mines, Museums." Manuscript in possession of the author, 1996.

———. "Archaeological Heritage: Values and Uses in the Local and the National Context in Peru." In *Peru: Beyond the Reforms.* Field Reports. Lima: PromPerú Summer Internship Program, 1997.

Hornberger, Nancy H. "Bilingual Education Policy and Practice in the Andes: Ideological Paradox and Intercultural Possibility." *Anthropology and Education Quarterly* 31, no. 2 (2000): 173–201.

Hudson, Chris, and Colin McEwan. "Focusing Pride in the Past: Agua Blanca, Ecuador." *Museum* 154, no. 2 (1987): 125–28.

Hudson, Kenneth. *Museums of Influence.* Cambridge, England: Cambridge University Press, 1987.

ICOM (International Council on Museums). "Statutes." icom.museums/statutes/html (accessed spring 2004).

ICOMOS (International Council on Monuments and Sites). "The Norms of Quito." http://www.icomos.org/docs/quito67.html (1967).

———."The Nara Document on Authenticity." http://www.international.icomos.org/naradoc_eng.htm (1994).

———. "The Declaration of San Antonio." *http://www.icomos.org/docs/san_antonio.html* (1996).

———. Copán designation for UNESCO. http://whc.unesco.org/archive/advisory_body_evaluation/129.pdf.

INAH (Instituto Nacional de Antropología y Historia). Museum of Mural Painting images. http://www.inah.gob.mx/pinturamuralteotihuacana/index.html (accessed 2005).

INC (Instituto Nacional de Cultura del Perú). "84%: La cifra que, para el Estado, representa a la cultura." Press release. http://inc.perucultural.org.pe/inst4.shtml (accessed spring 2004).

International Journal of Cultural Property. "The Universal Declaration on Cultural Diversity." *International Journal of Cultural Property* 11, no. 1 (2002): 129–36.

Jennings, Justin. "Seducing Adventure Tourists by Damaging Sites, a Peruvian Example." *SAA Archaeological Record* 2, no. 5 (2002): 21–23.

———. "Ruins on the Rapids: A White-Knuckle Down-River Ride to Save Peru's Past." *Archaeology* 56, no. 6 (2003): 30–35.

———. "Rafters, River Magic, and Ruins: Ethical Dilemmas in Adventure Tourism, Site Preservation, and Rural Development." Manuscript in possession of author, n.d.

Jonas, Lillian M. "Making and Facing Danger: Constructing Strong Character on the River." *Symbolic Interaction* 22, no. 3 (1999): 247–67.

Jones, Jane Peirson. "The Colonial Legacy and the Community: The Gallery 33 Project." In *Museums and Communities: The Politics of Public Culture,* edited by Ivan Karp, Christine Mullen Kreamer, and Steven D. Lavine, 221–41. Washington, D.C.: Smithsonian Institution Press, 1992.

Jones, Sian. *The Archaeology of Ethnicity: Constructing Identities in the Past and Present.* London: Routledge, 1997.

Jornada de Oriente. "Nuevo Intento de la Tosepan Titataniske. El Café Orgánico. Una Apuesta para la Sobrevivencia." *La Jornada de Oriente* (México), 14 junio 2001, p. 9.

Joyce, Rosemary A. "Solid Histories for Fragile Nations: Archaeology as Cultural Patrimony." In *Ethical Locations: Anthropological Moralities on the Boundaries of the Public and the Professional,* edited by Lynn Meskell and Peter Pels. Oxford, England: Berg, forthcoming, n.d.

Kaplan, Flora. "Mexican Museums in the Creation of a National Image in World Tourism." In *Crafts and the World Market: The Impact of Global Exchange on Middle American Artisans,* edited by June Nash, 103–25. Albany: State University of New York Press, 1993.

———, ed. *Museums and the Making of "Ourselves": The Role of Objects in National Identity.* London: Leicester University Press, 1994.

Karp, Ivan, Christine Mullen Kreamer, and Steven D. Lavine, eds. *Museums and Communities: The Politics of Public Culture.* Washington, D.C.: Smithsonian Institution Press, 1992.

Karp, Ivan, and Steven Lavine, eds. *Exhibiting Cultures.* Washington, D.C.: Smithsonian Institution Press, 1991.

Kidder, Alfred V., III. "Preliminary Notes on the Archaeology of Pucara, Puno, Peru." *Actas y Trabajos Científicos del XXVII Congreso Internacional de Americanistas* (Lima, 1939), 341–45. Lima: Libreria e Imprenta Gil, 1940.

———. "Digging in the Titicaca Basin." *University Museum Bulletin* 29, no. 3 (1956): 16–29.

Kirkpatrick, Sidney D. *Lords of Sipán: A True Story of Pre-Inca Tombs, Archaeology, and Crime.* New York: William Morrow, 1992.

Kirshenblatt-Gimblett, Barbara. *Destination Culture: Tourism, Museums, and Heritage.* Berkeley: University of California Press, 1998.

Kohl, Philip L., and Clare Fawcett, eds. *Nationalism, Politics, and the Practice of Archaeology*. Cambridge, England: Cambridge University Press, 1995.

Kolata, Alan L. *The Tiwanaku*. Cambridge, Mass.: Blackwell, 1993.

Larco Hoyle, Rafael. "Breve Historia del Museo Rafael Larco Herrera de Chiclín." *Turismo* 137 (1939). Lima: Touring Club Peruano.

———. *Los Mochicas*. Lima: Museo Arqueológico Rafael Larco Herrera, 2001.

Lathrap, Donald W. *Ancient Ecuador: Culture, Clay, and Creativity, 3000–300 B.C.*. Chicago: Field Museum of Natural History, 1980.

Lathrap, Donald W., Jorge G. Marcos, and James A. Zeidler. "Real Alto: An Ancient Ceremonial Center." *Archaeology* 30 (1977): 2–13.

Layton, Robert, ed. *Conflict in the Archaeology of Living Traditions*. London: Unwin Hyman, 1989. [1989a]

———. *Who Needs the Past: Indigenous Values and Archaeology*. London: Unwin Hyman, 1989. [1989b]

Layton, Robert, Peter G. Stone, and Julian Thomas, eds. *Destruction and Conservation of Cultural Property*. One World Archaeology 41. London: Routledge, 2001.

LeCompte, Margaret D., Jean J. Schensul, Margaret R. Weeks, and Merrill Singer. *Researcher Roles and Research Partnerships*, vol. 6, *The Ethnographer's Toolkit*. Thousand Oaks, Calif.: AltaMira Press, 2001.

Lefebvre, Henri. *The Production of Space*. Oxford, England: Blackwell, 1991.

León, Ignacio, and Juan Carlos Sánchez. "Las Gemelas y el Jaguar del Sitio El Azuzul." *Horizonte* 5–6 (1991–92): 56–60.

Lerner, Shereen, and Teresa Hoffman. "Bringing Archaeology to the Public: Programmes in the Southwestern United States." In *Cultural Resource Management in Contemporary Society: Perspectives on Managing and Presenting the Past*, edited by Francis McManamon and Alf Hatton, 247–75. New York: Routledge, 2000.

Lindao Quimí, Roberto, and Karen E. Stothert. *Así Fue Mi Crianza: Recuerdos de Un Nativo de la Parroquia Chanduy*. Guayaquil: Pro-Pueblo, La Cemento Nacional, 1995.

———. *El Uso Vernáculo de los Arboles y Plantas en la Península de Santa Elena/La Costumbre de Poner Apodos a los 'Viudos' en la Parroquia Julio Moreno, Provincia del Guayas*. Guayaquil: Fundación Pro-Pueblo, La Cemento Nacional y Subdirección Programas Culturales, Banco Central del Ecuador, 1994.

Litto, Gertrude. *South American Folk Pottery*. New York: Watson- Guptill Publications, 1976.

Lofgren, Orvar. *On Holiday: A History of Vacationing*. Berkeley: University of California Press, 1999.

Lowenthal, David. "Identity, Heritage, and History." In *Commemorations: The Politics of National Identity*, edited by John R. Gillis, 41–57. Princeton, N.J.: Princeton University Press, 1994.

Lumbreras, Luis Guillermo. *La Arqueología Como Ciencia Social*. Lima: Ediciones Histar, 1974.

Lury, Celia. "The Objects of Travel." In *Touring Cultures: Transformations of Travel and Theory*, edited by Chris Rojek and John Urry, 75–95. London: Routledge, 1997.

Lynott, Mark J. "Ethical Principles and Archaeological Practice: Development of an Ethics Policy." *American Antiquity* 62, no. 4 (1997): 589–99.

Lynott, Mark J., and Alison Wylie, eds. *Ethics in American Archaeology: Challenges for the 1990s.* Washington, D.C.: Society for American Archaeology, 1995.

———, eds. *Ethics in American Archaeology.* 2nd rev. ed. Washington, D.C.: Society for American Archaeology, 2000.

Manzanilla, Linda. "Teotihuacan: Urban Archetype, Cosmic Model." In *Emergence and Change in Early Urban Societies,* edited by Linda Manzanilla, 109–31. New York: Plenum Press, 1997.

———. "La Zona del Altiplano Central en el Clásico." In *Historia Antigua de México,* vol. 2, *El Horizonte Clásico,* edited by Miguel Angel Porrúa, 203–39. 2nd rev. ed. Mexico City: INAH/UNAM, 2001.

Marliac, A. "Archaeology and Development: A Difficult Dialogue." *International Journal of Historical Archaeology* 1, no. 4 (1997): 323–37.

Martínez-Carrasco, Néstor, and Lucero Morales-Cano. "El Discurso del Desarrollo Sustentable en el Turismo." In *Dimensión Social del Patrimonio Cultural del Mundo Maya,* 259–77. Memorias Jornada Académica: Dimensión Social del Patrimonio Cultural y Natural del Mundo Maya. Mexico City: Departamento de Etnología y Antropología Social del Instituto Nacional de Antropología e Historia, 1999.

Matero, Frank, Kecia I. Fong, Elisa del Bono, Mark Goodman, Evan Kopelson, Lorraine McVey, Jessica Sloop, and Catherine Turton. "Archaeological Site Conservation and Management: An Appraisal of Trends." *Conservation and Management of Archaeological Sites* 2, no. 3 (1998): 129–42.

Matos, Eduardo. *Museo de la Cultura Teotihuacana: Guía.* Mexico City: INAH/Instituto Cultural Domecq, 1995.

Mayrand, Pierre. "A New Concept of Museology in Quebec." *Muse* 2, no. 1 (1984): 33, 36–37.

———. "The New Museology Proclaimed." *Museum International* [UNESCO] 148 (1985): 200–201.

Mbunwe-Samba, Patrick. "Should Developing Countries Restore and Conserve?" In *Destruction and Conservation of Cultural Property,* edited by Robert L. Layton, Peter G. Stone, and Julian Thomas, 30–41. One World Archaeology 41. London: Routledge, 2001.

McClellan, Andrew. *Inventing the Louvre: Art, Politics, and the Origins of the Modern Museum in Eighteenth-Century Paris.* Berkeley: University of California Press, 1994.

McEwan, Colin. "Sillas de Poder: Evolución Sociocultural en Manabí, Costa Central del Ecuador." In *500 Años de Ocupación—Parque Nacional Machalilla,* edited by Presley Norton, 53–70. Quito: Ediciones Abya-yala, 1992.

———."Archaeology and Community." In "And the Sun Sits in His Seat: Creating Social Order in Andean Culture." Ph.D. diss., Department of Anthropology, University of Illinois at Urbana-Champaign, 2003.

McEwan, Colin, Chris Hudson, and María-Isabel Silva. "Archaeology and Community: A Village Cultural Center and Museum in Agua Blanca, Ecuador." *Practicing Anthropology* 16, no. 1 (1994): 3–7.

McEwan, Colin, and María-Isabel Silva. "Que Fueron a Hacer los Incas en la Costa Central del Ecuador?" In *Relaciones Interculturales en el Area Ecuatorial del Pácifico Durante la Epoca Precolombina,* edited by J. F. Bouchard and M. Guinea. BAR International Series 503. Oxford: British Archaeological Reports, 1989.

———. "Arqueología y Comunidad: Un Centro Cultural y Museo en la Comuna de Agua Blanca, Ecuador. Case Study." In *Interpretación Ambiental: Una Guia Práctica para Gente con Grandes Ideas y Presupuestos Pequeños,* edited by Sam H. Ham. Golden, Colo.: Fulcrum Publishing, 1993.

———."La Presencia Inca en la Costa Central del Ecuador y en la Isla de la Plata." In *Compendio de Investigaciones en el Parque Nacional Machalilla,* edited by M. Iturralde and C. Josse. Quito: Corporación CDC and Fundación Natura, 2000.

McManamon, Francis. "The Protection of Archaeological Resources in the United States: Reconciling Preservation with Contemporary Society." In *Cultural Resource Management in Contemporary Society: Perspectives on Managing and Presenting the Past,* edited by Francis McManamon and Alf Hatton, 40–54. New York: Routledge, 2000. [2000a]

———. "Archaeological Messages and Messengers." *Public Archaeology* 1, no. 1 (2000): 5–20. [2000b]

Medina, Maria Clara. "Articulation between Archaeological Practice and Local Politics in Northwest Argentina." In *Cultural Resource Management in Contemporary Society: Perspectives on Managing and Presenting the Past,* edited by Francis P. McManamon and Alf Hatton, 160–67. One World Archaeology 41. London: Routledge, 2000.

Merkel, John, Izumi Shimada, C. P. Swann, and Roger Doonan. "Pre-Hispanic Copper Alloy Production at Batán Grande, Peru: Interpretation of the Analytical Data for Ore Samples." In *Archaeometry of Pre-Columbian Sites and Artifacts,* edited by D. A. Scott and P. Meyers, 199–227. Marina del Rey, Calif.: Getty Conservation Institute, 1994.

Mesa Redonda. "Visiones del Centro Histórico del Cusco." *Crónicas Urbanas* (Cusco) 6–7 (1998): 51–62.

Meskell, Lynn, ed. *Archaeology Under Fire.* London: Routledge, 1998.

Mexican Tourism Board. Teotihuacan museums. http://www.visitmexico.com/wb/Visit-mexico/Visi_Teotihuacan/_aid/4439 (accessed 2005).

Mgomezulu, Gadi. "Editorial: The Site Museum." *Museum International* 223 (2004). http://portal.unesco.org/culture/en/ev.php-URL_ID=23104&URL_DO=DO_TOPIC&URL_SECTION=201.html#by.

Millon, René. *Urbanization at Teotihuacan, México,* vol. 1, *The Teotihuacan Map.* Austin: University of Texas Press, 1973.

Moguel, Patricia, and Víctor M. Toledo. "El Mérito Ecológico 2001: Otra Enseñanza Indígena." *La Jornada de Oriente* (México), 5 junio 2001, p. 16.

Mohr-Chávez, Karen L. "Traditional Pottery of Raqch'i, Cusco, Peru: A Preliminary Study of Its Production, Distribution, and Consumption." *Ñawpa Pacha* 22–23 (1987): 161–210.

Molyneaux, Brian. "Introduction: The Represented Past." In *The Presented Past,* edited by Peter G. Stone and Brian Molyneaux, 1–28. London: Routledge, 1994.

Moore, Jerry D. *Architecture and Power in the Ancient Andes.* New York: Cambridge University Press, 1996.

Morales-Cano, Lucero. "El Turismo Etnico en San Cristóbal de las Casas." *Boletín Oficial del Instituto Nacional de Antropología e Historia,* n.s., 48 (1997): 23–31.

———. "El Discurso de la Teoría del Desarrollo en la Protección del Patrimonio Cultural y Natural: El Caso del Sitio Arqueológico de Chinkultik en Chiapas." *Mesoamérica* 37 (1999): 51–71.

Morales-Cano, Lucero, and Avis Mysyk. "Cultural Tourism, the State, and Day of the Dead." *Annals of Tourism Research,* forthcoming, n.d.

Mortensen, Lena. "Las Dinámicas Locales de un Patrimonio Global: Arqueoturismo en Copán, Honduras." *Mesoamérica* 42 (2001): 104–34.

Moseley, Michael E., and Kent C. Day, eds. *Chan Chan: Andean Desert City.* Albuquerque: University of New Mexico Press, 1982.

Moser, Stephanie, Darren Glazier, James E. Phillips, Lamya Nasr El Nemr, Mohammed Saleh Mousa, Rascha Moatty Nasr Aiesh, Susan Richardson, Andrew Conner, and Michael Seymour. "Transforming Archaeology through Practice: Strategies for Collaborative Archaeology and the Community Archaeology Project at Quseir, Egypt." In *Museums and Source Communities: A Routledge Reader,* edited by Laura Peers and Alison K. Brown, 208–26. London: Routledge, 2003.

Mosquera, Marcela. "Geologia Arqueológica de la Zona de Agua Blanca, Puerto Lopez, Provincia de Manabi." Tesis de Grado, Escuela Politecnica Nacional, Quito, 1989.

Muringaniza, Svinurayi Joseph. "Heritage That Hurts: The Case of the Grave of Cecil John Rhodes in the Matopos National Park, Zimbabwe." In *The Dead and Their Possessions: Repatriation in Principle, Policy, and Practice,* edited by Cressida Fforde, Jane Hubert, and Paul Turnbull, 317–25. One World Archaeology 43. London: Routledge, 2002.

Nagin, Carl. "The Peruvian Gold Rush." *Art and Antiques* (May 1990): 98–145.

National Park Service. *Colorado River Management Plan.* Washington, D.C.: United States Department of the Interior, 1989.

Neirotti, Lisa Delpy. "An Introduction to Sport and Adventure Tourism." In *Sport and Adventure Tourism,* edited by Simon Hudson, 1–25. New York: Haworth Hospitality, 2003.

Nelson, Margaret C., and Brenda Shears. "From the Field to the Files: Curation and the Future of Academic Archeology." *Common Ground* 1, no. 2 (1996): 35–37.

Nelson, Sarah M. *Gender in Archaeology.* Walnut Creek, Calif.: AltaMira Press, 1997.

Newsweek. National Museum of Anthropology. Mexico City. New York: Newsweek, 1971.

Nicholas, George P., and T. D. Andrews, eds. *At a Crossroads: Archaeology and First Peoples in Canada.* Brunaby, Canada: Simon Fraser University, Archaeology Press, 1997.

Nieto Degregori, Luis. "Una Aproximación al Cusqueñismo." *Allpanchis* 26, no. 43/44 (1994): 441–76.

Norton, Presley, ed. *500 Años de Ocupación—Parque Nacional Machalilla.* Quito: Ediciones Abya-yala, 1992.

Olsen, Bjornar J. "The End of History? Archaeology and the Politics of Identity in a Globalized World." In *Destruction and Conservation of Cultural Property*, edited by Robert Layton, Peter G. Stone, and Julian Thomas, 42–54. One World Archaeology 41. London: Routledge, 2001.

Omland, Atle. "World Heritage and the Relationship between the Global and Local." M.A. thesis, 1997. http://folk.uio.no/atleom/master/contents.htm.

Onuki, Yoshio. "Ocho Tumbas Especiales de Kuntur Wasi." *Boletín de Arqueología PUCP* 1 (1997): 79–114. Fondo Editorial, Pontificia Universidad Católica del Perú, Lima.

———. "Una Perspectiva del Período Formativo de la Sierra Norte del Perú." In *Historia de la Cultura Peruana* 1 (2001): 103–26. Lima: Fondo Editorial del Congreso del Perú.

———. "The Kuntur Wasi Museum and Participation of the Local Community." Paper presented in the symposium "Site Museums in Latin America," 69th Annual Meeting of the Society for American Archaeology, Montreal, 2004.

Onuki, Yoshio, Yasutake Kato, and Kinya Inokuchi. "Las Excavaciones en Kuntur Wasi: La Primera Temporada, 1988–1990." In *Kuntur Wasi y Cerro Blanco: Dos Sitios del Formativo en el Norte del Perú*, edited by Yoshio Onuki, 1–126. Tokyo: Hokusensha, 1995.

Onuki, Yoshio, Yasutake Kato, and Yuji Seki, eds. *El Tesoro del Templo Kuntur Wasi.* Tokyo: Nihon Keizai Shinbunsha, 2000.

Onuki, Yoshio, Waltero Tosso, and Elmer Atalaya. "La Restauración y Conservación del Templo Kuntur Wasi: Un Caso de Estudio Sobre La Autenticidad." In *¿Credibilidad o Veracidad? La Autenticidad, un Valor de los Bienes Culturales*, edited by La Representación de UNESCO en Perú, 51–68. Lima: UNESCO, 2004.

Orbasli, Aylin. *Tourists in Historic Towns: Urban Conservation and Heritage Management.* London: E & FN SPON, 2000.

Palumbo, Gaetano. "Threats and Challenges to the Archaeological Heritage in the Mediterranean." In *Management Planning for Archaeological Sites*, edited by Jeanne Marie Teutonico and Gaetano Palumbo, 3–12. Los Angeles: Getty Conservation Institute, 2002.

Paredes, Rolando. "Excavaciones Arqueológicas en Pukara, Puno." Tesis de Licenciatura. Cusco: Universidad Nacional San Antonio Abad, 1985.

Pasztory, Esther. *The Murals of Tepantitla, Teotihuacan.* New York: Garland, 1976.

———. "A Reinterpretation of Teotihuacan and Its Mural Painting." In *Feathered Serpents and Flowering Trees: Reconstructing the Murals of Teotihuacan*, edited by Kathleen Berrin, 45–77. San Francisco: Fine Arts Museum, 1988.

———. *Teotihuacan: An Experiment in Living.* Norman: University of Oklahoma Press, 1997.

Patterson, Michael E., Alan E. Watson, Daniel R. Williams, and Joseph R. Roggenbuck. "An Hermeneutic Approach to Studying the Nature of Wilderness Experiences." *Journal of Leisure Research* 30, no. 4 (1998): 423–52.

Paucar, Angel, R. Andrade, M.-I. Silva, C. McEwan, and C. Zambrano. *Diagnóstico del Parque Nacional Machalilla de la Republica del Ecuador.* Quito: Ministerio de Agricultura y Ganaderia Direccion Nacional Forestal, 1987.

Pearce, Susan M. *Archaeological Curatorship.* London: Leicester University Press, 1990.

Pedersen, Asbjorn. "El Ajuar Funerario de la Tumba de la Huaca Menor de Batán Grande, Lambayeque, Perú." *Actas del 41 Congreso Internacional de Americanistas* (México) 2 (1976): 60–73.

Peers, Laura, and Alison K. Brown, eds. *Museums and Source Communities: A Routledge Reader.* London: Routledge, 2003.

Peralta, Ronald. "Comments" cited in "Visión del Centro Histórico del Cusco." *Crónicas Urbanas* (Cusco) 6–7 (1998): 52–54.

Piperno, Dolores R., Thomas C. Andres, and Karen E. Stothert. "Phytoliths in Cucurbita and Other Neotropical Cucurbitaceae and Their Occurrence in Early Archaeological Sites from the Lowland American Tropics." *Journal of Archaeological Science* 27 (2000): 193–208.

Piperno, Dolores R., and Karen E. Stothert. "Phytolith Evidence for Early Holocene Cucurbita Domestication in Southwest Ecuador." *Science* 299 (2003): 1054–57.

Pozorski, Sheila G. "Prehistoric Subsistence Patterns and Site Economics in the Moche Valley, Peru." Ph.D. diss., Department of Anthropology, University of Texas at Austin, 1976.

Pratt, Mary Louise. *Imperial Eyes: Travel Writing and Transculturation.* London: Routledge, 1992.

PromPerú. *Productos Turísticos Sostenibles: Experiencias en el Perú.* Lima: Comisión de Promoción de Perú, 2001.

Pyburn, Anne K. "Opening the Door to Xibalba." *Indiana Journal of Hispanic Literatures* 13 (1998): 125–30.

———. "Native American Religion vs. Archaeological Science: A Pernicious Dichotomy Revisited." *Journal of Science and Engineering Ethics* 5 (1999): 355–66.

———. "Archaeology for a New Millennium: The Rules of Engagement." In *Archaeologists and Local Communities: Partners in Exploring the Past,* edited by Linda Derry and Maureen Malloy, 167–84. Washington, D.C.: Society for American Archaeology, 2003. [2003a]

———. "We Have Never Been Postmodern." In *Continuities and Changes in Maya Archaeology: Perspectives at the Millennium,* edited by Charles W. Golden and Greg Borgstede, 285–91. New York: Routledge, 2003. [2003b]

———. *Ungendering Civilization: Rethinking the Archaeological Record.* London: Routledge, 2004.

Pyburn, Anne K., and Richard R. Wilk. "Responsible Archaeology Is Applied Anthropology." In *Ethics in American Archaeology: Challenges for the 1990s,* edited by Mark J. Lynott and Alison Wylie, 71–76. Washington, D.C.: Society for American Archaeology, 1995.

Quilter, Jeffrey. "Moche Politics, Religion, and Warfare." *Journal of World Prehistory* 16, no. 2 (2002): 145–95.

Ramírez, Susan E. *El Mundo al Revés: Contactos y Conflictos Transculturales en el Perú del Siglo XVI.* Lima: Fondo Editorial, Pontificia Universidad Católica del Perú, 2002.

Ravines, Rogger. *Los Museos del Perú: Breve Historia y Guía.* Lima: Instituto Nacional de Cultura, 1989.

Riviére, Georges Henri. "The Ecomuseum: An Evolutive Definition." *Museum International* [UNESCO] 148 (1985): 182–83.

Rockwell, E. "Constructing Diversity and Civility in the United States and Latin America: Implications for Ethnographic Educational Research." In *Ethnography and Education Policy Across the Americas,* edited by B.A.U. Levinson et al., 3–19. Westport, Conn.: Praeger, 2002.

Rowan, Yorke, and Uzi Baram, eds. *Marketing Heritage: Archaeology and the Consumption of the Past.* Thousand Oaks, Calif.: AltaMira Press, 2004.

Rubin de la Borbolla, Daniel F., and Pedro Rivas. *Honduras: Monumentos Históricos y Arqueológicos.* Mexico City: Instituto Panamericano de Geografía e Historia, 1953.

Rucabado, Julio, and Luis Jaime Castillo. "El Período Transicional en San José de Moro." In *Moche: Hacia el Final del Milenio,* edited by Santiago Uceda and Elías Mujica, vol. 1, 14–42. Actas del Segundo Coloquio sobre la Cultura Moche, Trujillo, 1 al 7 de Agosto de 1999. Lima: Universidad Nacional de Trujillo and Pontificia Universidad Católica del Perú, 2003.

Ruíz Gordillo, Omar. "Nueva Cabeza Colossal en San Lorenzo Tenochtitlán." *Cuadernos de los Centros Regionales, Centro Regional de Veracruz,* 1–12. Mexico City: Instituto Nacional de Antropología e Historia, 1982.

Sabloff, Jeremy A. "Distinguished Lecture in Archaeology: Communication and the Future of American Archaeology." *American Anthropologist* 100, no. 4 (1998): 869–75.

Said, Edward. *Orientalism.* New York: Vintage, 1979.

Salvat Editores Ecuadoriana. *Arte Precolombino del Ecuador.* Quito: Salvat Editores Ecuadoriana, 1977.

Samanez Argumedo, Roberto. "La Conservación del Patrimonio Inmueble en el Umbral del Tercer Milenio." *Crónicas Urbanas* (Cusco) 6–7 (1998): 97–104.

Sánchez Salazar, María Teresa, and Oralia Oropeza Orozco. *Atlas Regional del Istmo de Tehuantepec.* Mexico City: Instituto de Geografía, Universidad Nacional Autónoma de México, 2003.

Saville, Marchall H. *The Antiquities of Manabi, Ecuador,* vol. 1, *Preliminary Report.* Heye Foundation Contributions to South American Archaeology. New York: Heye Foundation, 1907.

———. *The Antiquities of Manabi, Ecuador,* vol. 2, *Final Report.* Heye Foundation Contributions to South American Archaeology. New York: Heye Foundation, 1910.

Schaedel, Richard P. "2000 Años de la Continuidad Cultural de los Muchik en la Costa Norte del Perú." *Ibero-Amerikanisches Archiv,* N.F. 13 (1987): 117–28.

———. *La Etnografía Muchik en la Fotografías de H. Brüning, 1886–1925.* Lima: Ediciones COFIDE, Corporación Financiera de Desarrollo, 1989.

Schensul, Jean J., and Steven L. Schensul. "Collaborative Research: Methods of Inquiry for Social Change." In *The Handbook of Qualitative Research in Education,* edited by M. D. LeCompte, W. L. Millroy, and J. Preissle, 161–200. New York: Academic Press, 1992.

Schmidt, Hartwig. "The Impossibility of Resurrecting the Past: Reconstructions on Archaeological Excavation Sites." *Conservation and Management of Archaeological Sites* 3, no. 1 (1999): 61–68.

Schmidt, Peter R., and Thomas C. Patterson, eds. *Making Alternative Histories: The Practice of Archaeology and History in Non-Western Settings.* Santa Fe, N.Mex.: School of American Research, 1995.

Schuster, Angela M. "Faux Maya." *Archaeology* (January/February 1999): 88.

Shackel, Paul A. "Working with Communities: Heritage Development and Applied Archaeology." In *Places in Mind: Public Archaeology as Applied Anthropology,* edited by Paul A. Shackel and Erve J. Chambers, 1–16. New York: Routledge, 2004.

Shackel, Paul A., and Erve J. Chambers, eds. *Places in Mind: Public Archaeology as Applied Anthropology.* New York: Routledge, 2004.

Shaffer, Marguerite S. *See America First: Tourism and National Identity, 1880–1940.* Washington, D.C.: Smithsonian Institution Press, 2001.

Shanks, Michael, and Christopher Tilley. *Re-Constructing Archaeology.* London: Routledge, 1992.

Sharan, Yael, and Shlomo Sharan. "Group Investigation in the Cooperative Classroom." In *Handbook of Cooperative Learning Methods,* edited by Schlomo Sharan, 97–114. Westport, Conn.: Praeger/Greenwood, 1994.

Shaw, Jonathan. "Maya Museum: Reviewing a Century of Harvard Connections to Copán." *Harvard Magazine.* http://harvard-magazine.com/jf97/maya.2.htm (accessed 1997).

Shennan, Stephen. "Introduction: Archeological Approaches to Cultural Identity." In *Archeological Approaches to Cultural Identity,* edited by Stephen Shennan, 1–13. London: Unwin Hyman, 1989. [1989a]

———, ed. *Archaeological Approaches to Cultural Identity.* London: Unwin Hyman, 1989. [1989b]

Shimada, Izumi. "Temples of Time: The Ancient Burial and Religious Center of Batán Grande, Peru." *Archaeology* 34, no. 5 (1981): 37–45. [1981a]

———. "The Batán Grande–La Leche Archaeological Project: The First Two Seasons." *Journal of Field Archaeology* 8 (1981): 405–46. [1981b]

———. *Pampa Grande and the Mochica Culture.* Austin: University of Texas Press, 1994.

———. *Cultura Sicán: Dios, Riqueza y Poder en la Costa Norte del Perú.* Lima: Banco Continental, 1995.

Shimada, Izumi, David Goldstein, W. Häusler, J. Sosa, and Ursel Wagner. "Early Pottery Making in Northern Coastal Peru: Part II: Field Firing Experiments." In *Mössbauer Spectroscopy in Archaeology,* edited by Ursel Wagner, 91–105. Hyp. Interact. vol. 2. New York: Kluwer Academic, 2003.

Shimada, Izumi, and John F. Merkel. "Copper Alloy Metallurgy in Ancient Peru." *Scientific American* 265 (1991): 80–86.

Shimada, Izumi, and Jorge Montenegro. "El Poder y la Naturaleza de la Elite Sicán: Una Mirada a la Tumba de Huaca Loro, Batán Grande." *Boletín de Lima* 15, no. 90 (1993): 67–96.

Shimada, Izumi, Ken-ichi Shinoda, Julie Farnum, Robert S. Corruccini, and Hirokatsu Watanabe. "An Integrated Analysis of Pre-Hispanic Mortuary Practices: A Middle Sicán Case Study." *Current Anthropology* 45, no. 3 (2004): 369–402.

Shimada, Izumi, and Ursel Wagner. "Peruvian Black Pottery Production and Metal

Working: A Middle Sicán Craft Workshop at Huaca Sialupe." *Materials Research Society Bulletin* [Warrendale, Penn.] 26, no. 1 (2001): 25–30. Special issue, "Preserving Art through the Ages," edited by Pamela Vandiver.

Sillar, Bill. *Shaping Culture: Making Pots and Constructing Households: An Ethnoarchaeological Study of Pottery Production, Trade, and Use in the Andes.* BAR International Series 883. Oxford: British Archaeological Reports, 2000.

Sillitoe, Paul. "The Development of Indigenous Knowledge: A New Applied Anthropology." *Current Anthropology* 39, no. 2 (1998): 223–52.

Silva, María-Isabel. "Toponymic Reconstruction as a Basis for Analysing Social, Economic, and Political Relationships among Contact Period Settlements on the Central Coast of Ecuador." Paper presented at the 11th Annual Midwest Conference on Andean and Amazonian Archaeology and Ethnohistory, Bloomington, Indiana, 1983.

———. "Pescadores y Agricultures de la Costa Central del Ecuador: Un Modelo Socio-economico de Asentamientos Precolombinos." M.A. thesis, University of Illinois at Urbana-Champaign, 1984.

———. "Dual Division Quadripatition and Hierarchical Organization among the Manteño Polities of Late Pre-Columbian Coastal Ecuador." Paper presented at the International Congress of Americanists, Bogota, 1985.

Silva, María-Isabel, and Colin McEwan. "Machalilla: El Camino de la Integración." *Colibrí* [Fundación Natura] 2, no. 5 (1989): 71–75.

———. "Arqueologia y Comunidad en el Parque Nacional Machalilla: Breve Historia y Reflexiones." In *Compendio de Investigaciones en el Parque Nacional Machalilla,* edited by M. Iturralde and C. Josse, 5–8. Quito: Corporación CDC and Fundación Natura, 2000.

Silverman, Helaine. "The Paracas Problem: Archaeological Perspectives." In *Paracas Art and Architecture: Object and Context in South Coastal Peru,* edited by Anne Paul, 347–415. Iowa City: University of Iowa Press, 1991.

———. "Touring Ancient Times: The Present and Presented Past in Contemporary Peru." *American Anthropologist* 104, no. 3 (2002): 881–902.

———. "Embodied Heritage, Identity Politics, and Tourism." *Anthropology and Humanism,* 30, no. 2 (2005): 141–55. [2005a]

———. "Two Museums, Two Visions: Representing Cultural Heritage in Cusco, Peru." *SAA Archaeological Record* 5, no. 3 (2005): 29–32. [2005b]

Silverman, Helaine, and Donald A. Proulx. *The Nasca.* Malden, Mass.: Blackwell, 2002.

Sivan, Renée. "The Presentation of Archaeological Sites." In *The Conservation of Archaeological Sites in the Mediterranean Region,* edited by Marta de la Torre, 51–59. Los Angeles: Getty Conservation Institute, 1997.

Solomon, Deborah. "Forget the Art—It's All about the Building." *New York Times Magazine,* December 9, 2001.

Spence, Michael. "From Tzintzuntzan to Paquime: Peers or Peripheries in Greater Mesoamerica?" In *Greater Mesoamerica: The Archaeology of West and Northwest Mexico,* edited by Michael S. Foster and Shirley Gorenstein, 255–62. Salt Lake City: University of Utah Press, 2000.

Spurling, Geoffrey E. "The Organization of Craft Production in the Inka State: The Potters and Weavers of Milliraya (Peru)." Ph.D. diss., Department of Anthropology, Cornell University, 1992.

Stanish, Charles. *Ancient Titicaca: The Evolution of Complex Society in Southern Peru and Northern Bolivia.* Berkeley: University of California Press, 2003.

Stephens, John L., and Frederick Catherwood. *Incidents of Travel in Central America, Chiapas and Yucatán,* vol. 1. 1841. New York: Dover Publications, 1969.

Stirling [Pugh], Marion. Personal letter to Margarita Bravo, 1945. Archives of the San Lorenzo Tenochtitlán Archaeological Project.

———. "An Intimate View of Archaeological Exploration." In *The Olmec and Their Neighbors,* edited by Elizabeth P. Benson, 1–14. Washington, D.C.: Dumbarton Oaks Research Library and Collection, 1981.

Stirling, Matthew. "On the Trail of La Venta Man." *National Geographic* 91 (1947): 137–72.

———. *Stone Monuments of the Río Chiquito, Veracruz, Mexico.* Anthropological Papers 43. Washington, D.C.: Bureau of American Ethnology, Smithsonian Institution, 1955.

Stocking, George W., Jr. "Essays on Museums and Material Culture." In *Objects and Others: Essays on Museums and Material Culture,* edited by George W. Stocking Jr., 3–14. Madison: University of Wisconsin Press, 1985.

Stone, Peter G., and Brian L. Molyneaux, eds. *The Presented Past: Heritage Museums and Education.* London: Unwin Hyman, 1994.

Stone, Peter G., and Philippe G. Planel. *The Constructed Past: Experimental Archaeology, Education, and the Public.* London: Routledge, 1999.

Stonich, S. C. "Political Ecology in Tourism." *Annals of Tourism Research* 25, no. 1 (1998): 25–54.

Stonich, S. C., J. H. Sorensen, and A. Hundt. "Ethnicity, Class, and Gender in Tourism Development: The Case of Bay Islands, Honduras." *Journal of Sustainable Tourism* 3, no. 1 (1995): 1–28.

Stothert, Karen E. "The Preceramic Las Vegas Culture of Coastal Ecuador." *American Antiquity* 50, no. 3 (1985): 613–37.

———. *La Prehistoria Temprana de la Península de Santa Elena, Ecuador: La Cultura Las Vegas.* Miscelánea Antropológica Ecuatoriana, Serie Monográfica 10. Guayaquil: Museos del Banco Central del Ecuador, 1988.

———. "Early Economies of Coastal Ecuador and the Foundations of Andean Civilization." *Andean Past* 3 (1992): 43–51.

———. "The New Role of the Ancient Lovers of Sumpa." In *Working Together: Native Americans and Archaeologists,* edited by Kurt E. Dongoske, Mark Aldenderfer, and Karen Doehner, 199–208. Washington, D.C.: Society for American Archaeology, 2000. Orig. pub., *SAA Bulletin* 16, no. 2 (1998): 24–27.

Stothert, Karen E., and Ana Maritza Freire. *Sumpa: Historia de la Península de Santa Elena (Museo Los Amantes de Sumpa).* Guayaquil: Banco Central del Ecuador and Plan Internacional Guayaquil, 1997.

Stothert, Karen E., Dolores R. Piperno, and Thomas C. Andres. "Terminal Pleistocene/

Early Holocene Human Adaptation in Coastal Ecuador: The Las Vegas Evidence." *Quaternary International* 109–110 (2003): 23–43.

Strong, William Duncan, and Clifford Evans Jr. *Cultural Stratigraphy in the Viru Valley, Northern Peru: The Formative and Florescent Epoch.* New York: Columbia University Press, 1952.

Stuart, David. "Hieroglyphs and History at Copán." http://www.peabody.harvard.edu/Copán/text.html (accessed 1996).

Swidler, Nina, Kurt Dongoske, Roger Anyon, and Alan Downer. *Native Americans and Archaeologists: Stepping Stones to Common Ground.* Walnut Creek, Calif.: AltaMira Press, 1997.

Symonds, Stacey, Ann Cyphers, and Roberto Lunagómez. *Asentamiento Prehispánico en San Lorenzo Tenochtitlán.* Mexico City: Instituto de Investigaciones Antropológicas, Universidad Nacional Autónoma de México, 2002.

Tchen, John Kuo Wei. "Creating a Dialogic Museum: The Chinatown History Museum Experiment." In *Museums and Communities: The Politics of Public Culture,* edited by Ivan Karp, Christine Mullen Kreamer, and Steven D. Lavine, 285–326. Washington, D.C.: Smithsonian Institution Press, 1992.

Tello, Julio C. "Los Trabajos Arqueológicos en el Departamento de Lambayeque." *El Comercio* (Lima), 29–31 de enero, 1937. [1937a]

———. "La Búsqueda de Tesoros Ocultos en las Huacas de Lambayeque." *El Comercio* (Lima), 11 de marzo 1937. [1937b]

———. "El Oro de Batán Grande." *El Comercio* (Lima), 18 de abril 1937. [1937c]

Tello, Julio C., and Toribio Mejía Xesspe. "Historia de los Museos Nacionales del Perú, 1822–1946." *Arqueológicas* 10 (1967): 1–268.

Thomas, David Hurst. "Roadside Ruins: Does America Still Need Archaeology Museums?" In *Public Benefits of Archaeology,* edited by Barbara J. Little, 130–45. Gainesville: University Press of Florida, 2002.

Thorsby, David. "Seven Questions in the Economics of Cultural Heritage." In *Economic Perspectives on Cultural Heritage,* edited by Michael Hutter and Ilde Rizzo, 13–30. New York: St. Martin's, 1997.

Tierney, Patrick. *Darkness in El Dorado: How Scientists and Journalists Devastated the Amazon.* New York: Norton, 2000.

Topic, Theresa Lange. "Excavations at Moche." Ph.D. diss., Department of Anthropology, Harvard University, 1977.

Torero, Alfredo. "Deslindes Lingüísticos en la Costa Norte Peruana." *Revista Andina* 8 (1986): 523–45.

———. *Idiomas de los Andes: Lingüística e Historia.* Lima: Instituto Francés de Estudios Andinos, 2002.

Tourtellot, Jonathon B. "Tourism Wars." *National Geographic Traveler* (October 2000): 110–19.

Trigger, Bruce. "Alternative Archaeologies: Nationalist, Colonialist, Imperialist." *Man* 19 (1984): 355–70.

Trotzig, Gustaf. "The 'Cultural Dimension of Development'—An Archaeological Approach." In *Archaeological Heritage Management in the Modern World,* edited by H. F. Cleere, 59–63. London: Unwin Hyman, 1989.

Turner, Christy G., II, and Jacqueline A. Turner. *Man Corn: Cannibalism and Violence in the Prehistoric American Southwest.* Salt Lake City: University of Utah Press, 1999.

Ubelaker, Douglas H. "Human Skeletal Remains from Site OGSE-80, a Pre-ceramic Site on the Sta. Elena Peninsula, Coastal Ecuador." *Journal of the Washington Academy of Sciences* 70 (1980): 3–24.

———. "Human Remains from OGSE-46, La Libertad, Guayas Province, Ecuador." *Journal of the Washington Academy of Sciences* 78 (1988): 3–16.

Uhle, Max. "Die Ruinen von Moche." *Journal de la Société des Américanistes* (Paris), n.s., 10, no. 1 (1913): 95–117.

———. "The Nazca Pottery of Ancient Peru." *Proceedings of the Davenport Academy of Sciences* 13 (1914): 1–16.

UNESCO (United Nations Educational, Scientific and Cultural Organization). Criteria for World Heritage Sites. http://whc.unesco.org/pg.cfm.

———. "Universal Declaration on Cultural Diversity," 2001. http://unesdoc.unesco.org/ images/0012/001271/127160m.pdf.

———. "The Effects of Tourism on Socio-Cultural Values." *Annals of Tourism Research* 4, no. 2 (1976): 74–105.

———. "Guidelines for World Heritage Convention." http://whc.unesco.org/world_ he.htm#debut.

United States Code. "Title 439—Public Lands: Interior." In vol. 2, part 83509, *Management Areas.* 2003.

USA Weekend. "How Adventure Travel Changed My Life." *USA Weekend* (September 12–14, 2003): 6–9.

Valcárcel, Luis E. "Un Valioso Hallazgo Arqueológico en el Perú." *Revista del Museo Nacional* (Lima) 6 (1937): 164–68.

Van den Berghe, Pierre. *The Quest for the Other: Ethnic Tourism in San Cristóbal, Mexico.* Seattle: University of Washington Press, 1994.

Vergo, Peter, ed. *The New Museology.* London: Reaktion, 1989.

Vester, Heinz-Gunter. "Adventure as a Form of Leisure." *Leisure Studies* 6 (1987): 237–49.

Vitelli, Karen D., ed. *Archaeological Ethics.* Walnut Creek, Calif.: AltaMira Press, 1996.

Vreeland, James M. "Algodón 'País': Un Cultivo Milenario Olvidado." *Boletín de la Sociedad Geográfica de Lima* 97 (1978): 19–26.

———. "The Ethnoarchaeology of Ancient Peruvian Cotton Crafts." *Archaeology* 35, no. 3 (1982): 64–66.

———. "Cotton Spinning and Processing on the Peruvian North Coast." In *The Junius B. Bird Conference on Andean Textiles, April 7 and 8, 1984,* edited by Ann P. Rowe, 363–83. Washington, D.C.: Textile Museum, 1986.

Walsh, Kevin. *The Representation of the Past: Museums and Heritage in the Post-modern World.* London: Routledge, 1992.

Watkins, Joe. "Cultural Resources as 'Owned Property': Archaeological Ethics and Land Ownership." *Public Archaeology Review* 2, no. 2 (1994): 5–7.

———. *Indigenous Archaeology: American Indian Values and Scientific Practice.* Walnut Creek, Calif.: AltaMira Press, 2000.

Watkins, Joe, Lynne Goldstein, Karen Vitelli, and Leigh Jenkins. "Accountability: Responsibilities of Archaeologists and Other Interests." In *Ethics in American Archaeology: Challenges for the 1990s,* edited by Mark J. Lynott and Alison Wylie, 33–37. Washington, D.C.: Society for American Archaeology, 1994.

Watkins, Joe, K. Anne Pyburn, and Pam Cressey. "Community Relations: What the Practicing Archaeologist Needs to Know to Work Effectively with Local and/or Descendant Communities." In *Teaching Archaeology in the Twenty-First Century,* edited by Susan Bender and George Smith, 73–81. Washington, D.C.: Society for American Archaeology, 2000.

Way, J. Edson. "The Modern Gallery Exhibition as a Form of Western-Indigenous Discourse." In *Imagery and Creativity: Ethnoaesthetics and Art Worlds in the Americas,* edited by Dorothea S. Whitten and Norman E. Whitten Jr., 108–27. Tucson: University of Arizona Press, 1993.

Wheeler, Jane, and Elias Mujica. *Prehistoric Pastoralism in the Lake Titicaca Basin, Peru: 1979–1980 Field Season.* Report submitted to the National Science Foundation, 1981.

Whelan, Tensie, ed. *Nature Tourism.* Washington, D.C.: Islan Press, 1991.

White, Timothy D. *Prehistoric Cannibalism at Mancos.* Princeton, N.J.: Princeton University Press, 1992.

Wilk, Richard R. "Whose Forest? Whose Lands? Whose Ruins?" *Journal of Science and Engineering Ethics* 5 (1999): 367–74.

———. "Miss Universe, the Olmec, and the Valley of Oaxaca." *Journal of Social Archaeology* 4, no. 3 (2000): 368–404.

Willey, Gordon R. *Prehistoric Settlement Patterns in the Viru Valley, Peru.* Bureau of American Ethnology, Bulletin 155. Washington, D.C.: Smithsonian Institution, 1953.

Wilson, Chris. *The Myth of Santa Fe.* Albuquerque: University of New Mexico Press, 1997.

Wolf, Eric R. *Europe and the People without History.* Berkeley: University of California Press, 1982.

Wylie, Alison. "On Ethics." In *Ethical Issues in Archaeology,* edited by Larry J. Zimmerman, Karen D. Vittelli, and Julie Hollowell-Zimmer, 3–16. Walnut Creek, Calif.: AltaMira Press, 2003.

Yamashida, Shinji. *Bali and Beyond: Explorations in the Anthropology of Tourism.* New York: Berghan, 2003.

Yriart, Juan Felipe. "Creating Fund-Raising Consciousness in Latin America." In *Women and Grass Roots Democracy in the Americas: Sustaining the Initiative,* edited by Dorrit K. Marks, 143–50. Miami: North-South Center Press, University of Miami, 1996.

Zeder, Melinda A. *The American Archaeologist: A Profile.* Walnut Creek, Calif.: AltaMira Press, 1997.

Zilhào, Joào. "The Rock Art of the Côa Valley, Portugal: Significance, Conservation, and Management." *Conservation and Management of Archaeological Sites* 2, no. 4 (1998): 193–206.

Zimmerman, Larry J., Karen D. Vitelli, and Julie Hollowell-Zimmer, eds. *Ethical Issues in Archaeology.* Walnut Creek, Calif.: AltaMira Press, 2003. [2003a]

Zimmerman, Larry J.. "Introduction." In *Ethical Issues in Archaeology,* edited by Larry J. Zimmerman, Karen D. Vitelli, and Julie Hollowell-Zimmer, xi–xvi. Walnut Creek, Calif.: AltaMira Press, 2003. [2003b]

Contributors

Luis Jaime Castillo Butters is associate professor and chair of the archaeology program at the Pontificia Universidad Católica del Perú, and director of the San José de Moro Archaeological Program, ongoing since 1991. Most of his research has focused on the Mochica of north coastal Peru. Recently he started a long-term excavation program in Pampa Grande, a Late Mochica settlement in the Lambayeque Valley.

Lawrence S. Coben is the director of Proyecto Inkallakta, a multidisciplinary project at the monumental Inca site of that name in Bolivia. He is the author of several papers and articles on the Inca, the use of space, and the role of performance and spectacle in ancient societies. His coedited (with Takeshi Inomata) *Theaters of Power and Community: Archaeology of Performance and Politics* examines the nature and political implications of theatrical performance at public events in these societies.

Ann Cyphers is a research scientist in archaeology at the Instituto de Investigaciones Antropológicas at the Universidad Nacional Autónoma de México. She has conducted archaeological fieldwork at various sites in Mexico, including Chalcatzingo, Xochicalco, San Lorenzo Tenochtitlán, and Laguna de los Cerros. She is the author of numerous reports, articles, and books dealing with the Olmec culture.

Carlos G. Elera has conducted extensive fieldwork on the north coast of Peru, investigating the long trajectory of cultural evolution from the first human occupations through the rise of complex societies as manifested in Cupisnique culture at the Puémape site, and, more recently, Sicán, and the Spanish Colonial period. He recently began long-term research and protection and conservation efforts directed at the cultural heritage of the Poma National Historical Sanctuary, located close to the Sicán National Museum, where he is director.

Graciela Fattorini Murillo has worked on archaeological field projects throughout Peru and on issues of conservation, collections management, and museum development. She is presently directing the restoration of the Museo Lítico Pukara and serves as the representative of Puno museums to the Regional Board of Culture, Lima. She has published many articles, including "Monolito Pukara" (*La Gaceta Arqueológica*) and "Sobre la Defensa y Conservación del Patrimonio Cultural" (*El Diario* newspaper) with Rolando Paredes.

Christine A. Hastorf is professor in the Anthropology Department at the University of California at Berkeley, where she oversees the McCown Archaeobotanical Laboratory and is curator of South American material at the Phoebe Hearst Museum of Anthropology. She has been conducting archaeological research in the Andes for over twenty years. Her fieldwork has been primarily conducted in the highlands of Peru and Bolivia, where she currently codirects a project on the Taraco Peninsula in the Lake Titicaca basin.

Ulla Sarela Holmquist Pachas, an archaeologist, currently teaches museology in the Humanities Department of the Pontificia Universidad Católica del Perú and is associated as a museologist with the San José de Moro Archaeological Project, as well as being an associated curator with the Rafael Larco Herrera Museum in Lima. She has been curator of the pre- Columbian collections at the Museo de Arte in Lima and assistant director of the Museo Nacional de Arqueología, Antropología e Historia del Perú.

Chris Hudson is a museum/exhibition designer. After working as British Volunteer Programme coordinator in Ecuador, he stayed on to design the Museo Arqueológico del Banco del Pacífico in Guayaquil and later returned to work on site museums at Salango and Agua Blanco (Ecuador) and at Ollantaytambo (Peru).

Justin Jennings is a visiting assistant professor in anthropology at Franklin and Marshall College and a research associate of the Cotsen Institute of Archaeology at the University of California at Los Angeles. His research focuses on state expansion and consolidation in the ancient Andes. He has worked extensively in the Cotahuasi Valley of southern Peru and is now conducting excavations at a Wari-influenced site there. His work on the archaeology of early states has appeared in several journals, and he has also written about tourism's impact on Cotahuasi's cultural heritage for *Archaeology*, the *SAA Archaeological Record*, and *Abenteuer Archäologie*.

Elizabeth A. Klarich has worked in the Lake Titicaca basin of Peru and Bolivia since 1994 on a variety of field projects and directed a geophysical survey and excavations at the site of Pukara in 2001–2002. Her research focuses on the origins of institutionalized inequality, the nature of urbanism, and monumental spaces as a reflection of site development. She is currently editing a volume on food preparation and feasting, and she is coediting *Advances in Titicaca Basin Archaeology II* with Charles Stanish.

Linda Manzanilla is a research scientist in archaeology at the Instituto de Investigaciones Antropológicas at the Universidad Nacional Autónoma de México and is professor at Mexico's Escuela Nacional de Antropología e Historia. She works on domestic archaeology in early urban developments, their changes through time, and their collapse.

Colin McEwan is head of the Americas Section in the Department of Africa, Oceania and the Americas at the British Museum, London. He is the author/editor of *Ancient Mexico in the British Museum* (1994), *Patagonia: Natural History, Prehistory, and Ethnography at the Uttermost End of the Earth* (1997), *Precolumbian Gold: Technology and Iconography* (2000), *Unknown Amazon: Culture in Nature in Ancient Brazil* (2001), and *Turquoise Mosaics from Mexico* (2006).

Lucero Morales-Cano has been a professor and researcher at the Instituto Nacional de Antropología e Historia in Mexico since 1992. She works with local communities in Chiapas and Puebla in cultural and natural heritage management and conservation.

Lena Mortensen is currently the assistant director of the Center for Heritage Resource Studies at the University of Maryland in College Park. She has conducted fieldwork in Honduras, studying archaeological tourism, and has worked with the Wildlife Conservation Society to create a management plan for the Copán Archaeological Park.

Yoshio Onuki is professor at the University of Tokyo, director of the Little World Museum of Man in Tokyo, and director of the Japanese Archaeological Mission to Peru. He has worked in the Andes for more than thirty years and is a specialist in the Formative period and museology.

G. Rolando Paredes Eyzaguirre has worked on numerous archaeological projects in coastal and highland Peru and served as director of the Dirección de Sitios Arqueológicos of the Instituto Nacional de Cultura in Lima in 1993. Since 1997, he has served as the director of the Puno office of the National Institute of Culture (INC–Puno). He has published many articles, including "Hacia una Cronología del Altiplano Puneño" with Graciela Fattorini Murillo and "Pukara Influence on Isla Soto, Lake Titicaca, Peru" with Joel Myres (both in press).

K. Anne Pyburn is professor of anthropology and gender studies at Indiana University in Bloomington and is core faculty in the graduate program in "Archaeology in Social Context." Her research centers on the lives of ordinary people living in the Maya Lowlands during the first millennium A.D.. She also writes about ethics and gender (most recently, *Ungendering Civilization: Rethinking the Archaeological Record*, 2004). She is the director of the Society for American Archaeology's MATRIX Project (http://www.indiana.edu/~arch/saa/matrix/) and the Chau Hiix Project in Belize (http://www.indiana.edu/~overseas/flyers/chauhiix.html).

Izumi Shimada is professor in the Department of Anthropology at Southern Illinois University. From 1978 to 2001 he directed the Sicán Archaeological Project, focusing on the developmental processes, internal organization, and material achievements of this culture. The results of this project formed the foundation of the Sicán National Museum. In 2003 he began investigations at the famed religious center of Pachacamac, outside the city of Lima. He has written over one hundred articles and authored or edited nine books published in Japan, Peru, and the United States.

María Isabel Silva served as national director of the Department of Anthropology, Archaeology, and History at the National Institute of Cultural Patrimony in Quito, Ecuador, from 1988 to 1990. Her research and publications concern the indigenous social and economic organization and ethnohistory of the coast of Ecuador; sustainable development and the management of cultural 294resources including tourism, archaeology, and community site museums; and museums and archaeology in social context. She codirected the Agua Blanca Archaeological Project.

Helaine Silverman is professor in the Department of Anthropology at the University of Illinois at Urbana-Champaign. She conducted various archaeological projects on the south coast of Peru between 1983 and 1996, focusing on the interplay of political organization, ritual practice, and expressions of identity among the Paracas and Nasca peoples of this region. In addition to numerous articles, she is the author of *Cahuachi in the Ancient Nasca World* (1993), *Ancient Andean Art: An Annotated Bibliography* (1996), *Ancient Nasca Settlement and Society* (2002), and *The Nasca* (2002, written with Donald A. Proulx). She has edited/co-edited four volumes dealing with Andean archaeology (*Andean Archaeology*, 2004; *Andean Archaeology I: Variations in Sociopolitical Organization*, 2002; *Andean Archaeology II: Art, Landscape, and Society*, 2002; *Andean Archaeology III: North and South*, 2006) and another treating mortuary landscapes (*The Space and Place of Death*, 2002). Currently she is studying archaeological tourism and the construction of local and national identities in Peru.

Karen E. Stothert is an investigator for the Anthropology Museum of the Central Bank of Ecuador in Guayaquil and is also a research associate at the Center for Archaeological Research at the University of Texas at San Antonio. Her research in coastal Ecuador has centered on the archaeology and ethnography of the Santa Elena Peninsula. She has published on preceramic food production and burial ceremonialism; prehistoric ideology, art, subsistence, and ceramic production; historical archaeology, including Colonial tar boiling; and ethnographic spinning, weaving, and bronze casting. She authored *Women in Ancient America* (1999) with Karen Olsen Bruhns.

Elka Weinstein is an independent museum consultant with her own company, Museologic. She specializes in education and interpretation for museum exhibits. She was most recently the acting museum advisor for eastern Ontario with the Ministry of Culture (Province of Ontario, Canada).

Index